Mass Theatre in Interwar Europe

KADOC Artes 15

Mass Theatre in Interwar Europe

Flanders and the Netherlands in an International Perspective

Thomas Crombez & Luk Van den Dries, eds

LEUVEN UNIVERSITY PRESS

Cover: Jozef Boon, *Credo!* (I believe), Brussels, 1936.
[Leuven, KADOC-KU Leuven: KFB1431]

© 2014
Leuven University Press / Presses Universitaires de Louvain / Universitaire Pers Leuven
Minderbroedersstraat 4, B-3000 Leuven

ISBN 978 90 5867 992 5
D/2014/1869/50
NUR: 676 - 694

Contents

A New Genre for a New Audience

Introduction

Thomas Crombez & Frank Peeters

It is 9 July 1938. On this Saturday night, an audience of thousands has gathered in the Antwerp marketplace for the first performance of *De Leeuw van Vlaanderen* (*The Lion of Flanders*). The open-air spectacle, written by Frans Meire, has been brought to the stage by Joris Diels, the successful director of the *Koninklijke Nederlandse Schouwburg*, KNS (Royal Dutch Theatre).

The Antwerp spectacle, as the rest of this chapter will argue, is the perfect example for introducing the genre of socio-theatrical events, a group term for the extremely popular genre of mass theatre during the interwar period in Europe.

The main difference between a regular theatrical performance and a socio-theatrical event is the context. This context is not primarily artistic, but clearly belongs to the social – and thus political and public – sphere. The idea that art has to take place in a context which is explicitly marked as 'artistic' is a premise of the late-modern art system. In his influential book *Theory of the Avant-garde* (*Theorie der Avantgarde*, 1974), Peter Bürger discusses this phenomenon within the theme of the art institution's 'autonomy' in bourgeois society.

At the fin de siècle, the autonomy of the art institution achieved its peak. In literature and art, this was expressed by aestheticism. The slogan of Victor Cousin, *l'art pour l'art*, was the most pronounced symptom of the position that art operated independently and that any artist or art lover owed responsibility only to himself and his own taste. The implication was that any claims for the social impact of art were to be abandoned.[1]

Not coincidentally, it was during approximately the same period that open-air theatre and mass spectacle were becoming increasingly popular. More and more artists were distancing themselves from the idea that artistic reality was its own cosmos. Bürger associated this project almost exclusively with those movements that are referred to as the 'historical avant-garde', including Dada, Surrealism, Constructivism and Futurism. In fact it was a widespread protest, which is illustrated in particular by the rapidly increasing incidence of socio-theatrical events.

A socio-theatrical event is designed to have a major impact on a clearly defined target group, and to 'activate' that group through artistic means. As the theoreticians of the genre would emphasize, it was theatre for the masses, by the masses. In the words of Dutch essayist and poetess Henriette Roland Holst: 'In these performances, the masses would understand more thoroughly the greatness of their own striving, they would better realize their own ideals'.[2]

To describe the impact of such events on a group of people, interwar critics and artists came up with terms such as 'conquest' or 'agitation'. For example, the Russian acronym *agitprop* refers to art that focuses on agitation and propaganda.

In this book, we use 'socio-theatricality' as a group term for various forms of mass theatre, which show a great variety in scale, location and design. The most traditional kind of socio-theatrical events were open-air theatre shows, often performed and designed by professionals, who wished to activate a larger community than was possible in the typical theatrical spaces of early twentieth-century bourgeois theatre. All other forms of socio-theatricality discussed in this book were not performed (exclusively) by profes-

1. Koninklijke Nederlandse Schouwburg, De Leeuw van Vlaanderen (The Lion of Flanders, F. Meire), 9 July 1938. Photo published in Het Antwerpsch Openluchtspel 'De Leeuw van Vlaanderen', *Antwerp, 1939. [Antwerp, Erfgoedbibliotheek Hendrik Conscience]*

1 Bürger, *Theory of the Avant-garde*, 19-25.
2 Roland Holst-Van der Schalk, *De voorwaarden tot hernieuwing der dramatische kunst*, 268.

sional actors and directors, but depended strongly on the participation of amateur performers.

Socio-theatrical events that involved non-professional actors may broadly be divided into two groups: choral and non-choral. Non-choral forms were often labelled as 'lay theatre' (*lekenspel* in Dutch or *Laienspiel* in German). The term was introduced by socialist youth movements and theatre groups to distance themselves from what was called 'amateur theatre' in the bourgeois sphere.

All choral forms of mass theatre were collectively referred to as 'choral drama' (*Chorspiel* in German). The smallest kind of events were most often designated by the term 'speech choir' (*spreekkoor* in Dutch, *Sprechchor* in German or *chœur parlé* in French), or alternatively 'movement choir' (*bewegingskoor*) if the performance was focused on collective rhythmical movements rather than reciting a text. Such events could overlap with the older nineteenth-century practice of *tableaux vivants*, a name which was occasionally still used.

These theatrical events involved between ten and hundred participants, and were often organized by schools, youth movements, political organizations or labour unions. Larger events were generically called 'mass spectacles' and grouped multiple speech and movement choirs.

Geographically speaking, this book will focus on socio-theatrical events in the European context, with a strong focus on two countries that have until now received little attention from historians and theatre scholars: the Netherlands and the Dutch-speaking part of Belgium (Flanders). However, the broader European context of socio-theatrical events from the interwar period will be closely studied, too. This includes events from former Soviet Russia, Germany, France and Switzerland.

Chronologically, most events discussed in this book took place between the end of the First World War (1918) and the onset of the Second World War (1939). Two important exceptions from before 1918 are the theatre reformers from the fin de siècle period,

10

which will be discussed in this introductory part, and the great national feasts in France and Switzerland, which took place in the wake of the French Revolution.

In the following, we will first see how three fundamental parameters of socio-theatricality shaped the political movements and cultural expressions of the early twentieth century. In the next part of this book, 'Mapping Mass Spectacle in Flanders and the Netherlands', our ambition is to survey the main organizations and ideological groups which were involved in Dutch and Flemish mass spectacles during the interwar period. Its promoters came from a broad political spectrum, comprising not only socialist and Catholic but also communist and national socialist leaders and artists. The last part, finally, zooms in on six case studies from this map. It collects two chapters on the origins of mass spectacle in the political and popular culture of the nineteenth century; three chapters on open-air and mass theatre during the 1920s and 1930s; and a concluding chapter on the fate of socio-theatricality in postwar Belgium.

The Lion of Flanders in Antwerp, 9 July 1938

On 9 and 10 July 1938, the *Guldensporenfeesten* (Commemoration of the Battle of the Golden Spurs) are being celebrated throughout Dutch-speaking Belgium, as the medieval victory of several Flemish cities over the French king is remembered. Moreover, exactly one hundred years have passed since Hendrik Conscience published the book that transformed the events of 1302 into a Flemish national myth, namely, *De Leeuw van Vlaanderen* (The Lion of Flanders, 1838). Meire's script is a dramatization of the book, and was the winning entry in a contest organized by the *Verbond van Vlaamse Cultuurverenigingen* (Federation of Flemish Cultural Societies).

Central to the drama is the contrast between the intrigues of the French court and

3. *Frans Meire,* De Leeuw van Vlaanderen, *Antwerp, 1938. [Antwerp, Erfgoedbibliotheek Hendrik Conscience]*

the harmonious unity of the Flemish leaders, who are able to relate to each other across the boundaries of class and guild. In the play, the contemporary problem of the division between the Flemish political parties is projected into the past and resolved there, on the basis of a political logic that relies on the concept of a unitary land for a unitary people. Speaking for this 'historically realized utopia' is the Dean of the Bruges weavers' guild, Pieter De Coninck:

> And thus it is in all of Flanders that we take after the same nature, the same blood, the same thinking. Any happiness or sorrow is shared by all. [...] We must therefore establish peace between us, and forget all the petty personal interests, the petulance and foolish audacity, in favour of a large and beautiful interest – the welfare of all.[3]

A second important aspect of the play is what might be described as its messianic dimension. This concerns in particular the

3   Meire, *De Leeuw van Vlaanderen,* 23.

4. Het Antwerpsch Openluchtspel 'De Leeuw van Vlaanderen', *Antwerp, 1939. [Leuven, KADOC-KU Leuven: KB35177]*

OPENLUCHTVERTOONINGEN
GROOTE MARKT — ANTWERPEN

9 EN 11 JULI 1939

"DE LEEUW VAN VLAANDEREN"

door

FRANS MEIRE

naar den roman van H. Conscience

Officieel Programma

Het Antwerpsch Openluchtspel

"De Leeuw van Vlaanderen"

door

Frans Meire

naar den roman van Hendrik Conscience

op de

Groote Markt

te

Antwerpen

ZONDAG 9 JULI TE 15 EN TE 20.30 U.
DINSDAG 11 JULI TE 20.30 UUR

BIJZONDERE OPVOERING VOOR DE SCHOOLJEUGD VAN
GROOT-ANTWERPEN OP DINSDAG 11 JULI TE 15.30 U.

role of the title figure, the 'Lion of Flanders'. In Conscience's narration of the historical events, as in Meire's dramatization, the son of the old Count Guy of Dampierre (who was lord of the County of Flanders and as such the highest power in the feudal system after King Philip IV) miraculously returned from his imprisonment in France. That son, Robert of Bethune, appears on the battlefield at the decisive moment, just as the tide was turning against the Flemish militia, in order to make his appearance as the heroic Lion of Flanders.

The ways in which the book and the play present this event certainly seem to endow it with a kind of supernatural quality. The Lion functioned as a *deus ex machina* that broke the course of events and gave them a radically different turn. As a nobleman, moreover, who (according to Conscience's version) sympathized with the guilds and the common people, he was able to function as the ideal symbol of Flemish unity and the bond with the land. In Meire's text, this is recounted as follows:

BREYDEL: My God, it was sad, it was hopeless … And then, suddenly, that radiant knight appeared, all dressed in gold, and riding on a dark trotter, a black giant of a beast. Sparks shot from the glittering costume of the mighty rider and his fiery horse, as they galloped over a dark ridge. [...] [T]hen, as they came closer, you could make out the figure of a black lion on the knight's golden armour, placed high in the centre of his chest, and on his round buckler he bore no other weapon or motto than the large black letters: 'Flanders the Lion!'[4]

Dynamics and Domination

It is Saturday, 9 July. The marketplace fills rapidly and it is remarkably chilly for a summer evening. There is some rain in the air, but that will only disturb the festivities on Sunday, when the *Rubens Cantata* by Peter Benoit is performed by the orchestra of the Royal Flemish Opera (led by Hendrik Diels, brother of the director), with the support of the Cathedral of Our Lady's carillon.

4   Meire, *De Leeuw van Vlaanderen*, 144-145.

This Saturday night, the audience is treated to scenes from a medieval past that, via a detour through nineteenth-century romanticism, have been translated to the stage and transformed into spectacle. No effort has been spared to make a lasting impression, both visually and acoustically: 'loudspeakers, bright spotlights, the glow of the fire, the thunderous music and trumpets, the trotting of the horses, the light of the torch bearers, the procession of banners, the colourful costumes, the many crowd scenes with moving groups'.[5]

Extras for the impressive crowd scenes had been recruited from no less than nineteen amateur groups from the Antwerp region. They came mainly, but not exclusively, from Catholic circles. Socialist organizations, such as 'Jean Jaurès', also collaborated in the spectacle. The extras were meant to constitute a richly decorated frame within which the star interpreters could shine. It was indeed an all-star cast, including Joris Diels himself in the title role of Robert de Bethune, the Lion of Flanders.

For more than one reason, the Antwerp open-air spectacle can be seen as a typical example of mass theatre, which achieved great popularity during the first half of the twentieth century in the Low Countries as in the rest of Europe. Conspicuous characteristics of the genre are, principally, its setting and its design.

Open-air theatre and mass spectacle typically took place in large public spaces such as parks and marketplaces. To make this space function in a theatrically effective way, the directors had to conceive of sets that were fundamentally different from classical theatrical staging. In an open-air space there was no proscenium arch, no theatrical scenery, and no wings.

The Antwerp marketplace was equipped with a rather minimally decorated stage, featuring only a few simple props to indicate whether the scene was set at court or in an inn. Diels divided the stage into two parts, connected by a bridge. This would allow for striking visual contrasts, for example, be-

tween the French court on one part of the stage and the Flemish townspeople on the other. The constriction formed by the bridge also accentuated the movements of large groups going from one stage to the other.

A second crucial element of Diels' production was the music. In almost every review of the performance, the powerful effect of the carillon was noted. In particular, the

5. *Two scenes of* De Leeuw van Vlaanderen *(F. Meire), 9 July 1938. Photos published in* Het Antwerpsch Openluchtspel 'De Leeuw van Vlaanderen', *Antwerp, 1939. [Antwerp, Erfgoedbibliotheek Hendrik Conscience]*

5   *Volk en Staat*, 7 Nov. 1938.

fact that the sounds of the performance were not generated by an orchestra, but by an instrument that was part of the living urban context itself – now transformed into theatrical scenery by the spectacle – guaranteed that the theatrical event not only took place in a public space, but actually *dominated* it. This was the term used frequently in the interwar period to indicate how an open-air spectacle interacted with the public space and with the mass of spectators. In this case, an enthusiastic (and Flemish nationalist) reviewer wrote that Diels' production 'dominated the space of the marketplace both acoustically and optically'.[6]

Domination invariably meant *activation* of the masses. It was not only the artistic impact of the spectacle that was of crucial importance to the organizers, but also the stirring up of national and political passions. In July 1938, especially, this appears to have been extremely important.

Politics and Pathos

During the 1930s, political tensions between Dutch-speaking and French-speaking Belgium rose to new heights. A context of national and international instability – Belgium had no fewer than ten different governments between 1931 and 1940, and the rise of fascism was increasing the tension between foreign powers – provided an environment in which both mass movements and radical political formations could thrive.[7]

The Flemish Movement was becoming radicalized under pressure from new parties such as the *Vlaams Nationaal Verbond* (Flemish National Association, VNV), founded in 1933 by Staf de Clercq. In the parliamentary elections of 1936, having formed a cartel with other Flemish nationalist parties, De Clercq won no less than 13.6 per cent of the votes in the Dutch-speaking region.[8]

Certain individual events kept the Flemish Movement in the news constantly. The 1932 law on the use of language for public administration officially introduced monolingualism, meaning that all public services and notices had to be offered in Dutch in the Flemish part of Belgium. However, many street signs and public notices in Flanders were still in French or at most bilingual. In 1937, activist Flor Grammens began a systematic campaign of painting over the signs. He frequently allowed himself be arrested in order to gain more publicity, and his example was soon followed by hundreds of students.

In the summer of 1938, newspaper headlines were dominated by Grammens' name. In late June, the Minister of Justice was even questioned in the Senate and in the House of Representatives over Grammens' imprisonment in the prison of Ghent. On 3 July, Ghent hosted the *Vlaams Nationaal Zangfeest* (Flemish National Song Festival), which was preceded by a mass demonstration demanding Grammens' immediate release.[9]

A few days later, this request was granted. By granting amnesty to Grammens and his collaborators, the Belgian government appeared to implicitly condone his interpretation of the new law: strict monolingualism in all administrative matters, including street signs.[10]

Even Grammens' most vocal supporters emphasized the purely symbolic and provocative nature of his actions. 'Grammens is the symbol of monolingualism for Flanders', said Reimond Tollenaere, representative for the VNV, during an interpellation in the Belgian Chamber of Representatives on 23 June.

That Tollenaere, regarded by many as an extremist politician, was enjoying widespread support from Catholic and pro-Flemish organizations was evidence of Flemish sensitivity over the issue of linguistic inequality (as well as – according to many – both social and economic inequality).

In the Belgian parliament, Tollenaere read a declaration by the Federation of Flemish Cultural Societies – the same organization that had organized the literary contest for *The Lion of Flanders* – in which the immediate release of Grammens and his supporters was demanded.

6 *Volk en Staat*, 7 Nov. 1938.
7 Dumont, "Fenomenologie van de massamanifestaties in België in de jaren dertig", 150-151.
8 De Wever, "Vlaamsch Nationaal Verbond (VNV)".
9 Elias, *Vijfentwintig jaar Vlaamse Beweging*, IV, 122-123.
10 Wils, "Flor Grammens".

Tollenaere was a young politician from an equally young and radical political party. By presenting the statement of the Federation, however, he was transformed into the representative of aggrieved Flanders. The Federation went on to unite such established organizations as the *Davidsfonds* and the *Verbond van Vlaamse Oud-Strijders* (Association of Flemish War Veterans, VOS).

On the same 9 July that would see the premiere of *The Lion of Flanders*, Prime Minister Paul-Henri Spaak received a delegation from the Federation. He was presented with a list of demands that included increased autonomy for Flanders, and amnesty for Grammens. That the effects of the Flemish agitation were felt is perhaps best illustrated by the fact that the socialist Prime Minister appeared the next day at the Groeninge festival in Kortrijk, another event celebrating the Battle of the Golden Spurs, but organized by Spaak's own party – the Belgian Workers' Party. The Belgian socialists had been organizing their own Golden Spurs commemorations since the beginning of the twentieth century, but it was the first time that a Belgian prime minister would speak at such an intensely symbolic pro-Flemish event.[11] A number of weeks earlier, when Spaak's new government was installed on 17 May, his inaugural statement had also stressed the legitimacy of the Flemish pursuit of cultural autonomy.

The front page of the Catholic and pro-Flemish newspaper *De Standaard* on 10 July shows just how closely these cultural and political events were connected. Historical articles on the Battle of the Golden Spurs, as well as reports on the weekend's festivities and a report on the meeting between the Federation of Flemish Cultural Societies and the Prime Minister, together made up a politico-cultural whole. The framework of these events inevitably had a significant effect on the production and reception of *The Lion of Flanders*, and on the other festivities that were taking place in Flemish cities at the time.

6. *Announcement of the manifestation demanding the liberation of Flor Grammens in* De Standaard, *9 July 1938.*
[Antwerp, Erfgoedbibliotheek Hendrik Conscience]

It was past midnight when the first performance of the open-air spectacle drew to a close (a second show was planned for Sunday afternoon). In press reviews, journalists and editors translated the exuberant audience responses into their own impassioned prose:

> The final apotheosis opens in the form of a broad wave of colours and flags, victory shouts and the clopping of the horses, while the heavy triumphal bell sounds, the bugles blare, the carillon rings and flags are unfurled from all the neighbouring houses of the Antwerp marketplace. The crowd stands up and sings the Flemish anthem, 'The Flemish Lion', with one voice.[12]

The Flemish Lion was the anthem of the Flemish Movement, dating back to 1845. It was a product of pompous nineteenth-century romanticism, in the same way that Conscience's *Lion of Flanders* was. In this performative context, however, it was the

11 Tollebeek, "De Guldensporen-vieringen"; Nörtemann, *Im Spiegelkabinett der Historie*.
12 Putman, *Tooneeldagboek 1928-1938*, 117-125.

7. *Joris Diels as Robert of Bethune in* De Leeuw van Vlaanderen *(F. Meire), 9 July 1938. Photo published in* Het Antwerpsch Openluchtspel 'De Leeuw van Vlaanderen', *Antwerp, 1938. [Antwerp, Erfgoedbibliotheek Hendrik Conscience]*

could be used to symbolize the ongoing conflict between the Nazi regime and the Catholic Church, as it was in Erwin Kolbenheyer's *Gregor und Heinrich* in 1935.

The contemporary parallel that was most manifestly accentuated in *The Lion of Flanders* was the truce element (*godsvrede*). Within the Flemish Movement, there was a strongly felt need to unite Flemish nationalists of all persuasions – from conservative Catholics to militant communists – under the same banner. In the spring of 1938, with the upcoming municipal elections on the horizon, several politicians (notably from the VNV) began to demand a new policy of concentration.[15] This will surely have provided a strong modern echo to the lines in the play where De Coninck calls for 'a stronger sense of self-consciousness and of new, unyielding solidarity'.[16]

Flemish national self-consciousness was a theme often repeated in the play, and it emphatically concerned the typically late-modern theme of national emancipation. The political logic that accompanied it was in fact closely related to medieval feudalism, which had had such a strong influence on the events of 1302. Within the new logic of sovereignty made popular during the 1930s, concepts such as people, land and nation (or race) were being presented as an unambiguous whole, a national self that had to know itself in order to exist as itself, and to defend itself from other nations. Concepts such as 'becoming itself', 'knowing itself' and 'self-affirmation' occupied a central role in that discourse.[17] Similarly, in *The Lion*, protagonist De Coninck speaks of 'a Flanders belonging to its own people', and states that 'Flanders is free and it knows itself'.[18]

The end of the drama – which, as mentioned above, was followed by a thunder of applause and the singing of the Flemish Lion – again emphasized the continued relevance of medieval Flanders' struggle for freedom. When, at the end of the battle, De Coninck concludes: 'The dead of Groeninghe are the seeds of the future', he is making reference to the Flemish poet and chaplain Cyriel

ultimate tool for transforming a theatrical event into a political demonstration. The medieval conflict between the Flemish cities and the French king was an ideal historical metaphor for venting contemporary feelings of inequality and oppression. As such, it is a clear case of *transposition*: a historical piece presented in such a manner or in such a context that parallels in the contemporary situation became impossible to overlook.[13]

In the turbulent interwar period, transposition was a favourite technique of politically engaged writers and dramatists. For his 1927 performance of *Gewitter über Gottland* (Storm over Gottland, by Ehm Welk), director Erwin Piscator radically transposed the historical play, whose plot concerned the 'proto-commune' of the medieval *Vitalianer Bund*, into the present using projections and film. In doing so, he made the revolt of the medieval rebels appear to flow directly into the Paris Commune, and from there into the First World War, the October Revolution, and the problems of contemporary Berlin.

National socialist drama, too, used the mechanism of transposition. The historical conflict between Pope Gregory VII and the German emperor Henry IV, for instance,

13 Ketelsen, *Heroisches Theater.*
14 Van der Logt, *Het theater van de nieuwe orde*, 121-124, 136-137, 343.
15 Elias, *Vijfentwintig jaar Vlaamse Beweging*, IV, 119.
16 Meire, *De Leeuw van Vlaanderen*, 24.
17 Sluga, *Heidegger's Crisis*, 121-122; Crombez, "The Sovereign Disappears in the Voting Booth".
18 Meire, *De Leeuw van Vlaanderen*, 24-25.

Verschaeve. Verschaeve's original verse –
'Here lie their bodies as seeds in the sand /
Hope for the harvest, O Flemish land' – had
recently been chosen to adorn the Yser
Tower (*IJzertoren*), an anti-war monument
erected in 1930 in Diksmuide, a Flemish
town that had been razed almost completely to the ground during World War I.
Simultaneously, the tower had also begun to
function as a memorial to the Flemish Movement.[19]

De Coninck refers even more explicitly
to the future of Flemish emancipation when
he utters his 'prophetic last words'. This, at
least, is the opinion of the journalist who
described the event for the nationalist Flemish newspaper *Volk en Staat*:

> It was an amazing moment, when Pieter
> De Coninck spoke his prophetic last
> words, and when Carolus, the carillon,
> and the trumpets filled the entire space
> with festive joy, and it all ended with a
> fiery Flemish Lion.[20]

What were those prophetic words?
De Coninck is, with an excess of dramatic
irony, speaking about precisely this kind of
future celebration:

> DE CONINCK: The battle has been won?
> Say, Breydel, has the Frenchman been
> defeated? – It is too powerful … too beau-
> tiful … My God! In the Flemish chronicles
> this will be noted as a happy day: 11 July,
> the day of the Holy Benedict, in the year
> of our Lord 1302 … […]
> Flanders will not forget this day.
> (*His words are carried by a trumpet call
> that drowns out the deep reverberations
> of the festive chimes.*) Minstrels will sing
> about this day for the future generations.
> And the people will always tell the story
> of this day, and if there are days when the
> old pride looks likely to perish – there will
> always be someone who has not forgotten.
> I see him thus in a frightened time: he
> will probably appear then as a silent,
> white-bearded sage, who writes a story
> full of beautiful symbols, like a bold call to
> arms.[21]

8. *Machteld of Bethune (Jet Naessens) in*
De Leeuw van Vlaanderen *(F. Meire),
9 July 1938. Photo published in* Het
Antwerpsch Openluchtspel 'De Leeuw
van Vlaanderen', *Antwerp, 1938.
[Antwerp, Erfgoedbibliotheek Hendrik
Conscience]*

That 'silent, white-bearded sage' is of course
Conscience himself, the author of the book
on which this drama is based. Such anachronistic references alert the spectator, via
historical fiction, to the current and political
dimensions of 'Flanders'. Other performances that took place during the 11 July celebration of 1938 also accentuated the historical
parallels. It was not only in Antwerp that an
open-air theatre performance with strong
historical and Flemish aspects was performed. In Aalst, Ghent, Brussels, Mechelen
and a number of other cities, festivities were
held that featured lectures, poetry readings,
dancing and singing choirs, collective recitals of the Flemish Lion, and Conscience-
inspired theatrical performances, such as
Dampierre by Ferdinand Vercnocke.

Perhaps the most remarkable of these
was a series of 'plastic images' (a neologism
probably devised to avoid the customary
French term *tableaux vivants*) performed by
the nationalist-inspired gymnastic circle, the
Vlaamse Nationale Blauwvoetbond:

> [I]n exemplary plastic groups, ten scenes
> from *The Lion of Flanders* were brought

19 See also the chapter 'The Pilgrimages of the Yser'.
20 *Volk en Staat*, 11 July 1938.
21 Meire, *De Leeuw van Vlaanderen*,
   144-147.

back to life, while a simple but eloquent short text was read out by a speaker. The audience called a couple of the groups back for an encore, and it was striking how each national Flemish symbol was received with a hurricane of cheers. The current spirit was felt in the room, there was an ironic cheer when we were reminded that Pieter De Coninck was imprisoned because he had incited the locals NOT to pay new taxes. But Jan Breydel with his butchers freed him.[22]

In this gymnastic performance, too, there are manifest allusions to current events. De Coninck, the Dean of the weavers' guild, was suddenly transformed into a symbol of the imprisoned activist Flor Grammens, an allusion which was afterwards reinforced by guest speaker Germain Lefever, chairman of the Association of Flemish War Veterans.

Three Parameters of Socio-Theatricality

The performance of *The Lion of Flanders* in the Antwerp marketplace in July 1938 combines almost all of the distinctive elements of mass spectacle during the 1930s. They may be labelled as parameters of socio-theatricality.

Mass open-air theatre is not usually an isolated artistic phenomenon, but an event linked to a broader political and social context, which is explicitly addressed and activated by the performance. In this case, 'performativity' concerns what is happening on stage just as much as what is happening in the audience. The performance of *The Lion of Flanders* required cooperation among the established professional artists of the KNS, but also among the hundreds of volunteers from amateur groups. In almost every form of mass theatre, professionals collaborated with amateur groups, but in different kinds of constellations. It should therefore not be described as a single genre, but as a heterogeneous amalgam of numerous sub-genres, ranging from small speech or movement choirs with ten or fewer performers to enormous mass demonstrations involving thousands of people. This is outlined in more detail below in 'Participants and Spectators'.

In addition to formal diversity, mass theatre took place in most diverse ideological contexts. The Soviet mass spectacles of the early 1920s are probably best known. Mass theatre was practiced with equal intensity, though, by nationalist and fascist groups, and within the militant circles of Catholic Action, and in socialist and communist circles. Questions raised by the ideological character of mass theatre are examined more closely in 'Ideological Diversity and the Question of Technique'.

An open-air location is almost always a public space, which creates new opportunities but also introduces special requirements for staging and set design. Combined with music or singing, this may create a performance which, as in Antwerp, 'dominates the space both acoustically and visually'. It is not only the empty space that is dominated by the spectacle, but obviously also the audience, which is transformed into a *mass*, a *nation*, or a *community* depending on the tone of the observer who describes the event. The issue of space will be discussed at length in 'Mass Spectacle and Public Space'.

Participants and Spectators

An open-air performance with large numbers of participants and spectators, such as *The Lion of Flanders*, is a typical example of a broader phenomenon from the interwar period: the organization of socio-theatrical events.

The social dimension of the performing arts was a central topic to early-twentieth-century debates and reforms. Vsevolod Meyerhold, who led the nationalized Russian theatres after the October Revolution, spoke of the audience as the 'fourth dimension' of theatre, after the dramatist, the director, and the actor. Therefore, a theatre production in itself was always unfinished, and could only be fully realized in confrontation with an audience. There, a 'fusion' between actor and spectator took place. To reinforce his argument, Meyerhold often referred to an aphorism by Pushkin: 'The theatre was created in the marketplace'.[23] It is precisely the 'marketplace' – often literally an open space in the city, but also more broadly the context of public space – that can turn a theatrical event into a socio-theatrical event.

In order to zoom in on the close relationship between these kinds of theatrical events and their broader political and social context, two 'canonical' cases of mass spectacle from the 1920s will be analysed in this section: the political spectacles of Soviet Russia, and the German choral drama movement.

Mass Spectacle in Soviet Russia

The Soviet mass spectacles make up what is perhaps the best known form of mass theatre from the first half of the twentieth century. Initially termed *massovoe deistvo* ('mass action'), they were introduced by the 'Plan for Monumental Propaganda' that Lenin and Lunacharsky developed in 1918.[24] In their utopian vision, a new festive culture was to be established, which would include new rituals and art forms functioning as essential elements of the future socialist society.

One of the largest and most frequently cited examples of this practice is *The Storming of the Winter Palace*, a mass spectacle staged in Petrograd (the former, and current, Saint Petersburg) on 7 November 1920. Directed by Nikolai Evreinov, and designed by Yuri Annenkov, it commemorated a crucial event in the course of the October Revolution, when not so much the Tsarist forces but the reformist transitional government of Kerensky was overcome.

The Storming of the Winter Palace involved no fewer than 8,000 performers, and the audience numbered at least 100,000. Erika Fischer-Lichte, who has thoroughly analysed this performance, writes that in such events 'a community was represented as well as brought forth'.[25] Mass spectacle is not just a spectacle for the masses, but a

spectacle in which the mass represents itself *as* itself and *for* itself.

Soviet mass spectacle began in March 1919 with the performance of *The Overthrow of Autocracy* by the newly formed Red Army Studio, headed by Nikolai Vinogradov-Mamont. The play, which celebrated the victory of the February Revolution, was first performed by Red Army soldiers for an audience of 600 people. Two typical characteristics of mass spectacle evident in this performance are firstly the desire to have the performers occupy all of the performance space (in this case the Rozhdestvensky House of the People's Volodarsky Hall in Petrograd), and secondly the use of two stages, connected by a pathway to emphasize the dynamics of the two warring groups and the

23 Braun, *Meyerhold on theater*, 256; Leach, *Vsevolod Meyerhold*, 17, 30.
24 Bowlt, "Constructivism and Russian Stage Design", 76; Tolstoy, Bibikova and Cooke, eds, *Street Art of the Revolution*.
25 Fischer-Lichte, *Theatre, Sacrifice, Ritual*, 105.

9. *Nikolai Evreinov and Yuri Annenkov,* The Storming of the Winter Palace, *1920.*
[*Tolstoj, Bibikova and Cooke,* Street Art of the Revolution*]*

10. Yuri Annenkov, The Mystery of Liberated Labour, *1920*.
[Tolstoj, Bibikova and Cooke, Street Art of the Revolution*]*

11. Yuri Annenkov, Toward a World Commune, *1920*.
[Tolstoj, Bibikova and Cooke, Street Art of the Revolution*]*

26 Fischer-Lichte, *Theatre, Sacrifice, Ritual*, 103-104.
27 Ibid., 106-107.
28 Braun, *The Director and the Stage*, 137.
29 Worrall, *Modernism to Realism on the Soviet Stage*, 8.

violence of their confrontations.[26] The role of the audience, as Meyerhold describes, was also crucial to the course of the performance.

The spectators responded again and again with frenetic applause, shouting, 'hurrah'. In the funeral procession, when the soldiers carried their dead comrades around the Hall, the spectators spontaneously rose from their seats and united and joined the soldiers in a choral rendition of the hymn 'As a martyr, you fell'. [...]. After the performance, hundreds of spectators shed tears of emotion and enthusiasm. They surrounded the somewhat dazed performers, embraced and cheered them.[27]

Following the extraordinary success of *The Overthrow of the Autocracy*, it was allegedly performed more than 250 times by the same troupe. Its director wrote that the performances obtained a ritual character: whenever a regiment of the Red Army was sent to the front, a manifestation was held that included a performance of the play.

Numerous other avant-garde directors who favoured the Revolution also contributed to the development of the genre in the following years. Mass spectacles were considered celebrations of the new regime's holidays, following the model of the liturgical calendar. Thus the *Mystery of Liberated Labour* was performed in Petrograd on Labour Day 1920, directed by Yuri Annenkov and Alexander Kugel, for an audience of 35,000. Other examples include *Russia's Blockade* (20 June 1920, 150 performers and 10,000 spectators) and *Toward a World Commune* (19 July 1920).

Even performances in the classic theatres came to be modelled on mass spectacle. For the performance of *Earth Rampant* (written by Sergei Tretyakov) in 1923, Meyerhold and his designer Liubov Popova deliberately avoided any aesthetic stylization. Their set design maximized the topicality of the play: the only props were real objects used by the Red Army, such as cars, motorcycles, machine guns, a field kitchen, a thresher, and so on. For lighting, only huge searchlights were used. The uniforms of the soldiers were authentic and the actors did not wear any make-up.[28] In the auditorium, extra wide passageways had to be cleared, which would allow the performers to drive military vehicles onto the stage. Afterwards, the production – in fact a mass spectacle performed inside a theatre – was staged by Meyerhold as a 'real' mass spectacle on the Lenin Hills near Moscow, for which military detachments were recruited.[29]

For Ilya Selvinsky's *Commander of the Second Army*, directed by Meyerhold in

1929, the chorus were equipped with megaphones. The stage itself was taken over by banners bearing revolutionary slogans, as well as giant constructions, everyday objects and projection screens.

The Soviet Example as a Model for Europe

Several features that stand out in the performance of *The Lion of Flanders* can also be found on a somewhat larger scale in the Soviet mass spectacles. To explore the aspects of context, narrative and space in particular, I will use the example of *The Storming of the Winter Palace*.

In the same way that the theatrical effect of *The Lion of Flanders* was magnified by its being performed among the late-medieval buildings of the Antwerp marketplace, along with the musical accompaniment of the carillon, the impact of *The Storming of the Winter Palace* was determined first and foremost by the fact of its taking place on the actual site of the historic events depicted in the play.

The atmosphere was further enhanced by the careful use of light, particularly from the spotlights installed in the plaza for the audience, but also from lights taken from the battleship *Aurora*, which had participated in the

original events of 1917 and was now moored on the river Neva.

> The searchlights of the battleship 'Aurora' [...] backlit the building, so that it seemed to become transparent, melting in light. Then, together with the searchlights in the Square, they shifted to a spot on top of the Palace where a huge red banner was lifted, now flooded with light, and in the windows of the Palace, red lights flashed on.[30]

The end, like the beginning, attempted once more to embed the representation of the event in its original context, in order to erase the boundaries between theatrical fiction and everyday reality as far as possible. After the defeat of Kerensky, the spotlight was once again directed at the red flag flying at the top of the Palace, accompanied by a fireworks display. The performance ended with singing and a festive procession by the actors, which the audience was invited to join.

The narrative, too, featured an equally naive and manicheistic structure as that of *The Lion of Flanders* and other forms of political theatre from the 1920s and 1930s. The two stages in the set design reflected the dramatist's choice. Facing the group of 'Whites' on one stage – which included Kerensky and his supporters, members of the transitional

12. Vsevolod Meyerhold, Earth Rampant *(Sergey Tretyakov), 1923.*
[Braun, Meyerhold: a Revolution in Theatre*]*

13. Vsevolod Meyerhold, Commander of the Second Army *(Ilya Selvinsky), 1929.*
[Braun, Meyerhold: a Revolution in Theatre*]*

30 Fischer-Lichte, *Theatre, Sacrifice, Ritual,* 113.

government, landowners, bankers, and soldiers of the White Army – stood the workers, women, children and mutilated soldiers of the proletariat on the other stage. The dichotomy was radical. No gray zones existed, and the narrative consisted of a series of partial victories that ultimately resulted in the grand finale where the conclusive victory of the Red Army was celebrated.

Of particular note is the fact that Fischer-Lichte detects a *messianic* element in the Petrograd spectacle. Just as in the well-known scenes from medieval mystery plays, in which the damned souls in hell implore the actor representing Christ to help them, the group of women, children and the wounded on the square pray to the Red stage for help. First, the performers begin to sing the International, after which more and more voices crying for Lenin are heard, and finally, on an elevated platform, the familiar silhouette of a man in a long coat appears, encouraging the workers to take up arms against their oppressors.[31]

This narrative of violent confrontation between two groups, transforming oppression into the festive victory of the oppressed, was visually translated onto the two stages. They were each divided into several platforms of different heights, and connected by a bridge. On this bridge, the first clash between the White and the Red groups took place. Subsequently, the scene of the action shifted to the Winter Palace itself. For this shift, a corridor running through the crowd was used, and brought the action – both the performers and their military vehicles – up close.

As may be evident from this discussion, socio-theatrical events such as *The Storming of the Winter Palace* are not only remarkable on account of their size, but also because of their strong link to a specific political and social context. This context is no longer a theatrical 'setting' in the traditional sense of the word. Telling details such as the role of the carillon in the Antwerp performance of *The Lion of Flanders*, or that of the battleship Aurora in the Saint Petersburg spectacle,

show how this context is truly part and parcel of the performative event. In these cases, in fact, location, history and social context seem to have become 'performative agents' in themselves.

Choral Drama in the Weimar Republic

If Soviet agitprop loudly introduced Europe to mass spectacle, it also prompted other socialist and communist organizations to launch socio-theatrical events. Among these was the renowned workers' theatre movement in Germany, which employed various theatrical forms ranging from semi-professional theatre productions on political issues (for example, the Proletarian Theatre of Erwin Piscator) to *Arbeitersprechchöre* (workers' speech choirs), street performances of the 'living newspaper', and mass spectacles of political revues.[32]

The rise of the workers' speech choir can be traced through the cultural events organized by socialist societies before the First World War. These evenings, involving singing and recitation, were in turn subject to impulses from the German youth movement, and especially from the *Wandervogel* movement. For example, the *Proletarische Feierstunden* or 'proletarian hours of festive joy', organized on Sundays in Berlin and in other German cities just after the First World War by departments of the *Unabhängiger Sozialdemokratische Partei* (Independent Social-Democratic Party, USPD), aimed to give a wider audience to certain highlights of bourgeois literature as well as to socialist songs. On the program of such evenings – taking place in Berlin's *Grosse Schauspielhaus* and attracting thousands of spectators – a performance of the International could easily be found alongside the poems of Goethe.[33]

From the 1920s onwards, this humanistic approach was considered little more than an ill-fated attempt to 'translate' bourgeois culture for the proletariat, and its promoters therefore began to search for authentic forms of 'proletarian culture'. Exclusively canonical poems from a privileged literary past

31 Fischer-Lichte, *Theatre, Sacrifice, Ritual*, 116.
32 Hoffmann and Hoffmann-Ostwald, *Deutsches Arbeitertheater 1918-1933*.
33 Clark, *Bruno Schönlank und die Arbeitersprechchorbewegung*, 72-84.

were no longer recited by the workers choirs. Instead, special texts were written for these mass spectacles and for the workers' choirs, which were referred to as *Chorspiele* (choral dramas).

The most eminent and prolific authors of such texts were Ernst Toller and Bruno Schönlank, though many others who sympathized with the socialist struggle also contributed one or more scripts. The list includes, for example, Karl Vogt *(Der Krieg, 1929)* and Albert Talhoff *(Totenmal,* 1930). The fact that professional authors committed themselves in this way to a form of theatrical practice chiefly produced by amateurs clearly demonstrates once again the hybrid character of socio-theatrical events.

Choral dramas such as *Der gespaltene Mensch* (The Divided Man) by Schönlank were staged by Karl Vogt, Vera Skoronel and Berthe Trümpy at the Berlin Volksbühne with a chorus numbering up to seventy performers.[34] At the opening of the 1925 International Workers' Olympics in Frankfurt, Auerbach's *Kampf um die Erde* (The Battle for Earth) was performed before an audience of 100,000.[35] Talhoff's plays, too, were produced in a specially designed *Chorische Bühne* (choral stage) in Munich.[36]

As in Soviet Russia, the belief that socio-theatrical events were both a contribution to a community and a product of that community began to emerge. Director Albert Florath described the chorus as an artistic tool 'that brings art from the masses through the masses to the masses' ('das Kunst aus der Masse durch die Masse für die Masse bringt').[37]

Early on, Germany produced a comprehensive body of theory about the genre of mass theatre. Writers of choral drama such as Karl Vogt documented their own practice and discussed the genre's potential in critical essays. Socialist organizations such as the *Reichsausschuß für sozialistische Bildungsarbeit* (Committee for Socialist Educational

34 Clark, *Bruno Schönlank und die Arbeitersprechchorbewegung*, 113-123; Toepfer, *Empire of Ecstacy*, 244.

35 *Festbuch zur Ersten Internationalen Arbeiter-Olympiade*, 57.

36 De Vleeschauwer, "Het spreeken bewegingskoor III", 172.

37 Schönlank, "Proletarische Sprechchöre", 180.

14. Bruno Schönlank, De Moloch, transl. by Marie W. Vos, Amsterdam, 1927.
[Antwerp, Erfgoedbibliotheek Hendrik Conscience]

15. Karl Vogt, Der Krieg: Ein Chorspiel, Berlin, 1929.
[Antwerp, Erfgoedbibliotheek Hendrik Conscience]

16. *Physical exercises at the First International Workers Olympiad, Frankfurt, 1925.*
[Bonn, Archiv der sozialen Demokratie der Friedrich-Ebert-Stiftung]

Work) organized conferences on choral drama, the first of which took place in March 1926.[38]

Several lecturers on elocution and speech training (*Sprechkunde*) at German colleges and universities were also closely involved in the debate. It was their ambition to use choral drama as an educational tool for language proficiency. The protagonists of this movement included Friedrich Karl Roedemeyer (Frankfurt), Richard Wittsack (Halle) and Vilma Monckeberg (Hamburg).[39]

As early as 1926 – when in Flanders, for example, the choral movement had yet to take off – Roedemeyer was already able to synthesize the main views arising from these debates in his thoroughly researched book *Vom Wesen des Sprech-Chores* (On the Essence of the Speech Choir), including an extensive bibliography.

The author adopted a primarily historical approach in order to achieve the most comprehensive view possible of choral drama as a literary phenomenon. Roedemeyer set out to discuss the use of the chorus in Greek dra-

ma (mostly tragedy), and in medieval Christian liturgy. He also had ample attention for literary rewritings of ancient choral songs, however, especially those found in German literature from the Baroque and Romantic periods.

Roedemeyer's differentiation of the speech choir from the singing choir would dominate European discussions of choral drama throughout the 1930s, including those taking place within the Catholic choral movement in Flanders. His argument was that choral drama had undergone its most significant phase of growth during the development of medieval drama out of liturgy. This occurred chiefly in the monastic schools of the ninth century, when Gregorian chant became the liturgical standard for most of Europe.[40]

One typical feature of Gregorian chant is the question and answer sequence (the antiphon or responsory) that is performed among subgroups of the chorus, or between the priest and the faithful. Coupled with the introduction of short snippets that were

38 Roedemeyer, *Vom Wesen des Sprech-Chores*, 59; Schönlank, "Proletarische Sprechchöre".
39 Funke, "Der Sprechchor als Kunstpädagogisches Mittel".
40 Roedemeyer, *Vom Wesen des Sprech-Chores*, 10-11, 21-22.

VOM WESEN
DES SPRECH-CHORES

VON

PROF. FRIEDRICH KARL ROEDEMEYER
UNIVERSITÄTSLEKTOR

ZWEITE AUFLAGE

IM BÄRENREITER-VERLAG ZU KASSEL
1 9 3 1

added to aid memorization of the music (tropes), all the necessary elements were in place to allow the musical structure to evolve in an increasingly narrative and theatrical direction. The chorus could thus escape its strictly musical role, and (again) start to function as a dramatic whole. It was precisely this *dramatic* character of choral recitation that would be rediscovered during the first half of the twentieth century.

Still, Roedemeyer's theory was character-ized by a fundamentally classicist approach. Despite the importance that he attributed to medieval drama, he continued to emphasize the influence of the Greek tragic chorus. With a statement that is strongly reminiscent of the renewed interest, from 1910 onwards, in the Graecophile opinions of Romantic poets such as Friedrich Hölderlin (especially following Norbert von Hellingrath's dis-covery of new documents from Hölderlin's literary legacy), Roedemeyer claimed that all products of western culture, whether they consciously referred to Greece or not, were 'synthesized' by the Greek model ('jener

Synthesis alles Morgenländischen im Grie-chischen').[41]

The author took a very critical stance towards contemporary choral performance practices. He distinguished two key issues: first, the attempts to produce a modern staging solution to the problem of choral interventions in historical dramatic texts (such as the Greek tragedies, the baroque dramas or even later plays such as Friedrich Schiller's *Die Braut von Messina* [The Bride of Messina]); and second, the emergence of new choral dramas written by contemporary authors.

In Roedemeyer's eyes, the first of these issues held no potential for artistic success whatsoever. He also found numerous faults with the second issue, though he did seem at least to recognize its artistic potential. Despite his expression of admiration for the chorus *movements* in the large-scale pro-ductions of Sophocles' tragedies designed by Max Reinhardt, when it came to the recitation of the choral lyrics, Roedemeyer claimed that the absence of any musical score for these texts precluded their deeper understanding (let alone staging). 'There is no solution for the staging of Greek drama when it comes to the chorus.'[42]

In conclusion it should be noted that Roedemeyer even paid attention to the ideological diversity of choral drama. Still, he condemned the dichotomy between 'pro-letarian' and 'bourgeois' speech choirs that was in vogue within the socialist movement. For an author like Schönlank, on the other hand, that distinction had made it possible to distinguish the new practice of choral drama from the traditional bourgeois pastime of poetry readings:

> The movement of bourgeois choral dra-mas suffers from the fact that it is not sup-ported by an emotional world sufficiently compelling to generate a common experi-ence, and so remains purely artistic.[43]

Although Roedemeyer was evidently look-ing for a more generic definition of choral

41 Ibid., 23.
42 Roedemeyer, *Vom Wesen des
    Sprech-Chores*, 35.
43 Schönlank, "Proletarische
    Sprechchöre", 180.

drama, independent of the ideological choices made by Schönlank and his colleagues (Roedemeyer himself would later play an important role in the Nazi party), he did make a precise distinction between discussions about the usefulness of choral dramas in secular contexts (such as political movements) and within the Protestant and the Catholic contexts.

Such ideological diversity was swiftly curtailed in 1930s Germany, and the increasing censorship of all political tendencies other than National Socialism would also put an end to choral drama. This is also illustrated by the fate of a related phenomenon, namely the German open-air theatre movement. Like choral drama, it had been enjoying increasing popularity during the first decades of the twentieth century. From 1926 onwards, the Catholic communist Wilhelm Karl Gerst had tried to organize this movement by creating of a series of associations, and by devising new forms of mass open-air theatre.[44]

At the end of 1932, the *Reichsbund zur Förderung der Freilichtspiele* (Reich League for the Promotion of Open-air Theatre) was founded. The list of authors that would contribute to the project included well-known socialist writers of choral drama such as Ernst Toller and Bruno Schönlank.

Following the NSDAP coup, however, the League was replaced by the *Reichsbund der deutschen Freilicht- und Volksschauspiele* (Reich League for German Open-air Theatre and Folk Drama), an organization firmly controlled by the National Socialists. Authors such as Toller disappeared from the list of preferred authors. Gerst still played a prominent role in the new organization, though, and this would result in the construction of countless new open-air theatres (or *Thing-stätte*) in Germany.

The new kind of mass theatre that he originally had in mind, however, became restricted to a single very specific genre: the *Thingspiel*, a socio-theatrical event in which hundreds or even thousands of performers participated in the re-creation of an episode from recent political history, and which invariably ended with a tribute to Germany's contemporary 'resurrection'. After the movement's swift growth and numerous productions in the early 1930s, the *Thingspiel* was abruptly put aside, and eventually terminated, by Reich Minister of Propaganda Joseph Goebbels.[45]

44 Fischer-Lichte, *Theatre, Sacrifice, Ritual*, 126-127.

45 Ibid., 122-158; Reichl, *Das Thing-spiel*.

Ideological Diversity and the Question of Technique

The next section will discuss a conspicuous aspect of socio-theatricality, which already emerged from certain contexts discussed above, such as German choral drama: its ideological ambiguity. In the case of the Low Countries, which will be the central topic of the rest of this book, the ambiguity is even stronger.

After 1920, socio-theatricality exploded in Europe. It soon surpassed the predominantly socialist context in which it had originated, and was even adopted by anti-modern movements such as Catholic Action. In the case of Flanders, this was a highly remarkable phenomenon. Agitprop theatre was introduced from the Netherlands and Germany, but was soon dominated by Catholic and pro-Flemish groups.

The ideological heterogeneity is striking. How was it possible that the theatrical form of mass spectacle could be injected with such diverse ideological content? In this section, which stands apart from the rest of the book because of its theoretical (rather than strictly historical) orientation, I wish to reflect briefly on the philosophical topic of ideological diversity and *Gemeinschaft* (community).

Socialists believed that mass spectacle was ideal for expressing the new socialist community, while the Catholic movement, which had gone through a phase of rejuvenation following the encyclical *Rerum Novarum* (1891), insisted that an authentic mass spectacle could only be produced by a community of the faithful. At the same time, historical mass spectacles, featuring a strong nationalist aspect, were expressing an idealized image of the national or folk community. In the ideologically contested landscape of the interwar period, opposite groups laid claim to socio-theatrical phenomena.

The common explanation of this issue is that socio-theatricality was little more than a technique, which could be appropriated and deployed by any group. Yet this contradicts a deeply ingrained premise of Critical Theory

19. The Heidelberg Thingstatte *(2010).*

(which was foundational for the field of cultural studies), namely the methodological principle concerning the relationship between technology and ideology. This was discussed in detail in the writings of the Frankfurt School, and would eventually be labelled 'technological determinism' in the context of media studies after Marshall McLuhan.

The assumption that human thought and technology are intimately linked has its roots in a particular group of theories about literature and art, all of which date from the early twentieth century. These theories emphasize the *construction* of the artwork, and are exemplified in Russian Formalism (in the writings of Viktor Shklovsky), in Bertolt Brecht's theory of epic theatre, and in Constructivism.

Each of these approaches held that art consists of a series of 'tricks' that unsettle the reader's or spectator's daily perception of his or her environment. Shklovsky argued that a literary author did not aim to provide an adequate representation of the world. On the contrary, he explicitly intended to make it difficult for the reader to situate the events of the story in his or her familiar conception of reality. The reader must make an effort to

20. *Leni Riefenstahl,* Triumph des Willens (screenshot)*, 1935.*

which bring it into existence. The expression has its roots in a criticism made by Chekhov during a rehearsal of *The Seagull* at the Moscow Art Theatre. When an actor told him that the production would include realistic sound effects of croaking frogs and barking dogs, 'because that is real', Chekhov is said to have replied: 'The stage is art ... The stage requires a certain conditionality (*uslownost*). You have no fourth wall.'[47]

It is precisely in this process of defamiliarization or distancing that the value of the artistic medium lies – the form and content of a work of art become seamlessly fused. Depending on the technique an author or artist chooses, the field of meanings that his or her work can evoke is then either expanded or reduced. The missing link between form and content is the key expression *experience*. Certain forms provide a specific artistic experience and can therefore address only a specific semantic field. Classical literary forms create one kind of experience, while avant-garde forms address another.

Apart from Shklovsky's writings, the 1936 essay by Walter Benjamin on 'Das Kunstwerk im Zeitalter seiner mechanischen Reproduzierbarkeit' ('The Work of Art in the Age of Mechanical Reproduction') has an important place within Formalist aesthetic theory. In it, he took a radical stance to the interdependence of artistic technique and meaning. On the basis of the works of art produced in the contexts of fascism and communism, Benjamin drew a strict distinction between the aesthetic outlooks of the two ideologies. In the case of fascism, he examined elements such as the cult of the Führer, the choreographed mass meetings, and the filmed registrations (e.g., *Triumph of the Will* by Leni Riefenstahl). In the case of communism, mass meetings also played a role, but here they bore a revolutionary significance. Furthermore, he discussed the first products of the new collective experiments in art production, e.g., Asja Lacis' proletarian youth theatre, based on children's aesthetic 'activation', or novels such as Sergei Tretyakov's *Feld-Herren* (Lords of the Field), which had

recognize his own picture of reality in the distorting literary mirror.

> We see the object as though it were enveloped in a sack. We know what it is by its configuration, but we see only its silhouette. The object, perceived thus in the manner of prose perception, fades [...]. And so life is reckoned as nothing. Habitualization devours works, clothes, furniture, one's wife, and the fear of war. [...] And art exists that one may recover the sensation of life; it exists to make one feel things, to make the stone stony. The purpose of art is to impart the sensation of things as they are perceived and not as they are known.[46]

In response to Shklovsky's theory, and others, Soviet avant-garde theatre directors such as Vsevolod Meyerhold began to underline the formalistic aspects of their practice. Meyerhold was the first to draw attention to the 'theatricality of the theatre'. He called this 'conditional theatre' (*uslowny teatr*), or theatre that emphasizes the (artificial) conditions

46 Shklovsky, "Art as a Technique",
    22-26.
47 Chekhov quoted in Bochow,
    *Das Theater Meyerholds und die
    Biomechanik*, 21-23.

been written during a stay at a Soviet collective farm, or *kolkhoz*.

For Benjamin, the *technical* gap separating fascism from communism was identical to the gap in *ideological content*. The technical distinction was seen as a foundation for the ideological. Communism employed a higher artistic-technical ingenuity, because the collective was activated as a group that simultaneously produced and consumed art, while fascism merely wanted to 'control' the collective using a few brilliant directors.

Benjamin's well-known conclusion was that fascism aestheticized politics, while communism would politicize art. We can say that Benjamin's belief in the boundless possibilities of artistic technique was naive, in a sense. Like so many of his contemporaries, he had been intimidated by the technological impact of the First World War, by the advance of urbanization and the ubiquitous techno-economic system, expressed through mass media, public transportation and new architecture. In short, by the culture of modernism.

Concerning socio-theatrical phenomena, contemporary authors such as Susan Buck-Morss and Slavoj Žižek draw a sharp line between the mass spectacles of fascism and those of communism, just as Benjamin did.[48]

For example, in their discussion of *The Storming of the Winter Palace*, discussed above, they note that many of the players and spectators had themselves taken part in the original events (since the cast consisted mainly of sailors, Red Army soldiers, and students). Moreover, during the rehearsal period and the performance itself, the war against the White Army was still raging in the vicinity of Saint Petersburg. Reporting on the event, one writer noted that the Russian Revolution would be remembered as a series of brutal and bloody events while, simultaneously, 'all of Russia was acting'.

For Žižek, this was as an authentic realization of the Wagnerian total work of art (*Gesamtkunstwerk*) which enables a community to discover itself in the image created by the artwork they are then participating in. (The idea of a community staging itself through mass spectacle had already emerged in several of the events discussed above.) In Wagner's case, it was an idealized community of intellectual and wealthy art lovers, who would gather for a special festive occasion in a specially designed space – i.e., the Bayreuth *Festspielhaus*.

Žižek suggests that the Soviet community of amateur performers – workers, soldiers and students – actually comes much closer to an authentic *Gesamtkunstwerk*. The body of performers almost coincided with the body of characters they wished to represent, in that there were only small differences between their actual roles in the revolutionary events and the 'roles' they played in the mass spectacle. The coincidence of the community with itself, the confrontation of the community with its own image, was realized as literally as possible. This was done for *technical* reasons: in contrast to the hierarchical mass spectacles produced by the National Socialists (particularly the monumental Nuremberg party rallies), the Soviet mass works of art were

48 Žižek, "Heiner Müller Out of Joint", 47-49; Buck-Morss, *Dreamworld and Catastrophe*, 144.

effectively created by the masses. The collective consults with itself, and directs itself.

Using this theoretical detour, it is now possible to explore the problem mentioned at the beginning of this chapter in more detail. All three ideological tendencies that made use of socio-theatrical events between the wars in Flanders and the Netherlands apparently had a sufficiently large *ideological overlap* to be able to employ identical artistic and technical resources. This ideological overlap was situated primarily at the level of collectivism and the community. As pointed out before, the socialists wanted to promote the proletarian community through mass theatre, while the Catholic movement continually emphasized the resurgence of an authentic community of faith, and the nationalists strove for a close-knit national community.

Socio-theatricality was first and foremost an expression of the interwar mass movements, but it was also a medium through which the masses could begin to identify themselves as a collective. The strong formal parallels between events from such diverse ideological backgrounds – ranging from revolutionary communism in Soviet Russia to the militant Catholic movement in Western Europe – demonstrate how these movements had significantly more in common than initially meets the eye.

Mass Spectacle and Public Space

Apart from the social dimension of the theatrical event, and the ideological ambiguity of certain forms of mass theatre, a third conspicuous aspect of the *Lion of Flanders* performance introduced above was its relation to public space. In the following section, this aspect will be analysed through the ideas of two important reformers from Germany (Georg Fuchs) and Flanders (Jan Oscar de Gruyter).

In some way, choral drama and mass spectacle served to artificially *create* a community, fulfilling that typically modern ambition to control not only the physical but also the social. But how? Several examples are found in the overview of socio-theatrical events in Europe, above. Of crucial importance was the idea that the masses – both the collective represented by the chorus and the mass audience – would fill and 'dominate' the public space.

This idea of the particular relationship between public space and the theatrical event can be traced back to an earlier movement in theatre reform, namely, that of open-air theatre and community art.

At the end of the nineteenth and the beginning of the twentieth century, a number of artists emerged who denounced the prevailing literary theatre as undemocratic and as conflicting with the essence of theatre as a community experience. Their impetus was demophilic: they viewed theatre as a 'feast', a cultic ritual in which the individual spectator undergoes a metamorphosis and becomes a 'transindividual' human being. The people, not the individual, is seen as the cornerstone of society.[49]

Long before the dramatic text would be relegated to the margins of the theatrical event by the post-dramatic theatre of the 1970s and 1980s, a number of theatre makers were already advocating a break from purely text-based and psychological-realist theatre, such as Adolphe Appia, Georg Fuchs, Max Reinhardt, Edward Gordon Craig, Vsevolod Meyerhold, Alexander Tairov and Jacques Copeau.

In their vision of a future theatre, the distance between spectators and performers would be drastically reduced and the text largely abandoned in favour of rhythm and movement. As Fuchs writes in *Die Schaubühne der Zukunft* (The Theatre of the Future, 1905): 'The drama is possible without a word and without a sound, without a stage and without decorations, purely as a rhythmic movement of the human body.'[50]

49 Fischer-Lichte, *Kurze Geschichte des deutschen theaters*, 274.
50 Fuchs, *Die Schaubühne der Zukunft*, 41.

Re-theatricalizing the Theatre

Fuchs holds that the theatre should depart from its role as Guckkastenbühne or 'viewing box theatre', which is crammed with theatrical machinery and ingenious techniques for imitating reality as closely as possible.

> The development of the conventional theatre itself has proven to us that the whole proscenium stage, together with the wings and the soffits, together with the panorama views and set pieces [...] stands in the way of any real development of modern art. Therefore: away with the flies! Away with the spotlights![51]

The theatre of the fourth wall, which has as its premise the complete separation of performers from spectators, stands in the way of an authentic theatrical experience. In contrast, Fuchs argues that the theatre should be a feast in which performers and spectators participate equally. He calls for an event that unites both agents in a 'great, intoxicating upheaval'. The contemporary literary theatre can never be a feast, because it is based around the individual spectator enjoying the spectacle in a darkened auditorium, isolated from the other spectators. Fuchs has a completely different vision in mind, which Fischer-Lichte traces back to the philosophy of Friedrich Nietzsche. Fuchs sees the process of individuation as the root of all evil, a process which must be broken in order to restore the lost primordial unity of nature. This unity can never be experienced by the individual, since it requires the rare event of a mass of people commonly sharing a passion.[52]

For Fuchs, the Passion Play in Oberammergau (Bavaria), which was performed every decade, was therefore a good example of how such a theatrical feast might be manifested. There was another motive for his advocacy of a theatre in which thousands of spectators might simultaneously participate: the literary theatre was too expensive, excluding all but a small elite from the artistically significant events taking place on the stage.[53]

51 Ibid., 33, 38-39.

52 Fischer-Lichte, *Kurze Geschichte des deutschen Theaters*, 273-274.

53 Fuchs, *Die Sezession in der dramatischen Kunst und das Volksfestspiel*, 78.

22. Georges Moynet, Trucs et décors: La Machinerie théâtrale, *Paris, 1893.*
[Collection F. Peeters]

23.Georg Fuchs, Die Schaubühne der
Zukunft, Berlin, 1905.

24. Jozef Simons, Naar Oberammergau, Tongerlo, 1933.
[Collection T. Crombez]

25. Advertisement for the Ober-
ammergau Passion Play of 1930 in
Tooneelgids, 15 July 1930.
[Leuven, KADOC-KU Leuven]

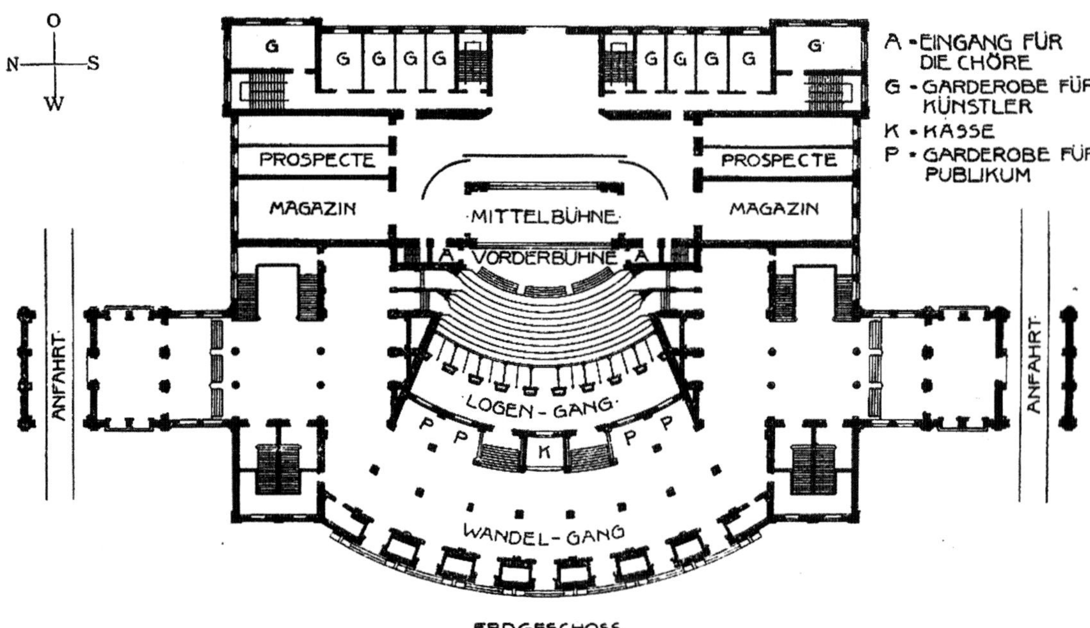

O
N S
W
A - EINGANG FÜR
DIE CHÖRE
G - GARDEROBE FÜR
KÜNSTLER
K - KASSE
P - GARDEROBE FÜR
PUBLIKUM
G
PROSPECTE
MAGAZIN
MITTELBÜHNE
PROSPECTE
MAGAZIN
A · VORDERBÜHNE · A
ANFAHRT
ANFAHRT
LOGEN - GANG
P P K P P
WANDEL - GANG
ERDGESCHOSS

jozef simons
Naar
Oberammergau

J N
R J
OBERAMMERGAUER
PASSIONSSPIEL

26. Photographs of the 1930
Oberammergau Passion Play from the
archives of Jozef Boon.
[Leuven, KADOC-KU Leuven]

As an architectural model, the Greek amphitheatre remained the ultimate venue for this kind of event. Yet Fuchs was aware that the German climate would render such an open-air theatre unplayable for most of the year, so he preferred the option of a *Doppel-Amphitheater* with 1500 seats.[54] As an eloquent appeal, Fuchs adds the phrase 'Retheatricalize the theatre' to the title page of his book *Die Revolution des Theaters* (The Revolution of the Theatre, 1909). As he maintains, the theatre will either move the masses or disappear into the artistic arrière-garde and prove its own superfluity.

54 Fuchs, *Die Schaubühne der Zukunft*, 45 (images: 64, 80).

27. *Photographs of the 1930 Ober-ammergau Passion Play from the archives of Jozef Boon.* [Leuven, KADOC-KU Leuven]

Jan Oscar de Gruyter's Open-Air Theatre Project

The story of Ghent director Jan Oscar de Gruyter and his various initiatives for producing open-air theatre in Flanders and the Netherlands leads back to Fuchs through the Russian avant-garde artist Alexander Tairov. De Gruyter, educated in Germanic languages at Ghent University, had been following the developments in contemporary European theatre closely. His own theatre practice was a moderate form of modernism, but from the testimony of Michel Van Vlaenderen, we know that he had read the works of Georg Fuchs and the key work of the Russian Constructivist director Tairov in its German translation (*Das entfesselte Theater*, 1927).[55]

Tairov endorses the idea of a synthetic theatre in which its various components come together organically, and where the text is no longer the first and most privileged layer of signification. Meanwhile, on the basis of his messianic vision of the role that theatre should fulfil in Flanders, De Gruyter would continue to defend the primacy of the dramatic source text. His efforts have therefore been called evolutionary rather than revolutionary, in contrast with the later and more explicitly modernist experiments of the Flemish Popular Theatre (which De Gruyter

helped to found) under Dutch director Johan de Meester Jr.

Tairov, for his part, was also influenced by Fuchs' work, and especially by *The Theatre of the Future* (1905). Its anti-intellectualism, in particular, appealed strongly to Tairov. Unlike Fuchs, however, Tairov did not feel that the spectator should participate. As Carlson notes: 'Tairov sees the spectator only as a witness to the art, in no way essential to it.'[56] De Gruyter, finally, saw theatre as the art form *par excellence* for allowing the Flemish people to become an integral part of modern European civilization. Public participation was out of the question. The mental feebleness of the Flemish spectator, though, was De Gruyter's primary reason for producing theatre, and he saw Flemish writers and theatre makers as 'the physicians of our people'.[57] Theatre, for De Gruyter, was much more than an artistic activity: it was a civilizing project.

Despite the differences that characterize this set of theatre makers, it is clear that views on theatre were going through dramatic shifts in much of Western Europe around the turn of the century. Community art; questioning the status of the text; experimenting with style and staging; rejecting the *théâtre à l'italienne* but also fourth-wall theatre – all of these issues were being taken up

55   The English translation (under the title *Notes of a Director*) would only be published in 1969.

56   Carlson, *Theories of the theater*, 358.

57   De Gruyter quoted in De Loore, *Dr. Jan Oskar de Gruyter (1885-1929)*, 12.

by a leading generation of young artists and scenographers.

As mentioned above, De Gruyter was no revolutionary. As a philologist, language was very important to him and the dramatic text would remain throughout his life the focal point upon which the theatrical spectacle was constructed. De Gruyter had developed a strategy for making the Flemish people 'healthy and strong' again, as though it were a kind of therapy. Theatre was a key instrument in his approach, with the explicit provision that the actors speak proper Dutch, untainted by Flemish accents or dialects. His inflexible attitude in this regard would cost him the sympathy of many pro-Flemish intellectuals and politicians. But De Gruyter was unmoved and kept his long-term vision in mind:

> This is again, after all, an issue of power. The focus of Dutch life is undeniably Holland. Hence, the current general colloquial language is a civilized form of the Dutch dialect [...]. Under the penalty of standing outside of general Dutch cultural life, we have to submit to that.[58]

In the spirit of Fuchs, De Gruyter saw open-air theatre as the ideal location for realizing this ideal form of a popular culture. He knew that the Antwerp city council was planning to construct an open-air theatre in one of the city's many parks. This would be the perfect opportunity to realize

> a genuine popular theatre, where the people, the *true* people of Antwerp, would enjoy the great creations of world literature free of charge, where the public – by following the drama, and nothing but the drama, in the most sober natural setting – would undergo a healing cure for the illness caused by the inartistic, downright ugly staging equipment that still burdens our theatres.[59]

Through De Gruyter's influence, Holland influenced not only the language of Flanders, but also the theatre. He was especially interested in Willem Royaards and Eduard Verkade, who had set up a remarkable collaboration on the occasion of the *Zomerspelen* (Summer Plays) in 1907 in the idyllic artistic village of Laren (North Holland). According to De Gruyter, this collaboration had demonstrated what modern drama could be.

The collaboration was remarkable because these two giants of Dutch theatre were in fact alien to each other in every respect. The introverted Verkade and the exuberant Royaards nevertheless combined their efforts in a historical performance of *Elkerlyc* (Everyman), conducted in the spirit of Edward Gordon Craig. Verkade played the character of Death, and Royaards that of Everyman. Even after more than a century, photos of the production do not look dated. Later, Verkade would go on to produce Joost van den Vondel's *Adam in ballingschap* (Adam in Exile, 1664) and Shakespeare's *Romeo and Juliet* (1597) with the Haghespelers at Valkenburg's open-air theatre. In the same theatre, De Gruyter would later put on Vondel's *Jozef in Dothan* (Joseph in Dothan, 1640) and Sophocles' *Philoctetes,*

28. Alexander Tairov, Das entfesselte Theater, *Berlin, 1923.*
[Leuven, KU Leuven, Centrale bibliotheek]

58 De Gruyter quoted in Peeters, *Jan Oscar de Gruyter en het Vlaamse Volkstoneel*, 195.

59 De Gruyter, *Dr. Jan Oskar de Gruyter*, 375.

29. Advertisement for Lanseloot ende Sanderyn *and* Elckerlic *by Eduard Verkade and Willem Royaards at the Laren summer plays, 1907. Published in* De Telegraaf, *14 July 1907.*

30. Eduard Verkade in Lanseloet, *1908. [Antwerp, Letterenhuis]*

in June 1921. Royaards, for his part, played *Oedipus* in Sonsbeek Park in Arnhem.

Arguably, De Gruyter never directed a true mass spectacle, although some of his open-air shows attracted a great crowd. Among these, his performance of *Philoctetes* with the *Vlaamse Vereniging voor Toneel- en Voordrachtkunst* (Flemish Society for Theatre and Recitation) on 22 August 1909 in Sint-Martens-Latem is particularly memorable.[60]

But it was especially as the leader of the Flemish Popular Theatre, during its second season (1921-1922), that he produced a number of extraordinarily successful open-air spectacles in the Netherlands, the extras for which were actually provided by the villages where the show was put on (Sluis, Domburg and Hulst). Jozef Goossenaerts, his secretary, friend and factotum of the company, remembers two outdoor performances of *Joseph in Dothan* that were particularly successful. During the performance on 16 August 1922 in Domburg, he writes, 'the au-

dience stormed over the fence and sat next to the players'. Earlier that year, too, on 15 June 1922 in Sluis, the Flemish Popular Theater apparently succeeded in realizing a form of community art using a mix of parade and open-air theatre.

And [the performers of] *Joseph* would go along the old, beautiful walls [...]. The mayor [...] had indeed taken measures so that an additional flock of sheep [...] passed through the town to the pasture where the play took place, and stayed there to graze while the performance lasted. Oskar took much pleasure in that, even to the extent that he, with his whole company, and all in makeup and costume, immediately followed the flock on its journey through the village. Sluis was in all respects a complete success.

The fiftieth performance of *Joseph in Dothan* in Sint-Martens-Latem on 1 July 1923, where De Gruyter had staged *Philoctetes* in 1909, is

60   Peeters, "22 augustus 1909. Openluchtvoorstelling van *Philoktetes* door de Vlaamsche Vereeniging voor Tooneel- en Voordrachtkunst te Sint-Martens-Latem", 568-573.

31. William Shakespeare, Romeo en Julia, *directed by Eduard Verkade in Frankendael, 1924.*
[Antwerp, Letterenhuis]

32. Sophocles, Philoctetes, *directed by J.O. De Gruyter, Sint-Martens-Latem, 1909, from the De Gruyter archives.*
[Antwerp, Letterenhuis]

33. Joost van den Vondel, Jozef in
Dothan, *directed by J.O. De Gruyter,
Valkenburg, 1921, from the De Gruyter
archives.*
[Antwerp, Letterenhuis]

*34. Herman Teirlinck and Jan Oscar
De Gruyter after the performance* Jozef
in Dothan, *directed by J.O. De Gruyter,
Sint-Martens-Latem, 1923, from the
De Gruyter archives.*
[Antwerp, Letterenhuis]

a benchmark in the history of Flemish open-air theatre.[61] On an iconic photograph we see how Jan Oscar De Gruyter is addressed by Herman Teirlinck after the performance. The revolutionary Teirlinck honours the evolutionary De Gruyter, and the changing of the guard is assured.[62]

Conquering Public Space

The fin de siècle ideas of Fuchs, De Gruyter and like-minded reformers proved to have lasting effects. During the 1920s and 1930s, the same question of how to activate the community through art was posed by the practitioners of mass spectacle. However, their answers would be different, and would move from specialized open-air theatres to public space conceived as a theatre.

In large public spaces, a director could not rely on the resources of the classic theatrical space: the deep stage with both proscenium stage and backstage, the framing provided by the proscenium arch, the decorative possibilities of theatrical scenery, and the dynamics provided by actors entering and exiting via the wings.

At the end of the nineteenth century, the 'Theatre Duke', as he was named, Georg II of Meiningen, had introduced the use of modular building blocks in set design in order to create height variation and produce more dynamic crowd scenes. In the early twentieth century, representatives of modernist theatre took this approach even further and radicalized it, this time for the sake of a non-realistic theatre concept.

Joris Diels, the director of the open-air play *The Lion of Flanders* discussed above, noted in an interview at the end of his career that many Flemish directors had taken their inspiration from the Russian director Alexander Tairov when they began to use the 'stepped stage' or *Treppenbühne*, as this kind of set design had become well known in Germany through the abstract staging of Leopold Jessner.[63]

A stage featuring a number of height levels made it possible to accentuate the visual dynamics of a group of extras, or a chorus in motion. It also required expert application, for example in the introduction of contrast between open and narrow spaces.

In the Antwerp marketplace, Diels divided the stage in two parts, which were then connected by a bridge, to allow for striking visual contrasts. Because of the constriction formed by the bridge, the movements of large groups were given special emphasis. It was a technique first introduced by Meiningen in 1875, for the staging of *Die Hermannschlacht* (Heinrich von Kleist). The Roman army had been marched onto

61 Peeters, *Jan Oscar de Gruyter en het Vlaamse Volkstoneel*, 417.
62 See the chapter 'The Machine on Stage'.
63 Van Kerkhoven and Mallems, "Joris Diels", 57.

35. Diagrams for the scenography of Jozef Boon, De Vuurberg, *designed by J. Lauwers, in* Toneelgids, *15 August 1930.*
[Leuven, KADOC-KU Leuven]

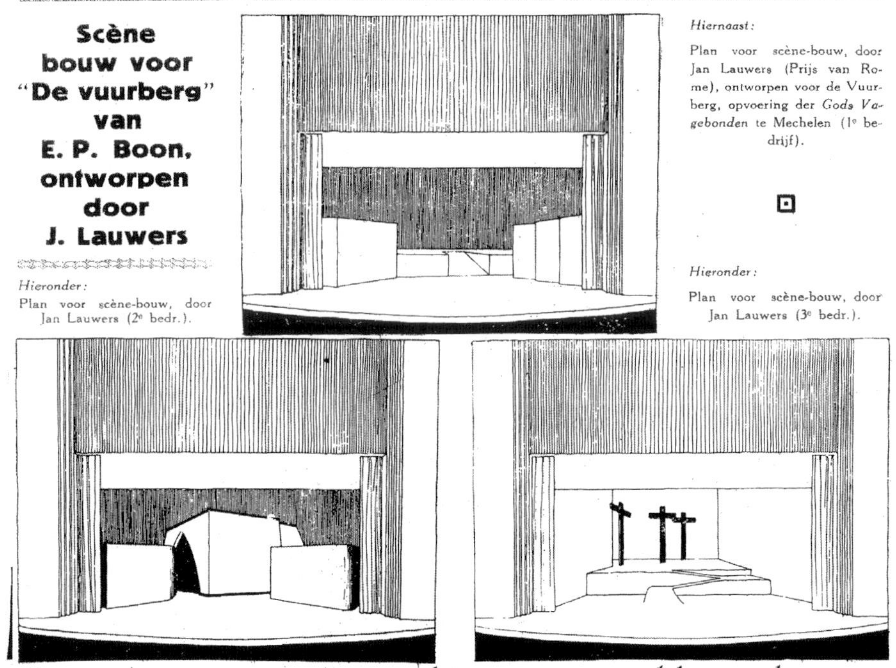

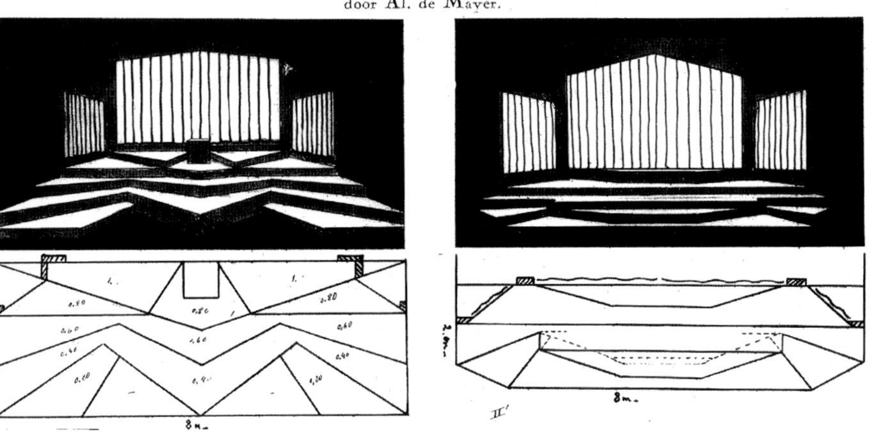

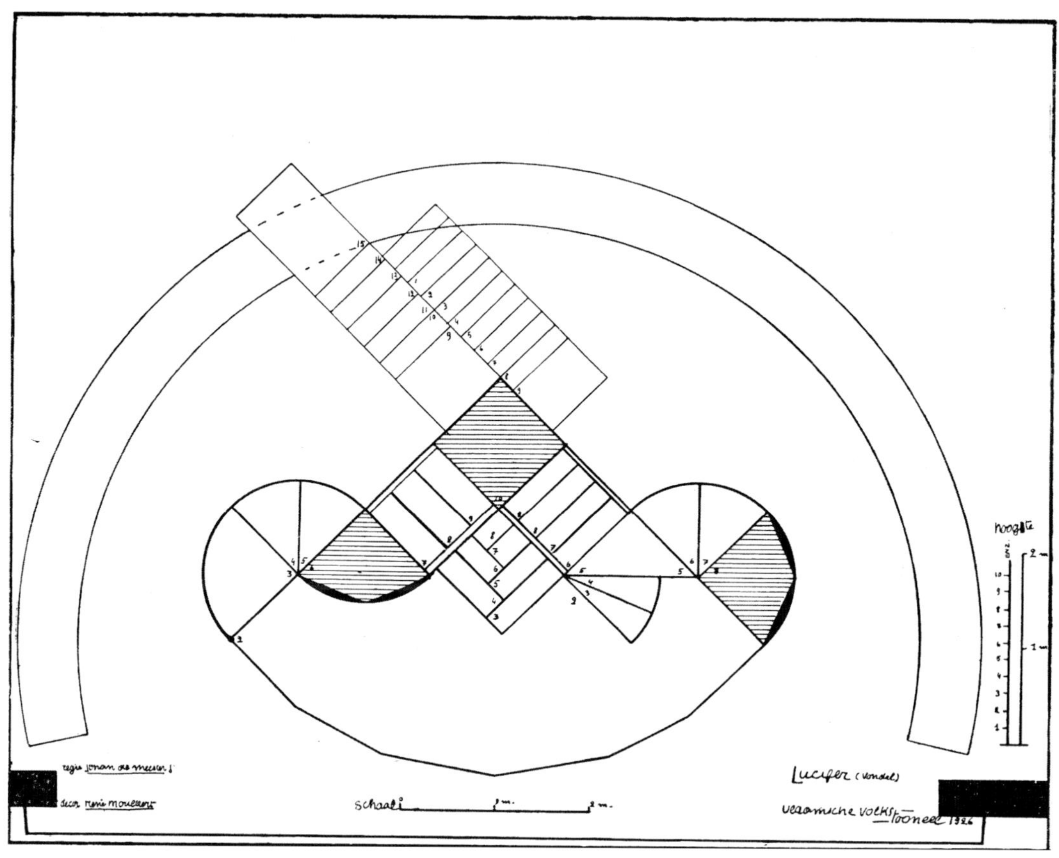

the front stage from the wings, and then made to disappear into the back through the small huts and narrow corridors of a German village, thus accentuating the size of the army using the constrained frame.[64]

While the director's filling of the visual space was crucial, music and sound also played an important role. In discussing *The Lion of Flanders*, we saw how particularly powerful the effect of the carillon had been. The soundscape of the spectacle was thus not generated by an external source, but by an instrument that was part of the urban context itself. Hence the striking observation that Diels' production had 'dominated the space of the marketplace both acoustically and optically'.[65]

This physical, visual and auditory 'domination' of space in socio-theatrical performances has been extensively analysed by Erika Fischer-Lichte using Max Reinhardt's work as an example. At the beginning of the twentieth century, Reinhardt staged a number of successful mass spectacles and open-air theatre shows in various places across Europe.

In 1910, Reinhardt directed Sophocles' *Oedipus Rex* (translated and adapted by Hugo von Hofmannsthal) for the arena stage of the redesigned *Musikfesthalle* in Munich, on the occasion of Georg Fuchs' *Volks-Festspiele* (Popular Theatre Festival).

In 1911, he would follow this up with a production of the *Oresteia* by Aeschylus. Both productions also came to the Schumann Circus in Berlin, and then went on tour in Europe. For the first Salzburg Festival in Austria in 1911, he again asked von Hofmannsthal to adapt a classical story, namely the late-medieval play *Jedermann* (Everyman). Another adaptation of medieval source material was *The Miracle*, written by Karl Vollmoeller and, after its German premiere in 1911, this was also performed in London (1912) and the United States of America (1924).

For each of these large-scale productions, Reinhardt assigned a central role to

64   Grube, *Geschichte der Meininger*, 83.

65   *Volk en Staat*, 11 July 1938.

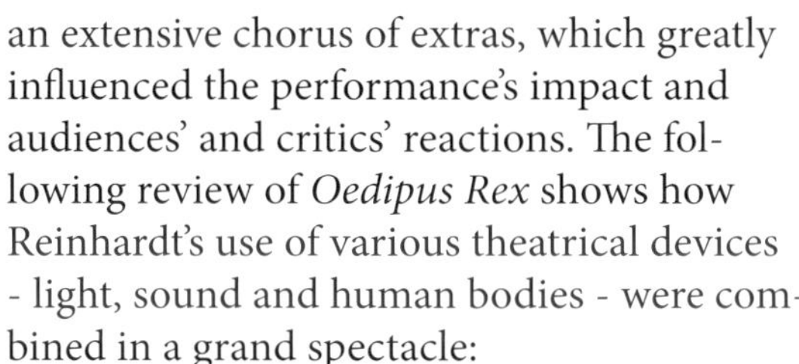

an extensive chorus of extras, which greatly influenced the performance's impact and audiences' and critics' reactions. The following review of *Oedipus Rex* shows how Reinhardt's use of various theatrical devices - light, sound and human bodies - were combined in a grand spectacle:

> Blue light falls in the ring that has become the orchestra: bell-like sounds clang, swell, voices moan, becoming louder, surging, and the people of Thebes swarm in through the central entrance opposite the built-up stage. Running, stampeding, with raised arms, calling, wailing; the space is filled with hundreds of them and their bare arms stretch to the sky.[66]

According to Fischer-Lichte's interpretation, the impact of such scenes on the audience was so high because the performers of the mass chorus constituted a collective, 'non-semiotic' body. Unlike other traditional components of the theatrical idiom of signs – dialogue, facial expressions, body language, the visual codes of costumes and scenery, etc. – this group of hundreds of performers was an overwhelming physical and energetic entity. The frantically moving chorus broke through the fourth wall, crossing the boundary between stage and auditorium, and thus generated an energy that

filled the whole room. 'The energy emanating from the performers' bodies seemed to circulate in the space, infect the spectators and energize them.'[67]

To some, the dominant physical presence of the chorus appeared not only overwhelming but even intimidating.

> [The performers] used their bodies in order to dominate and occupy the space. In doing so, they demanded the full attention of the spectators, forcing them to direct their attention to their bodies – not to the semiotic qualities of their bodies, i.e., not to their bodies as texts composed of signs telling a story or revealing a particular psychology which must be deciphered by the spectators. Rather, the attention of the spectator was drawn to the phenomenal bodies of the performers, attracted in particular by the energy that seemed to emanate from them, pour into the space and spread and circulate among the spectators.[68]

The 'conquest' of a public space by the impressive physical presence of a large chorus, then, was a crucial characteristic of mass theatre, together with its social context and the closely-knit integration of ideological content.

66 Norbert Falk quoted and translated in Fischer-Lichte, *Theatre, Sacrifice, Ritual*, 51.
67 Fischer-Lichte, *Theatre, Sacrifice, Ritual*, 62.
68 Ibid., 62-63.

Mapping Mass Spectacle in Flanders and the Netherlands

Ad van der Logt & Thomas Crombez

Mass theatre was a popular expression of 'community art' in many European countries around 1900. Theatre visionaries focused on ever larger groups for the purposes of spectacle and entertainment (e.g., in the case of Max Reinhardt) as well as for creating political agitation.

With regard to the Low Countries, the new trend of socio-theatrical events was imported from Germany and Russia via the socialist movement. There, workers' choirs (both singing and speech choirs) had quickly risen in favour.

With regard to the Low Countries, it is especially interesting to observe how the mass theatre phenomenon displayed a high ideological heterogeneity. The following sections will explore this diversity through a thorough overview of the main ideological settings in which socio-theatrical events were organized.

In the Netherlands, choral drama and mass spectacle mainly took place in socialist and communist circles. Dutch translations of German texts by Bruno Schönlank were published by the *Arbeiders Jeugd Centrale* (Young Workers' Centre, AJC). But mass theatre was also adopted by the Catholic modernization movement known as the *Graalbeweging* (Grail movement), as well as by certain Protestant groups.

In Flanders, some socialist choral dramas were written by Daan Boens, including the mass spectacle *Koning Arbeid* (King Labour), which was staged during the Labour Day celebrations of 1932 at the Vooruit in Ghent, directed by Michel van Vlaenderen. Eight hundred participants from numerous amateur groups and socialist youth groups were involved in this production. The second performance, in the Ghent velodrome, was watched by more than 6,000 spectators.[1]

It was Flemish Catholicism in particular, though, that would soon appropriate the socialist idea of lay theatre and choral training. Their spokesmen defended the modernization of Catholicism, which was at the same time traditionalist and radically contemporary. Nationalist movements, too, were quick to realize that agitprop-esque theatrical forms were an excellent means of mobilizing the masses.

In the following sections, the case of the Netherlands will be discussed first. We will situate socio-theatrical events in socialist, communist, national socialist and Catholic circles. Next, socio-theatricality in Flanders will be analysed, first from the socialist and then from the Catholic perspective.

Socialist Lay Theatre in the Netherlands

Aside from the socio-theatrical activities of the Catholic Grail movement, Dutch choral drama and mass spectacle mainly took place in socialist and communist circles. Yet the attitude of the largest socialist party, namely the *Sociaal Democratische Arbeiderspartij* (Social Democratic Labour Party, SDAP), and in its wake the *Nederlands Verbond van Vakverenigingen* (Dutch Federation of Trade Unions, NVV), towards lay theatre can only be described as somewhat ambiguous.

On the one hand, neither organization had any wish to encourage the production of lewd plays in smoky town halls – a stereotype that clung persistently to the notion of 'popular theatre' at that time. The leadership

1. Ben Groeneveld practices Roland Holst's choral play De opstandelingen *(The Rebels).*
[Amsterdam, Internationaal Instituut voor Sociale Geschiedenis, Collectie AJC]

1   Mortelmans, "Hendrik de Man", 230-231.

2   *Arbeidersontwikkeling*, 13.

of the SDAP had high demands of socialist theatre. Dilettantism and theatrical folklore were banished. Following the example of the *Freie Volksbühne* in Germany, they envisioned a large, quasi-professional popular theatre company. Socialist worker-actors were expected to be paragons of discipline and virtuous conduct, and directors of workers' theatre groups were expected to imitate the social-realistic and naturalistic style of the bourgeois theatre, cleaned up where necessary.

On the other hand, however, both the SDAP and NVV were driven by the changing circumstances of the mid-1920s to reorient their struggle for the material improvement of labourers' lives. Once the eight-hour day had been enforced, a growing need to improve the spiritual life of the working classes became apparent.

> However, the task of proletarian development work is not only to contribute uniformly to the intellectual knowledge of the participants, but also to contribute to their social, spiritual and moral growth, to show them the way to a society of a higher social and spiritual structure [...]. That is why the artistic development of the workers is be taken up enthusiastically.[2]

Educating workers in a new culture tended to have the side effect of strengthening their class consciousness, and of protecting them from the temptations of capitalist mass culture. To that end, socialist leaders such as Koos Vorrink and Hendrik De Man began from a behaviourist model of education. If the sense of inferiority to bourgeois culture could be lifted, an elite of intellectuals and artists could teach the workers what constitutes good art and how to respond to it.

In the *Rapport Arbeidersontwikkeling* (Report on the Workers' Development), a 1924 SDAP and NVV publication, the labour movement was therefore characterized as a *cultural* movement. As a result, subsequent years saw the introduction of many new initiatives, such as the *Instituut voor Arbeidersontwikkeling* (Institute for the Development of Workers, IVAO), the public broadcaster VARA (*Vereniging van Arbeiders Radio Amateurs*, Association of Worker Radio Amateurs), the Workers' Sports Association, and the *Arbeiders Jeugd Centrale* (Young Workers' Centre, AJC).

In the early 1930s, a change in direction occurred when socialist artists were invited to develop a new workers' theatre, aimed especially at performances for festive occasions such as Labour Day.

Traditional Workers' Theatre in the Netherlands

Although the SDAP focused primarily on achieving its political and socio-economic aims, the workers' movement had a long history of forming artistic and cultural associations. In 1902, the *Bond van Arbeiders-Zangverenigingen* (Federation of Workers' Choir Societies) was founded in the Netherlands. In 1910, this example was followed by the Dutch Federation of Workers' Musical Societies, and in 1917 by the Federation of Workers' Theatre Societies.

According to the latter federation's periodical, *Het Arbeiders Tooneel* (The Workers' Theatre), which was printed between 1930 and 1936, the association united 107 distinct

2. Dramatic Club The Deed (Workers' Theatre Club of the SDAP) after the performance of Heijermans' *Allerzielen* (All Souls' Day). Uitgeest, 13-16 January 1932.
[Uitgeest, Beeldbank Historische Vereniging Oud Uitgeest; www.oudoudgeest.nl]

Author	Title (English)	Title (Dutch)	Performances
1. Herman Heijermans	*All Souls' Day*	*Allerzielen*	38
2. Herman Heijermans	*Trusting Our Fate to God*	*Op Hoop van Zegen*	27
3. William Hartley (Jaap van der Poll)	*It Has Been Written*	*Er staat geschreven*	24
4. Herman Heijermans	*Pray and Work*	*Ora et labora*	22
5. Herman Heijermans	*The Seventh Commandment*	*Het zevende gebod*	14
6. Arie Pleysier	*They Who Stayed Behind*	*Zij die nableven*	14
7. Herman Heijermans	*Links in the Chain*	*Schakels*	13
8. H. Kesnig	*Factory Workers*	*Fabrieksmenschen*	12
9. Maurice Rostand / Alfred Savoir	*The Man I Killed*	*Ik heb een mensch gedood*	12
10. Herman Heijermans	*The Girls*	*De meiden*	11

theatre groups. The editor in chief of *Het Arbeiders Tooneel*, Hessel Jongsma, taught his readers to choose popular contemporary plays (by Herman Heijermans, for example) and to stage them in the modern-realistic style of Jacques Copeau and Georges Pitoëff.

An analysis of the six volumes of *Het Arbeiderstooneel* yields the list above of the ten most-performed plays. Unsurprisingly, Heijermans dominates the list. Certain established names from contemporary drama are conspicuously absent, such as Jan Fabricius and Henrik Ibsen, and the majority of the dramatists whose work was performed did not become part of the dramatic canon. Plays such as these were performed during socialist meetings, in addition to *tableaux vivants*. On the evening of 1 May 1929, for example, performances of *Man and Superman* by G.B. Shaw and *De opgaande zon* (The Rising Sun)

3. The ten most-performed plays by the Federation of Workers' Theatre Societies, 1930-1936.

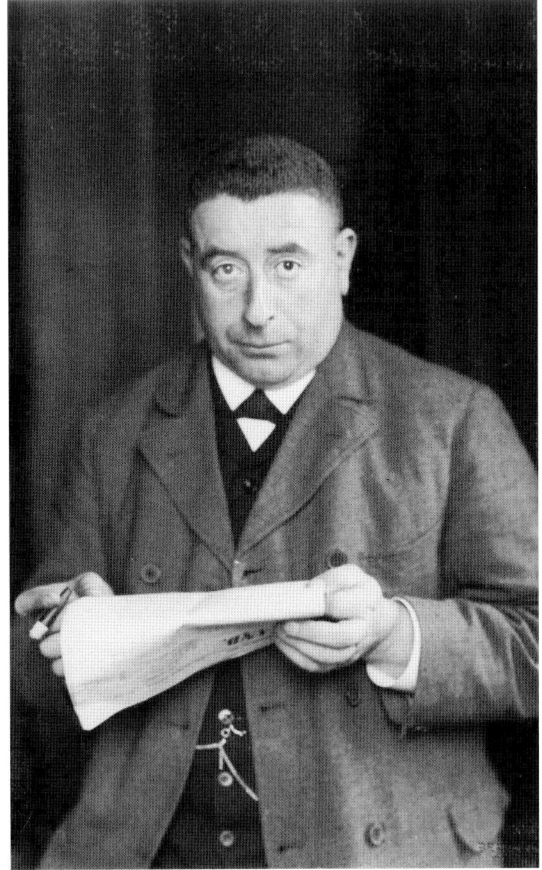

4. Title page of the magazine Het Arbeiderstooneel *(The Workers' Theatre), 1932.*
[Amsterdam, Internationaal Instituut voor Sociale Geschiedenis]

5. Herman Heijermans.
[The Hague, Letterkundig museum]

by Heijermans took place. Besides plays with a serious message, there were also comic revues and satires, performed solely for the purpose of entertaining the workers attending the meeting, or in order to ridicule political opponents.

The Development of Lay Theatre

During the interwar period, the three distinctive elements of social-democratic manifestations were drama, speeches by political leaders, and mass demonstrations. Rulof identified the following development:

> What had started as an experiment in lay theatre during the first years of the twentieth century evolved into an attempt not only to reform the theatre into a momentous event that would captivate large numbers of players and spectators, but also to design the manifestation itself as if it were a theatre production, fusing dance, speech, singing and acting into an organic whole.[3]

In the early 1930s, socialist lay theatre underwent a number of transformations, until old-fashioned naturalistic drama characterized by dialogue was replaced by speech and movement choirs. The impetus for such a radical change was prompted by the Amsterdam Federation of the SDAP's decision to hold the 1929 Labour Day celebrations at the Olympic stadium.

This experiment was also endorsed by party members who opposed the attempt of workers' theatre groups to follow the example set by professional theatre groups. They were convinced that subjects taken from bourgeois theatre bore no relation whatsoever to their target audience: the socialist working classes. They also believed that worker-actors had sufficient inherent acting qualities to allow them not to slavishly imitate professional actors.

The entertainment value of farces and satires, then, had to be exchanged for instructive pieces on the history of socialism and the labour movement. Socialists such as Kees Vorrink and Hendrik De Man considered the stage an excellent pedagogical tool for teaching the audience to rise up and participate in the fight for a better (socialist) future. On the subject of the large-scale Labour Day celebrations on 1 May, Rulof writes:

> The mobilization of the audience required an identification with the events on the stage or in the arena of the stadium. Since such identification was hampered by the breaks between the different episodes of an event, it was soon decided to model the mass manifestation itself as a play. The individual components of the May Day rally – the arrival of the participants, the opening speech, the songs, the great May speech, the May spectacle and the finale of singing the International together – were included as much as possible in the script of the May spectacle itself.[4]

Directors such as Albert van Dalsum, who directed the Expressionist socialist-inspired play *Gas I* by Georg Kaiser (with 250 extras from the AJC), also strove to eradicate the separation of the audience from the performers. This ambition was at odds with the experimental theatre of alienation that Brecht was pursuing, which implied that spectators ought to be *prevented* from identifying too intensely with the characters. In socialist mass spectacle, identification was precisely what was aimed for: the audience had to feel as if they were one with the socialist heroes of the past that symbolized the entire movement.

The characters in the play were therefore stripped of individuality and psychological motivation. They became one-dimensional, abstract symbols of social and political groups, such as 'the Capitalist', 'the Communist' and 'the Nazi', and, of course, 'the Socialist'. The event was a work of art in its entirety, in which dialogue alternated with choral passages as well as with mime and symbolism, and in which political parades would blend into dance and vice versa.

At both the local and the national level, young politicians with a background in the AJC took over a number of branches of the party during the early 1930s. It was this

3   Rulof, *Een leger van priesters voor een heilige zaak*, 199.

4   Ibid., 219-220.

group that played a major role in the May committees of the Amsterdam Federation, as well as in the *Cultuurraad* (Cultural Council) of the SDAP and NVV, founded in 1933. From his position as Council chairman, Vorrink would deeply influence the socialist artists who were commissioned to develop a new working-class theatre. Their inspiration came from the workers' theatre as it had developed in Germany after the First World War. If the starting point had been to spread bourgeois culture among the workers, now the ambitions had shifted to learning the workers how to argue their political position through 'acting out' a social problem on the stage. Socialist lay theatre was increasingly politicized under the influence of communist agitprop theatre.

The Council, in the meantime, focused especially on the May spectacles, which were performed with great enthusiasm from 1934. Hendrik De Man played a leading role in this development with his mass spectacle *Wir!*, which was put on at the 1932 Labour Day rally in Frankfurt by 2,000 performers, and would have its first (partial) performance in Switzerland and the Netherlands one year later. According to De Man, it was because socialist art was supposed to instil a sense of community that it was necessary to break down the separation between stage and auditorium.

Another important example was Martin Gleisner's *Rotes Lied* (Red Song, 1933), also a mass spectacle involving movement and speech choirs similar to *Wir!* After fleeing from Germany, Gleisner would design the May spectacle *Naar de Nieuwe Tijd* (Towards a New Age) with Marie Vos, Ben Groeneveld and Piet Tiggers.

To summarize these developments, Vorrink published the brochure *Feest-cultuur* (Festive Culture) in 1934, followed by the report *Stellingen Feestcultuur* (Propositions for a Festive Culture), in which he described the Cultural Council's activities between 1933 and 1936.

In *Het Arbeiders Tooneel,* articles by Jan Lemaire Jr. informed lay players about the genre of choral drama, which socialist groups had initially rejected because it did not allow individual players to excel. Groeneveld's production of *Masse Mensch* (Toller), however, had disproved this idea. Ideologically, the chorus was appropriate to workers' theatre because it emphasized the collective. In this sense, the *Bond van Arbeiders-Tooneelvereenigingen* (Federation of Workers' Theatre Societies) would follow the same path as the Communist League of Workers' Theatres in Germany.

It was not only the groups united by the Federation who were performing socialist theatre. In the AJC, young socialists were putting on plays and looked for new dramatic forms. They found them in lay theatre, which involved fewer rehearsals and the combination of singing, music, dance and dialogue, giving every member of the cast an opportunity to express themselves.

In his book *Lekenspel* (Lay Theatre), Groeneveld gives the following definition of his title topic:

> Lay theatre is the direct and spontaneously discovered expression of a concept or an emotion, unmediated by professional study, where the central concern is to give shape to the thoughts and feelings of a specific, more or less closed community. Lay theatre takes a non-artificial, candid, spontaneous and natural form.[5]

5   Groeneveld, *Lekenspel*, 5.

6. *Roland Holst's lay theatre play* Wij willen niet *(We Are not Willing, 1932).* [*The Hague, Beeldbank Nationaal Archief / Foto Spaarnestad*]

7. Georg Kaiser, Gas I *(1928), directed by Albert van Dalsum.*

The director and the performers had to focus on positive elements in the play, such as the sense of community, accepting responsibility, self-examination, and fostering character traits such as honesty, loyalty and sincerity.

The most prominent AJC lay theatre play was *Goudvreugde's ontwaken* (Goldjoy's Awakening), written by Marie W. Vos in 1924 and performed annually. The story is derived from the Edda, and tells the story of how Daybearer finds Goldjoy with the help of the ring Comradepower and the New Youth. He frees Goldjoy from her banishment, after which a new and better era begins.

At the end of the 1930s, *Goldjoy's Awakening* was replaced by *Dagdragers beproeving* (Daybearer's Ordeal), whose far less optimistic narrative testified to the worsening international situation.

In searching for a new style, the AJC also introduced the chorus, borrowed from the Proletkult movement in Soviet Russia through German examples. Perhaps the most impressive of these new choral dramas was *Moloch* by Bruno Schönlank, translated by Marie W. Vos and performed by Koos Vorrink and Line Tiggers during the SDAP's Easter Congress on 14 February 1925.

On another occasion, 250 AJC members were involved in the 1928 production of *Gas I* (Kaiser) by Albert van Dalsum. Members of the AJC also adapted the anti-war poem *Het slagveld* (The Battlefield) by Bram van Collem into a mass spectacle, which was published as *De soldaten* (The Soldiers) in 1927.

Labour Day Celebrations

The SDAP May spectacles from the 1930s, in particular, are prime examples of socialist mass spectacle in the Netherlands. After the First World War, the organizers returned to the familiar forms and elements that had been used before 1914. A brief welcome speech was followed by the singing of socialist songs, and a speaker gave a festive speech, which was then followed by music, declamation, lectures, and sometimes a play.

The term 'lay theatre' (*lekenspel*) was explicitly chosen by the socialists to distance themselves clearly from what was called 'amateur theatre' in the bourgeois world. The plays had a cultural-emancipatory goal: to emancipate the working classes from capitalist society, and to prepare a better, socialist society. Ultimately, this cultural-emancipatory goal was not achieved, because the party leaders made a political choice to fight *with* the bourgeoisie against their common enemies on the left and the right: communism and national socialism. Instead of separation, the AJC was forced to strive for integration.

Propaganda in the socialist choral dramas and mass spectacles was meant to be indirect in nature, as opposed to communist theatrical events. The viewers themselves were supposed to draw the right conclusions, rather than having them explained by the actors.

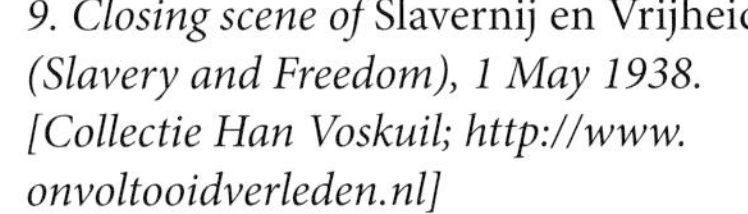

8. *Collaborators of the lay theatre play* Slavernij en Vrijheid *(Slavery and Freedom) written by Klaas Voskuil and Simon Carmiggelt, 1 May 1938. From left to right: director Paul Steenbergen, Mrs. and Mr. Diepenhorst (president of SDAP The Hague) and Klaas Voskuil. [Collectie Han Voskuil; http://www. onvoltooidverleden.nl]*

9. *Closing scene of* Slavernij en Vrijheid *(Slavery and Freedom), 1 May 1938. [Collectie Han Voskuil; http://www. onvoltooidverleden.nl]*

When, in 1921-1922, an atmosphere of crisis became dominant among the workers, the Amsterdam Federation of the SDAP concluded that the 1923 May festival should have a different character. In 1926, the Committee for the Reorganization of the May festival was installed, chaired by the Amsterdam politician Eliazer Polak. It concluded that the current interpretation of Labour Day failed to mobilize the workers. The proposed new structure clearly bore the stamp of AJC chairman Vorrink. In the brochure *De Meiroep* (The Call of May, 1926) Polak proposed a central manifestation featuring speech and movement choirs, plays, *tableaux vivants*, music and dance, in which the youth of the AJC in particular should play a major role.

In 1933, the May festival was finally realized in the form proposed by the Polak committee. It opened with standard bearers and a march by the AJC members. Speeches by party leaders figured as a transition to the cultural component, which included a mass spectacle or play. On the first occasion, this play, *Liberation* (Bevrijding), was composed from parts of *Wir!* (We!) by Hendrik De Man. It was this form that would predominate in the May spectacles from 1933

10. Henriette Roland Holst, De voorwaarden tot hernieuwing der dramatische kunst *(The Conditions for a
Renewal of Dramatic Art), Rotterdam,
1924.*
*[Kortrijk, KU Leuven, Campus Kortrijk,
Bibliotheek Humane Wetenschappen]*

until 1939, with titles such as *Naar de Nieuwe Tijd* (Towards the New Age, by Martin Gleisner); *Wij, Roode Valken* (We, Red Falcons, by Jo van de Walle) or *Van slavernij tot vrijheid* (From Slavery to Freedom, by Klaas Voskuil and Simon Carmiggelt).

The Reception of Socialist Mass Spectacle

From contemporary reviews, it is apparent that critics such as Menno ter Braak quickly recognized the characteristics of socialist mass spectacle. In his 1934 discussion of *Als jij het wil* (If You Want It) by Garmt Stuiveling, he remarked:

> Lay theatre, then, demands a certain dose of rhetoric; it is one of those forms of dramatic art that depends on declamation and speech choirs. As such the lay spectacle seems to me, in the shape that it has received from authors such as Henriette Roland Holst, Anthonie Donker and M.H.K. Franken (influenced especially by German Expressionism), to be a much more artificial product than the currently decaying genre of opera. In times past, Lucia di Lammermoor died with an aria on her lips, now we see that the conscience of the masses is swept from one extreme to another by the choirs, who attack each other in military fashion, wearing uniforms, with uniformed voices and uniformed ideas. Any connection to the choral songs of Greek tragedy, which Mrs Roland Holst likes to refer to, seems to be no more than a formal agreement. These modern chants are not spontaneous events, but experiments, deliberately modelled on individual declamation of the past.[6]

There are, however, a number of other elements that frequently return in socialist lay theatre: the struggle against capitalism, represented by socialdemocratic heroes of the past, who often fight in vain; the history of May Day; and the necessity of going to war against fascism and national socialism.

Besides the reviewers, socialist thinkers themselves were also trying to get to grips with the new genre. Just as in other countries, new theories were emerging alongside the new socio-theatrical practices. In 1924, Henriette Roland Holst published *De voorwaarden tot hernieuwing der dramatische kunst* (The Conditions for a Renewal of Dramatic Art), a work on theatrical reform that was strongly reminiscent of contemporary books such as *The Art of the Theatre* by Edward Gordon Craig (1911) or *Die Schaubühne der Zukunft* by Georg Fuchs (The Theatre of the Future, 1905).

Like Craig and Fuchs, Roland Holst attacked the commercial theatre of her time, which was ruled by convention and strove only for 'diversion, which means fleeing from the emptiness of their lives, coarse sensationalism, and sexual arousal'.[7] Like them – and one could add to this list the names of Adolphe Appia, Jacques Copeau, Vsevolod Meyerhold, Herman Teirlinck – she idealized the supposed 'popular theatre' of the Middle Ages, which was supposed to have been realized entirely for and by the community itself.

6   *Het Vaderland,* 2 May 1934.
7   Roland Holst-Van der Schalk, *De voorwaarden tot hernieuwing der dramatische kunst,* 200.

As Roland Holst saw it, the only chance to revive theatre as a 'community art' lay in the dramatic representations made by the oppressed classes themselves. They had perhaps not been initiated into classical bourgeois culture – and might even be considered 'factually cultureless' – but their increasing class consciousness allowed them to escape the disastrous tendencies of individualization and self-indulgence that had ruined bourgeois theatre.[8]

> We have reason to believe that community drama (either as an open-air spectacle or performed in small neighbourhood theatres by a few players) could be for the moving masses of this new era what the mystery plays were for the medieval masses: festive highlights in their lives, lovingly and carefully prepared, joyfully and solemnly celebrated, and gratefully remembered. In these performances, the masses would understand more thoroughly the greatness of their own striving, they would better realize their own ideals. As a great wind, the belief in their calling and in their power would blow through all the spaces of their collective consciousness.[9]

Over the next decade Roland Holst would work hard to actually realize her vision through her own work. *Kinderen van deze tijd* (Children of These Times) was written as a commissioned work for the *Vrijzinnig Christelijke Studenten Bond* (Liberal Christian Student Association), but – rather unusually – the author herself attended all rehearsals and continued to revise the text according to the performers' suggestions. In a letter to Hendrik De Man, she wrote that such productions offered special opportunities 'for the collective outpouring of inner movements, for collective purification and bonding'.[10]

Present-day historians such as Blockmans, who has re-evaluated socialist mass spectacles, conclude that the socialists did not quite succeed in their project.[11] This is partly because the leadership of the SDAP gradually came to occupy the position of the middle class in the political arena, and partly

because their intentions were not purely socialist, which made it possible for other parties, such as the *Nationaal-Socialistische Beweging* (National Socialist Movement, NSB), to copy them. The topics common to mass spectacles were subject to interpretation: community and solidarity, frugality, respect for nature, artistry and curiosity. Artistically, they lacked the originality and technical quality required for leaving a lasting impression. A third reason was the position of socialist culture. On the one hand, socialism ought to represent the struggle against capitalist domination, but on the other hand, the movement wished to elevate its cultural expression to the level of a bourgeois culture that despised modern cultural phenomena such as jazz music or nightclubs. In addition, socialist leaders underestimated the influence of the commercial entertainment industry.

Blockmans' verdict on mass spectacle is even more critical. The mass spectacles were naive and grotesque attempts to dramatize the emancipatory struggle of the working class, he wrote. The pathetically declaimed lyrics full of abstract themes, the shallowness of the dramatic action, and the accumulation of stereotypes and platitudes today seem laughable and amateurish.

Rulof, by contrast, considered these phenomena from the perspectives of cultural history and sociology. That a mass demonstration could be set up as a play, integrating the orator into the spectacle and abolishing the separation between actors and audience in order to mobilize the spectators for the socialist cause, was felt by Rulof to be a positive evolution. Yet he also noted that the performance of Maurits Dekker's May spectacle of 1939 had effectively undone much that had been achieved by the originally revolutionary forms of workers' theatre. Dekker's work symbolized a return to the workers' theatre of the past. Prominent features of lay theatre, such as dance, music, speech and movement choirs, had again been replaced by a mix of entertainment and education, in which the farcical element prevailed.[12]

8 Ibid., 277.
9 Ibid., 268.
10 Roland Holst quoted in Etty, *Liefde is heel het leven niet*, 504.
11 Blockmans, "Beziel tot hooger Leven!", 204-206.
12 Rulof, *Een leger van priesters voor een heilige zaak*, 219-222.

Communist Choral Drama and Mass Spectacle in the Netherlands

The communist equivalent of the socialist Federation of Workers' Theatre Societies was the *Arbeiders Theater Bond Holland* (Holland Workers' Theatre League, ATBH), an organization controlled by the Dutch Communist Party and modelled on the Proletkult movement that had arisen in the Soviet Union and Germany. Its chief aims were to realize agitprop theatre, which usually took the form of street theatre and intended to spread the Marxist-Leninist doctrine using agitation and propaganda. The brief texts called for immediate political action. Problems were represented in a direct and simplified manner, with songs and commentary explaining the performed events.

Agitprop troupes were not organized exclusively by the ATBH, but also by other political groups on the (far) left such as the *Onafhankelijke Socialistische Partij* (Independent Socialist Party, OSP) and the *Communistische Jeugdbond* (Communist Youth League, CJB).

During the early 1930s, the ATBH was divided into five districts, with more than thirty distinct agitprop groups. The Amsterdam district, for example, boasted eight groups, which were named *Alert*, *Ontwaakt* (Awake), *Maxim Gorky*, *Enthousiasme* (Enthusiasm), *W. Münzenberg*, *De Roode Vogels* (The Red Birds), *Heil Moskou* (Hail Moscow) and *Tribune Front*.

Agitprop spectacles gained popularity after 1930, and usually took place at the Sunday meetings of the *Vereeniging van Vrienden van de Sovjet Unie* (Association of Friends of the Soviet Union, VVSU). Such meetings usually began with a propagandist speech for the Soviet Union, followed by the screening of a Russian film and a montage of pro-revolution newsreels. Between these events came songs, declamation, dance, acrobatics or agitprop scenes. The scenes had diverse ambitions: to educate on political and economic developments from a Marxist perspective; to generate feelings of hostility towards class enemies through caricatures of political opponents; to reinforce proletarian solidarity among the workers; and to expand and strengthen the Communist party.

The first communist choral dramas were beginning to emerge by the end of the 1920s, and their main purpose was 'to represent the speeches and debate of the meeting in a clear and orderly fashion.'[13] The play usually ended with a call for organized struggle, or with the audience singing a revolutionary anthem.

The first choral dramas were rather static in form, and only after some time did individual players step forward to speak their parts, taking the role of protagonists. Agitprop groups consisted of young workers who wished to represent the current political issues on the stage, 'so that ordinary workers could directly recognize their own problems and discover a revolutionary perspective from which to solve the problems.'[14]

The first section of each agitprop scene was devoted to the exposition of the problem. Then followed the agitation section, and finally the propaganda. In the first part, the subject of the meeting was summarized, in order to excite the indignation of the workers in the second part by exposing the caricatured or ridiculed capitalist enemies, or by listing their shameful crimes.

The success of the Dutch agitprop movement may be explained by the performances of German agitprop groups such as the Blue Blouses in 1932, and by the participation of a Dutch agitprop group in the International Workers' Theatre Olympiad in Moscow in 1933.

Apart from agitprop and choral drama, few other socio-theatrical events were organized by the Dutch Communist party, mainly because of the party's small size. The only communist mass spectacle realized in the Netherlands was titled *De eerste mei en het monster* (The First of May and the Monster), which took place on 1 May 1930 and was written by Johan Visscher.

After the communist writers' collective and eponymous periodical *Links Richten* (Aim Left) was disbanded in November

13 Projectgroep Literatuursociologie, *Links Richten tussen partij en arbeidersstrijd*, 441.

14 Ibid., 442.

1933, it became very difficult for the ATBH and the agitprop movement to find new writers, which caused a swift decline.

National Socialist Spectacles in the Netherlands

Socialist and communist parties were not the only political groups to organize mass spectacles, choral dramas and theatrical manifestations during the interwar period. Socio-theatrical events had proven to be a great propagandist tool for raising a large audience's awareness of ideology. Once national socialist groups from the extreme right spectrum of the Dutch political arena had gained a sufficient number of adherents, it was clear that they would also turn to theatrical events.

This section will feature two particular forms of socio-theatrical event. First, we will focus on the *landspelen* (land spectacles) that were specific to the farmers' organization *Landbouw en Maatschappij* (Agriculture and Society), which was especially active in the north of the Netherlands. Their theatrical propaganda activities guaranteed the interest of Anton Mussert's growing *Nationaal-socia-listische Beweging* (National Socialist Movement, NSB), since the theme of these mass spectacles was closely related to national socialist ideology. Second, we will examine the cultic plays organized by the Dutch national socialists themselves.

The Land Days of the National League for Agriculture and Society

The economic crisis of the 1930s affected not only the urban proletariat and middle class. Farmers, too, saw their income decline. In 1931 they organized themselves into crisis committees, which later transformed into regional farmers' associations. These joined forces nationwide two years later, and established the *Nationale Bond Landbouw en Maatschappij* (National League for Agriculture and Society).

The political position of this association can be situated on the nationalist far right of the political spectrum. Ahead of the 1935 elections, the association gave its members a negative voting recommendation regarding socialist and liberal parties.

From 1935 onwards, the league promoted the organization of massive open-air spectacles during what were called *Landdagen* (Land Days), which were meant to emphasize the cultural significance of the peasantry for the general public. Before the Second World War, a total of six land spectacles (*landspelen*) were held.

Many of the land spectacles had a historical character, where the dramatic action was situated in a pre-industrial era. The main characters, such as Jan Eleveld in *Naar 't land terug* (Back to the Land) and Rudolf van Coevorden in *De oude strijd* (The Ancient Struggle), were true leaders who aimed to transcend the boundaries between city and countryside.

In other land spectacles, this type of leader was replaced by a character such as a parson or village elder, who symbolized ancient peasant values. The secondary characters were farmers who lived in closely-knit communities and felt an affinity with the land. The spectacles regularly involved between 150 and 500 performers, and attracted between 14,000 and 20,000 spectators.

Depending on the political views of the spectacle's author, the texts could have a rather outspoken national socialist character, such as in the case of Jan Hendrik Holm, who had been a member of the NSB since 1933. Such plays were reviewed by national socialist periodicals like *Volk en Vaderland* and *Het Nationale Dagblad*. In an interview with Agriculture and Society's own periodical, Holm stated:

> It is a symbolic play, in which Mother Earth represents our land. I live in the belief that man should know himself to be bound to the land. This is the law of nature, but also the law which the Creator has imposed on us, His creatures.[15]

15 Nijkeuter, *De 'pen gewijd aan Drenthe's dierbren grond'*, 356.

The play asserts that working the land is the highest form of labour, and that a nation can only be powerful and strong when it has learned that lesson. Holm is thus revealed to be an adherent of the 'blood and soil' faction of national socialism, as described in R.W. Darré's book, much admired by Holm, *Neuadel aus Blut und Boden* (1930).

While discussing the Frisian author S.D. de Jong's spectacle *Eenheid* (Unity), several national socialist journalists took advantage of the opportunity to emphasize that the NSB had the same objectives as Agriculture and Society. The spectacle's writer had succeeded, in three successive parts, in showing the peasantry 'in its devout attachment to the land, in a period of far-reaching materialism and spiritual dissolution, and finally in a craving for reflection and the lived experience of ancient values'.[16] Because these land spectacles contained only a small number of national socialist themes, and could therefore not be considered part of an explicitly national socialist tendency, NSB-minded journalists also had their doubts. The denouement of *Unity* was considered unrealistic. How could it be explained that the Germanic god Loki had to flee, immediately after an episode in which the communist leader had been converted to the farmers' cause? They also considered it politically unwise to advise farmers that the only path to a higher social level was through membership of Agriculture and Society.

The Cultic Plays

Though it existed for only 14 years, the NSB wasted almost no time in beginning to propagate its ideology by theatrical means after its founding in 1931. On 22 December 1933, a professional theatre company called Fascio, managed by Jan C. Vos Jr, performed *De dag die komt* (The Day that Comes) by George Kettmann Jr., who was an editor of the national socialist periodical *Volk en Vaderland*.[17]

Parallel to developments in Germany, the NSB developed various socio-theatrical

activities to which the generic term 'cultic play' was later applied, and which may be regarded as the Dutch version of the Nazi *Thingspiel*. This new Dutch national socialist drama was expected to become the dominant form of theatre, and had three distinct expressions.

The first group of national socialist cultic spectacles were the *Hagespraken* in Lunteren, which were the Dutch movement's smaller version of the Nazi party rallies at Nuremberg, based on heroic stories from the Dutch past. The second group were historical dramas, based on Dutch myths or on national topics from Dutch history, such as the revolt of William of Orange against the Spanish in *De rebel der Nederlanden* (The Rebel of the Netherlands) by Jaap A. van Kersbergen. The third and final group sprang from ancient Germanic seasonal celebrations, at this time referred to as winter and summer solstice declamations. Within the framework of this chapter, the *Hagespraken* and the declamations can be considered socio-theatrical events.

The theatrical activities at NSB party meetings and commemorations demonstrate

16   *Volk en Vaderland*, 23 July 1937.
17   Van der Logt, *Het theater van de nieuwe orde*, 175-192.

a particularly national socialist content and design. Vondung (1971) has shown how closely the structure of these meetings, based on linguistic and musical symbols, was derived from Christian liturgy, or developed in parallel to it. In their choral dramas, and during commemorations, the German National Socialists used stylistic formulas such as metrical forms, rhyme and repetition in order to lend a sacral and heroic character to the events. For example, structures such as liturgical antiphons and formulas such as confession and invocation were directly integrated. The musical compositions guaranteed that the space was filled with a powerful sound, in order to achieve a wonderful ambience and a mystical resonance. The architecture of these spaces resembled that of a church.

In the Dutch context, we will focus on the *Hagespraken* that took place before the Second World War – the last of which was held on 22 June 1940 – in Lunteren. The event consisted of a number of tightly scripted rites: the sounding of the huge bell, the marching in of the various NSB organizations, the singing of national anthems or

national socialist songs, the various speech choirs answering prompter Adriaan van Hees, and the parade of flags. All of these dramatic actions served as a frame for the various speeches, which gave the *Hagespraak* event the character of a national socialist liturgy. In a sacred place, national socialists professed their loyalty to leader Mussert and, by doing so, strengthened their mutual bond of solidarity.

Speech choirs were an integral part of the socialist and communist theatrical subcultures. Both at political rallies and indeed on almost every special occasion, opportunities to perform a choral speech or drama were rarely missed. As in Germany, the national socialists copied this socio-theatrical tradition from communism and socialism, and pasted it into a wholly different context.

With the exception of occasional choral dramas written by NSB celebrities such as George Kettmann Jr, whose works include *Het zaad kiemt* (The Seed Germinates), it was mainly members of the *Nationale Jeugd-storm* (National Youth Storm), the NSB's youth movement, who performed the speech choirs during propaganda evenings. The texts of the choral dramas were published in advance in their periodical *De Storm-meeuw* (The Storm Gull), so that all regional subgroups could rehearse them before the meeting.

A typical example of a text performed by the National Youth Storm is *Jong Dietsland Spreekt* (Young Dutchland Speaks). The term *Dietsland* refers to a political vision popular among both Dutch and Flemish national socialists, in which the current territory of the Netherlands would again be joined with Flanders and French Flanders. The text consists of six stanzas, and contains a characterization of the Youth Storm with particular emphasis on national socialist motives such as struggle, youth, strength and patriotism.

Perceived contrasts with political opponents were emphasized in the choral dramas. They were the 'cowardly' and the 'lukewarm' who had not dared to choose national socialism. Another subject of such choral dramas

13. *George Kettmann as a war correspondent (c. 1943). [www.dbnl.org]*

came together: singing, recitations of chants or poems, political speeches, parades of flags, and so on. In terms of dramatic design and staging, they recall the *Thingspiele* from the first years of the Reich, and the socialist May Day demonstrations.

Summer and winter solstice declamations constitute the third form of cultic plays. They were part of the midsummer and midwinter meetings of the Dutch ss and WA (*Weerbaarheidsafdeling*, the NSB's militia).

Such gatherings had a fixed structure. During the midwinter meetings, one of the local division's leaders, or a reciter, would step into the circle of ss and WA members and explain the significance of the winter solstice. He would then recite the opening lines of the choral drama *Midwinter Solstice* by NSB poet Jaap van Kersbergen.

Comrades! As we came here, through the darkness,
which, for those who dare, never is obscure;
as we came from the city and the countryside,
from the heath and from the waterfront,
from the marsh and the shadows and the towns
leaving our homes and the battles we've fought
so far – and which await again tomorrow,
as we are reflecting in quiet tonight,
so, comrades, has Dutchland traditionally gone:
As we stand here at the fireplace,
so the fathers stood, centuries ago,
at their fireplace. Ever since they fought here,
lived here and worked, – since here the first
Germanics dominated the sea and the moors,
since here our family finds its Dutchland,
the men have come, against the wind,
from hours afar, from here and there,
to stand together in a circle, in the dead of winter,
awaiting the hour of midwinter night,
to ignite the fire, which knows no bounds.[18]

The fire was then lit, and the reciter told his comrades that the fire had mythical powers. What was not worthy or characteristic of the nation, the fire would burn away, replied the chorus. The speaker continued with a hymn to the farmer, after which the midwinter horn was blown and the subject of the choral drama was introduced. The midwinter horn was blown again, and then all of the Dutch

was the close bond between the Dutch people and the Dutch dynasty.

On Nazi holidays, such as the Führer's birthday, choral dramas were recited. Kettmann mentions a *Feiergestaltung* for the Führer performed by participants at the Avegoor ss school. In the choral text, Hitler was described as a messianic figure sent by God.

The number of choral dramas apparently diminished during the Nazi occupation of the Netherlands, according to the sparse news reports that are available from the time. Propaganda for the Nazi cause was no longer directed outward to dissenters who might be persuaded to join the national community of the New Order, but instead became more internally focused, and played a role in the communal experience of national socialist solidarity.

The national socialist choral dramas were not isolated events, but were often performed during party meetings. These meetings therefore assumed the shape of a complete work of art, in which different disciplines

18 Van Kersbergen, "Midwinterzonnewende", 571.

heroes of the past were invited into the circle of the 'true patriots', i.e., the present WA members.

The choir, again consisting of the same comrades, confirmed this wish with the slogan: 'Into our circle!'

One at a time, these heroes appeared:
- Claudius Civilis, who had fought against the Roman domination.
- Radboud, King of the Frisians, whose lust for freedom was praised.
- Warriors from Flemish history: Jan Breydel, Pieter De Coninck, Gwijde van Dampierre, Jan Hyoens and Jacob van Artevelde, who had protected Dutchland from Latin (i.e., French) influences.
- The Counts of Nassau, 'of German blood – true to the Dutch Fatherland until death', with their leader, William of Orange.
- The unknown *Geus* (after the sixteenth-century noblemen who had protested against the Catholic occupation of the Netherlands), a 'hater of foreign influences'.
- Jan Pietersz. Coen, Peter Stuyvesant and Jan van Riebeek, the founders of the Dutch colonies overseas.
- Maarten Tromp and Michiel de Ruyter, representing all admirals, captains, boatmen and sailors who had fought against England and Spain.
- King William III, who had protected Dutchland from demise in 1672, while the unfaithful regents had lusted more after money than honour.
- William I, who had launched the Germanic struggle against Napoleon together with the British and the Germans.
- Chassé and Van Speyk, who had refused to surrender to the French.
- The Boers in South Africa for their struggle against the English: Krüger, Steijns, Larey, De Wet and Fourie.
- General van Heutz, the Governor-General of the Dutch East Indies and the military and civil governor of Aceh.
- Herman van den Reeck, a student who had been shot by a Belgian policeman during a pro-Flemish demonstration on the occasion of the Commemoration of the Battle of the Golden Spurs in 1920.

Thereafter, a number of nationalist Dutch songs would be performed. The meeting concluded with a short speech given by a local NSB leader, which would emphasize the greatness of leader Mussert. The WA men then went inside, drank a cup of coffee or had a meal together, and went home.

A number of dramatic texts were produced for the midwinter solstice celebrations. One example is the choral drama *Gedenk* (Remember), which was probably to be performed in the circle of the Dutch SS at the end of 1942. This text demonstrates the purpose of such ceremonies: the time of the midwinter solstice was a time of reflection, a time to remember those who had passed away during the previous year.

Remember also featured passages which were to be spoken by several groups from the national community – workers, peasants and civilians – who would look back on the previous year. This was the year that had ended in the sudden outbreak of war with the Soviet Union. After a brief review of the pernicious evils of democratic society, the poet wondered whether it marked the end of the nation, the empire, the fatherland. Tens of thousands had answered the Führer's call, and had joined the ranks of the black soldiers. They had become members of the SS, and many of them had fallen in the Russian war. The choral drama was then interrupted by a message from the army headquarters of the Führer, praising the Dutch Legion for its bravery in fighting the Bolsheviks at the battle north of Lake Ilmen. With the promise that the dead soldiers would live on, the choral drama was concluded.

This cultic play featured all of the typical themes of the German *Thingspiel*. The feeling of being part of a closely-knit community, the camaraderie, being part of a mighty whole, the national unity, and the figure of the leader were strongly emphasized. In dangerous times, a leader would always appear, to show the way. As with the *Thingspiel*, the division between performers and audience was removed. The meetings were ceremonial in a way that lent an almost mythical character to certain rituals: lighting the fire, speaking the fire spell, and blowing the midwinter horn. The cultic spectacles had an educational and propagandist value. The participants were thus strengthened in their belief in national socialism.

The Catholic Movement in the Netherlands

As far as religion was concerned, the main actors developing new theatrical forms were the *Vrijzinnig Christelijke Jongeren Bond* (Liberal Christian Youth Association), which was a Protestant organization, and its Catholic counterparts the *Jonge Wacht* (Young Guard), the *Kruisvaart* (Crusade) and the *Graalbeweging*.

The rise of socio-theatrical events is particularly conspicuous in the case of Catholicism. Around the time of the First World War, the Catholic Church was faced with increasing numbers of Catholics turning their backs on the Church. This growing apostasy could seemingly not be stopped by the clergy. The Church also had to respond to the growing popularity of socialist organizations by stimulating the creation of similar Catholic groups.

Concerned Catholics in several European countries began to consider it necessary to engage the laity in the fields of apostolate and pastoral care. Their aim was ratified by the papal encyclical *Ubi Arcano Dei Consilio* in 1922, calling for 'Catholic Action'. This society-wide initiative would 'restore all things in Christ' (following the motto of Pius X) through engaged lay groups.

First, we will look at the Grail movement, which organized its enormous Grail spectacles both at home and abroad, involving an unprecedented number of actors and spectators. A discussion of the mass spectacles put on by other Catholic groups will conclude this chapter.

The Grail Movement

During the period that the Catholic Action was initiated, a movement of large-scale conversion was taking place in the dioceses of Haarlem and Utrecht. One of its chief players was the Nijmegen professor of Dutch literature and linguistics, Jacques van Ginneken S.J.

In order to realize his ideas for a new Catholic impetus, Van Ginneken took his inspiration from the early Christians. Again, 'soldiers, preachers and martyrs for Christ' were to go out and convert the world. In his eyes, strong women were the most suitable candidates for this, because, in those chaotic times, their sense of personal sacrifice, perseverance and tenacity would give them a higher chance of success than men.

In 1919, Van Ginneken founded a group of laywomen, the 'Women of Bethany', with Maria Albers, Lou van Moorsel and Johanna Innemée. Two years later, in 1921, he founded a second group, the 'Women of Nazareth'. Among its first members were Liesbeth Allard, Mia van der Kallen, Lydwine van Kersbergen and Louise Veldhuis.

It was not only Van Ginneken's initiative that had inspired the radical Catholic efforts of these religiously inspired laywomen from the upper middle classes. Because they wanted neither to marry nor to enter the convent, they were seeking other opportunities to develop their talents and claim their place in society. Together they started the *Graalbeweging* (Grail movement) in the diocese of Haarlem in 1928. By 1935, no fewer than 23 per cent of all Dutch girls who were members of youth movements would be members of the Grail.

The Grail movement was led by the Women of Nazareth and its aim was to convert the world, beginning in the Netherlands. Besides being a religious movement, the Grail was also a social movement that wished to improve the fate of working class girls, and a cultural movement that wished to build an autonomous Catholic culture, reacting mainly against socialism and communism. *De zilveren trompet* (The Silver Trumpet), the movement's periodical, referred frequently to this latter objective.

> The International Workers' Theatre League, under the leadership of Comintern, currently encompasses over 500 amateur groups with more than 20,000 members. It has also begun to set up groups for children: the young communists have been working in this direction for some time. You see how our opponents are conscious of the tremendous influence of lay theatre. [...] What we lack now is a Catholic culture, i.e., a unity between the Catholic Spirit living in us and animating us and all our other expressions of life![19]

Prominent Dutch Catholic intellectuals, such as Ernest Michel, Anton van Duinkerken, and Gerard Brom, had a sceptical if not negative attitude toward the Grail. There were several reasons for this: the external manifestations of their idealistic message; the central position occupied by women in the emancipatory movement; and the fact that they were themselves no admirers of Jacques van Ginneken. In her recent evaluation, Derks concluded:

> Condemned to superficiality and evaluated as hysterical and exalted; marginalized; or characterized as an early feminist movement – that seems in short to have been the fate of the Grail movement in recent history.[20]

The movement was very visible in the early years of its existence. Processions with banners and mass spectacles involving thousands of Grail girls were held to prove their religious enthusiasm. They even performed their choral dramas in the streets, among the shoppers.

After the death of Haarlem bishop Aengenent in 1935, who had assumed control of the Grail movement, it became more introverted, as his successor,

Mgr. J.P. Huibers, gave back more control to the local clergy. The movement was incorporated into Catholic Action, which placed central importance upon womanhood and motherhood. On 1 January 1935, membership of the Grail movement numbered 11,138.

The Grail Spectacles

Under the changing conditions of the time, which influenced women more strongly than men, the Grail leadership saw it as their mission to find a new life purpose for every Catholic woman. This concerned both the natural destiny of woman as a mother as well as her supernatural role. In line with this new attitude, the Grail aimed to develop a matching stylistic expression, an art form (especially a performing art), a science, and a form of entertainment.

Van Ginneken wanted the Grail movement to spread the Catholic message using the latest developments in lay theatre, new forms of mystery plays, and liturgical song and dance. The Grail would extend its efforts not only to the members' own parishes, but also to those who had turned away from the church and sought entertainment in football stadiums, cinemas and dance halls. Catholic writers such as Marie Koenen and Annie van Wageningen-Salomons were invited for lectures, to read from their own work or to write scripts for mass spectacles.

In their drive to apostolize, the Grail leadership made extensive use of medieval stories, rituals and symbols, but also of modern technology. Moreover, they were charmed by the ostentatious style and modernist culture of the rival *Arbeiders Jeugd Centrale*, typified by their performances of choral dramas by writers such as Henriette Roland Holst. The Komsomol or communist youth organizations in the Soviet Union were a second source of inspiration.

For the Grail leadership, theatre was to act as an environment for the formation of personal character and for the cultural education of the Grail girls. At first, they rehearsed plays from the classic repertoire

19 *De zilveren trompet*, 5 April 1932.
20 Derks, *Heilig moeten*, 241.

and from medieval Dutch literature. Their aims were best served by heavily symbolical morality plays such as *Elckerlyc* (Everyman) or *Mariken van Nieumeghen*, and by modern plays such as *The Secrets of the Holy Mass*, adapted by Henri Ghéon from Pedro Calderón de la Barca's text. This was not felt to be sufficient, however, and it was therefore decided that special plays would be written and performed for their target audience, which would become known as *Graalspelen* (Grail spectacles).

The modernity of massive choral dramas was not the only reason this theatrical form of expression was appropriated by the Grail movement. Theatre was to make the Catholic ideal of womanhood more concrete for women, and because this expression of the ideal was considered of the utmost importance, traditional theatrical forms were gradually abandoned.

Early Grail Spectacles

The first phase in the development of Grail spectacles was a walk organized on All Saints' Day, in which 600 girls carried lighted candles along the canals of Amsterdam. Each of these girls had been assigned a holy woman over whom to meditate while they walked.

The first true Grail spectacle took place in the city theatre of Amsterdam in 1930. *Het mysteriespel Parcival* (The Percival Mystery Play) was an adaptation of the legend of Percival, written by Marie Koenen on the basis of her eponymous 1920 novel. The spectacle was performed a second time in Leiden in 1935, where the march of the Grail maidens, carrying the Grail dish and singing the *Laudate Dominum* by Palestrina, made a great impression on the audience.

The spectacle began with a number of religious songs, accompanied by dancing: *Attende Domine* and *Miserere*, followed by *The Cancticle of St. Francis* and *Sanctus*. In the Catholic interpretation of the saga, Percival was a Christ-like figure who saves mankind through his sacrifice. The pious and sacrificial redemption of this mystical Grail legend tied in closely with the convictions of Van Ginneken and the prominent Grail leaders. The Grail girls featured appropriately as the idealistic and strong-willed 'knights', who would save the world and herald a new feminine period in world history.

The Royal Cross of Easter (1931)

For the spectacle *Het Koninklijk Paaschkruis* (The Royal Cross of Easter), director Maria van der Kallen erected a large black cross on a podium in the centre of the Olympic stadium in Amsterdam, as a symbolic reference to Calvary. Under the arms of the cross, twenty groups of Grail girls together formed the shape of a rose. They wore white tunics, with the image of a cross emblazoned on the breast, and capes of different colours. As the girls moved, the colours appeared to flow among each other. On the roof of the stadium were trumpeters who set the tone and initiated the melody.

As the Catholic symbol of the cross was becoming less prominently displayed in modern society, the Grail girls wanted to salute and honour Christ's cross of suffering: 'We worship and praise you, Christ, because by your sacrifice on the cross you have redeemed the world' (*Leidsche Courant*, 14 March 1931). The approaching triumph of Catholicism seemed already to have been accomplished: 'Per crucem ad lucem – through the Cross to the Light'. The symbolism was even stronger for the 2,500 Grail girls participating because they had learned that, even as they were establishing the symbol of the cross then and there, it was being brought down by the communist revolution in Eastern Europe.

Two years earlier, two Grail leaders had attended the AJC Labour Day celebrations in the same Olympic stadium, in order to spy on the genre of choral drama. The experience was reported as follows:

Then came the choral drama, and that made a powerful impression on us. Strongly rhythmical, spoken by clear voices, hundreds were united with each other to testify to their own red ideas. To *testify*, indeed, it was a *testimony*. They did not merely recite a poem from memory, no, what they said came from their souls, it was their conviction that they were performing, these young people, who would perhaps each of them alone speak only reluctantly, but who dared very well here, gaining strength from each other, no, they *had* to shout out their conviction in the chorus lines, the sound bounced off the walls, echoing that cry from hundreds of young throats. [....] Here you feel the soul of the masses – united by a single conviction – whose joy of being able and allowed to express themselves, shines without fear from their faces.[21]

Later, Grail leaders were no doubt pleased to learn that their design had been successful, since many Grail girls had pinned quotations from *The Royal Cross of Easter* to their bedroom walls, which would help them remember the message in difficult times.

The reviews were generally positive. A mass choral drama put on by such a young organization was seen as a great achievement. When the Grail movement followed up with an even bigger event one year later, though, new performances of *The Royal Cross of Easter* were written off as 'quite nice'.

The reviewer of *Het Vaderland* (7 April 1931) was not as positive as his colleagues. Theatrically, he had the impression that the lyrics were being recited rather than performed, since in his opinion the tension that a mass chorus must possess in order to captivate the audience, as well as the nuance of voices, and imaginative intonation and rhythm, were entirely absent. Furthermore,

14. Performance of De Koninklijke weg des Kruizes *(The Royal Cross of Easter) at the Olympic Stadium in Amsterdam by 2,600 girls of the Grail movement on Whit Monday, 6 April 1931. [Nijmegen, Katholiek Documentatie Centrum]*

21 *Leidsche Courant*, 14 March 1931.

the speech choir was not felt to be a true movement choir, because their movements were limited to simple and stereotypical gestures.

The Royal Cross of Easter appears to have been performed again on several occasions. In late May 1931, a Rotterdam performance followed (Nenijtoterrein), involving 1,500 Grail girls in a slightly altered version. Fragments of the spectacle were probably included in private performances for the Grail members themselves in Leiden (1934) and Bodegraven (1935). Even during the Second World War, a (partial) performance given in Bodegraven was mentioned in regional newspapers.

Like the later spectacles *Everyman* and *Rorate*, *The Royal Cross of Easter* was eventually translated into German. Under the title *Kreuz Chor*, it was then performed at the Ufa Palast am Zoo in Berlin on 3 May 1936. This was an edited version that left the text intact, but did not include the religious songs and dances. The Grail movement even made itself heard in the Dutch East Indies, as in April 1934, Grail girls from the Catholic Girls Society in Batavia performed a show based on the Amsterdam version of *The Royal Cross of Easter*.

A few months later, on 6 September 1931, another Grail spectacle took place. It was a performance of the medieval mystery play *Everyman*, produced in the open-air theatre of Valkenburg near Maastricht. The Dutch Grail leadership saw *Everyman* as an excellent opportunity for promoting its ideals. To that end, the Dutch text was translated into German and English, and performed at the Circus Busch in Berlin and at the Royal Albert Hall in London.

Pentecostal Blessing (1932)

The 1932 Grail spectacle *Pinksterzegen* (Pentecostal Blessing) included group formations, speech choirs, and tentative stepping dances like *The Royal Cross of Easter*, but music and dance were also added, and these kept pace with the recited sections. Moreover,

the differences in the various songs' colour and character were much more marked. In *Pentecostal Blessing*, the angels' and devils' choirs have a different character altogether than that of the Grail choir. The opposition between the groups was thus emphasized, creating more dramatic action, and the Grail leaders concluded that they were increasingly gaining ground on Max Reinhardt's mass spectacles.

This Pentecostal spectacle symbolized a battle between good (the power of divine love) and evil (godless communism and socialism). More than 10,000 Grail girls were recruited, yet their movements were perfectly synchronized since *The Silver Trumpet* had published the scripts and choir formations beforehand.

Nine groups of Grail girls played a fairly dynamic role in the choreography, which made it necessary to let groups of 500 to 2,000 girls execute regular mass movements. Furthermore, there were three distinct groups of about 500 members that had to manoeuvre between the other teams in a disciplined and uniform manner.

All of this would have made it very difficult to control the spectacle centrally.
Because of the size and nature of the production, it was impossible to employ a central
conductor and two gestural leaders, as had
been the case for *The Royal Cross of Easter*.
Instead, the spectacle was controlled in a
decentralized way, where the leaders moved
between the other players and gave unob-
trusive clues to make all dances and chants
proceed evenly and smoothly.

Why the Grail movement wanted to include so many performers in this spectacle
was a question that vexed the critics. Such
a large mass was difficult to direct. Some
reviewers expressed a suspicion that the religious value of the event was deemed more
important than the artistic or cultural value.
Enormous numbers of performers were intended to impress not only Catholic circles,
but also the rival socialist and communist
groups.

The highlight of the spectacle was the
descent of the Holy Spirit. Seraphim and
Cherubim in blood-red robes with feathered
wings on their backs came down from the
stands into the arena. The kneeling Grail
girls threw off their veils, and moved their
hands in ecstasy as they prepared to let the
Holy Spirit descend into their hearts.

Pentecostal Blessing was also a response
to the rapid spread of socialism and communism. The communist opponents were symbolized by the appearance of Komsomol girls
on motorcycles and bicycles, who want to
lure the Grail girls into evil. At one stage, the
Grail girls appear to have been won over, but
the sudden appearance of Mary saves them.
The chorus firmly renounces the temptation. The communist girls flee, leaving their
vehicles behind. The conflict with socialism
is expressed through a dispute between 'the
world' in the stands, and the Grail girls in the
arena. The girls' response to the hatred and
contempt of the (socialist) world is love and
appreciation. Then, the socialist girls in the
stands take off their gray clothes and put on
colourful robes, and join the rest of the girls
in the arena in the celebration of Pentecost.

Rorate (1933) and Saint Lydwina (1933)

After *Pentecostal Blessing*, the Grail leadership received an invitation from Paul
Steinmann, vicar-general of Christian
Schreiber, the bishop of Berlin. He was impressed by the zeal and enthusiastic proselytizing that the Grail girls had displayed in the
spectacle, and saw some potential to transfer
the ideals of the Grail movement to Germany. In September of 1932, the first German
Grail House opened, and Van der Kallen and
Joan Overboss both took up residence there.

On 8 January 1933, the performance of
Rorate, a mystery play based on the message
of Christmas, took place in Berlin. The title
was taken from the Advent hymn *Rorate
coeli desuper*. Two trains carried 1,000 Grail
girls to Berlin in order to perform in the
spectacle with their German sisters. After
Mgr. Aengenent celebrated the Mass, 1,500
Dutch and German Grail girls marched on
the Alexanderplatz, and performed the Roman salute.

After the speech choirs' performance,
Mgr. Aengenent gave a speech in which he
emphasized that the Grail was a movement

16. Performance of the mystery play
Rorate *at the sport palace of Berlin,
8 January 1933.*
*[Nijmegen, Katholiek Documentatie
Centrum]*

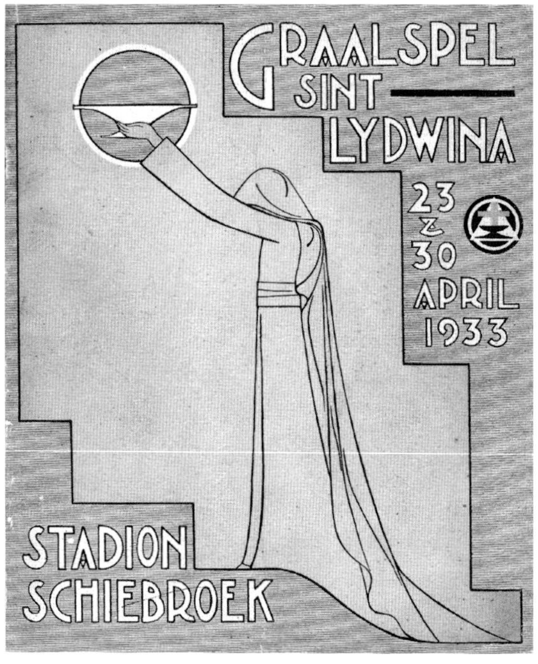

with three distinctive objectives. First, it had a religious aim: to teach women to take pride in their faith and also to propagate it in the world. They would transfer this belief to their children, so the Church would grow. Secondly, it was a social movement, responsible for training women to be good housewives. Finally, the Grail was a cultural movement: it strove for a Catholic culture, but one where the accent would not lie on cultural forms and experiments, but on the Catholic content of what was shown.

In the presence of numerous dignitaries, the gala performance of the Grail spectacle *Saint Lydwina* took place on 30 April 1933, in the Xerxes stadium of Schiebroek, in celebration of the 500th anniversary of the saint's death. Grail members had been responsible for all artistic aspects: the script was written by Liesbeth Allard, the music by Tabitha Vermeulen, and the production (involving 7,000 performers) was designed and directed by Procula Scholten.

Saint Lydwina tells the story of this sacred Schiedam woman in five parts. The first scene of the mystery play opens with the Sanctus chant, and is intended as a prelude. This scene is set in heaven, five years before the birth of Lydwina. As in Goethe's *Faust,*

a choir of angels asks God to intervene in the history of mankind, because of the brutal wars and the persecution of the Church.

Mary and the angels pray to God that a female martyr may attempt to atone for the problems the men were apparently unable to solve. God then selects a group of 'heroines of the cross', including Joan of Arc, St. Catherine of Sienna, Francesca Romana and Coleta, to help Mary in her mission. Mary, however, also wants to include a woman who will become God's 'heroine of suffering'. Eventually, a city in Holland, namely Schiedam, is chosen to bring forth this woman.

The next scenes narrate various episodes from the life of Lydwina, focusing on her struggle with the passions. The most important message for the audience is that Lydwina has to learn how to endure her suffering, following the example of Christ. Eventually, a choir of angels sings jubilantly about the insight she acquires, and afterwards Lydwina prays to Mary and sings a song about her choice to endure her suffering.

The fourth scene deals with 'the Sacrament of Penance and Reconciliation' and covers Lydwina's penance. A choir of angels sings of the history of this sacrament. Since the crucifixion of Christ, all of the sins of the world have been forgiven. And in every age, God has chosen a human being to do the same as Christ. As Lydwina has succeeded in re-living the suffering of Christ in the previous scene, she now has to do penance for another 33 years in order to amend for the sins of the world. Mary gives her a celestial crown, Jesus comforts her with visions, and pilgrims come to visit and honour her.

The final scene consists only of song and dance, and shows Lydwina's triumph: her coronation in heaven is accompanied by the hymn *Gloria in Excelsis Deo*, which is sung by all of the participants. During Lydwina's coronation, all of the performers representing her also stand under the cross in white bridal veils, signifying their marriage to Christ. The curtains of heaven are opened to reveal the coronation to the audience.

The *Jesu Corona Virginum* is sung, after which Lydwina descends from heaven and the Grail girls dance the *Magnificat* with her. Finally, all performers sing *Gloria in Excelsis*, which is danced by the angels.

In 1934, following the large-scale spectacles *Rorate* and *Lydwina*, the Grail movement performed both an Easter play, entitled *Now the Lord Passes by*, and a Christmas play. The Easter spectacle was set in Palestine at the time of Christ's life, and the texts were taken from the book of Exodus, the Gospel of St. John, the Song of Songs and the writings of Thomas à Kempis, Guido Gezelle, and others.

This intertextual approach was deliberately chosen for Easter, as it was thought that the collage of source material would make the audience more aware of the eternal beauty and nurturing power of doctrinal Catholicism. The makers of the spectacle chose as their starting point the idea that modern-day Catholics no longer had time to study dogma for themselves, because of the restlessness of their daily existence. Catholic dogma would only really begin to live for them when they saw how it could inspire young Grail girls to live a rich and varied life. Therefore, the separation between audience and players was partly removed, because both groups were expected to express their common Catholic faith. The performance then had more of a ritual character, and was more liturgical than dramatic in nature.

Light and sound effects were used to captivate the audience, and it was hoped that any lack of dramatic tension could be compensated for by the emphatic power of the

18. Performance of the Grail spectacle Sint Lydwina *(Saint Lydwina) at the Xerxes Stadium in Rotterdam-Schiebroek, 30 April 1933. [Nijmegen, Katholiek Documentatie Centrum]*

message portrayed by this Grail spectacle. Therefore, most scenes were to be viewed as successful examples of pedagogy, or as one reviewer put it: 'dressage of girls'.

Other Catholic Mass Spectacles

The Grail movement was not the only Catholic group to spread its ideals through theatre. The *Christengemeenschap* (Christian Community), inspired by Rudolf Steiner's anthroposophy, also performed Grail spectacles. Additionally, on Palm Sunday, 5 April 1936, a new church building in The Hague was inaugurated with a performance of *Percival* (after Wolfram von Eschenbach) by an unknown group.

Similarly, Grail spectacles were not the only theatrical activities performed by Catholic organizations. In the national and regional press, mass spectacles were frequently reviewed, in two distinct categories. Firstly, the reviewers devoted particular attention to performances that commemorated the anniversary of a saint. Secondly, the silver jubilee of a parish priest was frequently celebrated with a mass spectacle in which most of the village participated, directed by an artist of national renown. This was common in small villages before the outbreak of the Second World War. *The Secrets of Mass* by Calderon de la Barca (in a modern adaptation by Henry Ghéon), in particular, was performed dozens of times.

The battle between good and evil was the subject of the open-air spectacle *Offensief* (Offensive) by Jac. Schreurs M.S.C., staged on 1 August 1937 in Bodegraven. In the centre of the stage stood a large purple cross, in stark contrast to the white backdrop. At the beginning, a woman in a white gown and purple robe stands alone on stage, symbolizing the Catholic Church. On the stairs leading up to the cross, the sleepers and the indifferent are situated on the right-hand side, with the fighters on the left. A Grail choir sings *Rorate coeli desuper* to conclude the first act.

In the second act, the evangelical counsels appear on the right, with the three desires on the left: Mammon, Venus and Jupiter (money, lust and pride). The world is forced to choose between the cross of Christ and the flag of Satan. In the third act, the angels Michael and Lucifer appear, the latter draped in a dragon flag. Behind Michael stand the squires and soldiers (on the right-hand side) and behind Lucifer stands a choir all dressed in black, and the citizens of the world. A debate ensues between Michael and Lucifer on the subject of the world's contemporary problems, which is won by Michael.

To underline the glory of the Church, flowers fall from the sky and doves are released, and the woman's purple robe falls to the floor, making her shine in the dazzling white gown alone. The resulting feelings of joy are translated into an increasingly louder *Veni spiritus*. At the end, the entire world is urged to rally behind the cross.

As we saw with the Grail movement, organizers and directors were frequently inspired by the medieval drama tradition when designing their mass spectacles. For the performance of the 'sacrament spectacle' *Anno Santo* on 18 June 1933 in the Amsterdam Olympic stadium, 3,500 participants reconstructed a medieval miracle procession under the leadership of director Frank Luns. This was only one of numerous occasions when Catholic organizations used theatre to give a voice to their convictions and ideals, reaching out to larger and larger audiences.

Socialist Groups in Flanders

Socio-theatrical activity in the Dutch-speaking part of Belgium adopted different forms than in the Netherlands, but it was nonetheless organized along the same ideological lines. The following sections, therefore, will follow the same structure as above, and treat respectively socialist and Catholic groups. There was little Flemish mass theatre that could unequivocally be labelled as national socialist (as was the case in the Netherlands) but a number of explicitly nationalist spectacles did take place. One example of interwar mass spectacle was discussed above (see The Lion of Flanders in Antwerp, 9 July 1938). Additional examples from the postwar period, particularly the Flemish nationalist 'Pilgrimages of the Yser', will form the topic of the last case study in the concluding part of the book.

Both German and Dutch Labour Day celebrations of the 1930s grew gradually into mass spectacles. Spectacles by Hendrik De Man (*We!* in Frankfurt in 1932, *Liberation* in Amsterdam in 1933) included mass movement choirs, choral drama, and film. Additionally, the shows featured folk dance performances by socialist youth movements such as the AJC, and athletic performances by the socialist Sports Association.

That socialist socio-theatrical events were less common in Belgium, is evident from the fact that texts written by De Man, a leading Belgian socialist, were never performed in his own country. In Flanders, a few choral dramas were written by Daan Boens, including the mass spectacle *Koning Arbeid* (King Labour), which was staged at the Labour Day celebrations of 1932 at the Vooruit in Ghent, directed by Michel van Vlaenderen.[22] This section will discuss the performance of *King Labour*, as well as how such performances relate to the theories on moral education that were developed by De Man and others.

King Labour (1932)

Boens' mass spectacle *King Labour* was produced as part of the May Day festivities of 1932. The celebrations on 1 May began with a huge demonstration against rising unemployment. There were also demands for the 40-hour week, equal wages and general disarmament. The demonstration included a parade with floats and groups of costumed children, whose outfits referred to the socialist struggle for a better future for the weavers' children. The demonstration took place on the Vrijdagmarkt (Ghent) and in the surrounding streets. The flags of numerous socialist groups were visible in the parade. One of the floats was dedicated to physical education, another to the radiant glory of labour and peace.

The evening program included a carillon concert at the belfry, a 1 May banquet, a jazz concert and a free showing of *Er staat geschreven* (It Has Been Written), an antiwar play by William Hartley (pseudonym of Jaap van der Poll), performed by the Multatuli Circle, a socialist group of amateur players, at the Royal French Theatre.

King Labour was not performed as part of the May Day festivities themselves, but on the evening before. That night, the grand meeting hall of the Vooruit hosted a large celebration organized by the *Belgische Werklieden Partij* (Belgian Labour party, BWP). The first part of the program consisted of an opening play, *De Menschenhater* (The Misanthrope) by Jef Vander Meulen, and a jubilant march performed by the Vooruit orchestra.

The second part consisted of the performance of *King Labour*, which involved over 600 performers. The director, Michel van Vlaenderen, had also designed the stage sets. After the performance both the performers and the audience sang the International together. The May evening was concluded with a special carillon concert at the Ghent belfry.

In order to realize the mass spectacle, numerous socialist organizations were mobilized, and the correspondence of party secretary Emiel Vergeylen shows that preparations began in December 1931.

Among the organizations participating were the Vooruit orchestra, which numbered 30 musicians, and the *Marxkring* choir (Marx Circle), which numbered 90. The Ghent Gymnastic Federation was also invited to participate in the final apotheosis and to provide extras for the spectacle. Their athletes figured in a pantomime spectacle portraying a battle scene. The indispensable involvement of a number of youth groups, such as the *Socialistische Meisjeskring* (Socialist Girls' Circle), the *Arbeidersjeugdverbond* (Young Workers' Association, AJ) and the *Socialistische Jonge Wachten* (Social-

22 Mortelmans, "Hendrik de Man", 230-231.

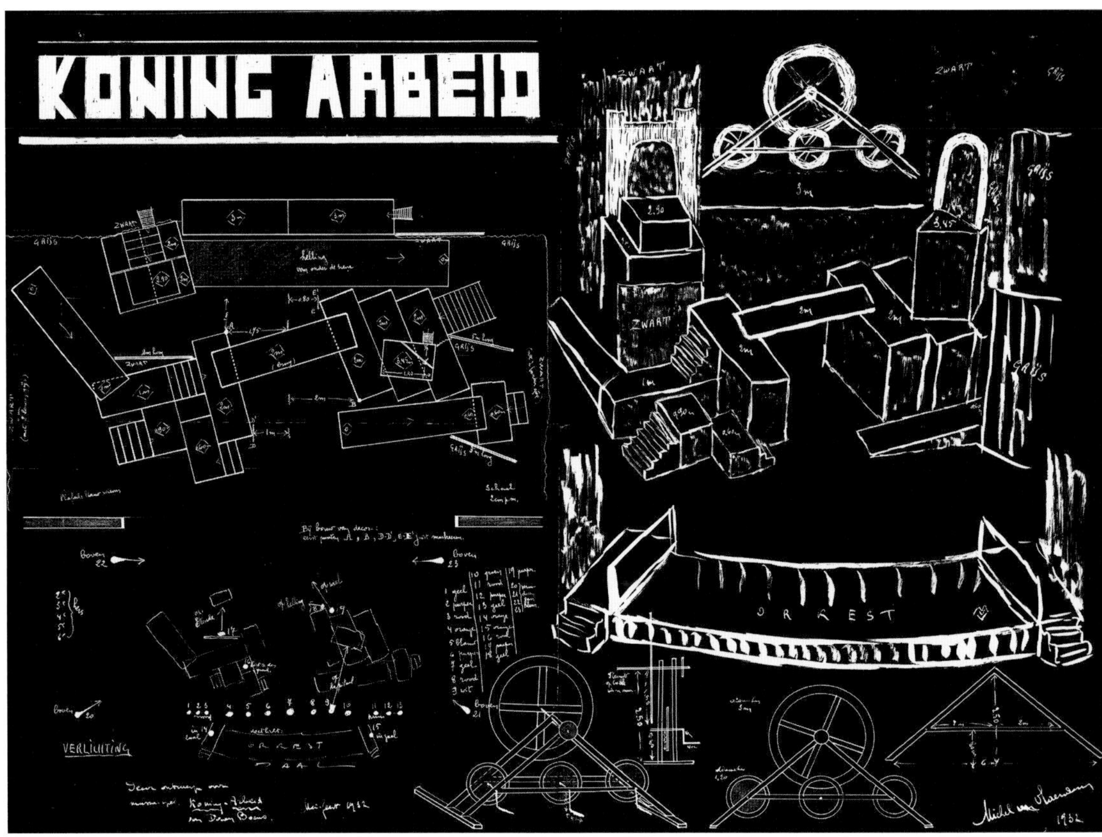

19. *Scenographic design for* Koning Arbeid.
[Antwerp, AMSAB]

ist Young Guards), also made it possible to form speech choirs and perform fragments of cantatas.

Adult students of the *Volkshogeschool* (Popular University) were also enlisted, particularly from their speech and movement choir. Children aged between ten and fourteen years old were recruited from fourteen different socialist groups in the Ghent region to take part in the choirs.

Of the socialist theatre groups, the Multatuli Circle was the most prominent Ghent organization participating in *King Labour*, assisted by performers from other amateur groups such as *Toneelkring Hooger Op*.

The evening concluded with a final chorus and an impressive parade, for which Van Vlaenderen had requested the assistance of 100 men from the *Arbeidersverweer* (Workers' Guard), a paramilitary socialist organization.

King Labour was labelled a 'workers community play' (*arbeidersgemeenschapsspel*) by the socialist periodical *Vooruit*,[23] and its narrative is typical for the ideologically charged socio-theatrical events of the period.

The play starts in the darkness of early morning, when the workmen go to the factory and are bound to the machines as slaves. Oppressed by the capitalist, their misery brings them to an awareness of their power and they cry out in their desire for freedom. Young people are the first to rise in protest, freeing the oppressed workers, who rally around the red flag and organize a strike against slave labour. Then, however, the strike is broken and they go back to work, ashamed of their acts of resistance.

Under the obligations of misery, humanity obeys the capitalist rule: they accumulate gold and goods. Unemployment, however, remains a problem. To escape the looming crisis, the capitalist stirs up hatred among different nations, using misery to stimulate the desire for war, and an armed conflict inevitably breaks out.

23 *Vooruit*, 17 April 1932.

Amid the inferno of destruction, under the thunder of the cannons and the sound of machine guns, men fight each other like beasts. That is, until the figure of a young woman appears. She is the woman of the future, standing between the men and calling to the women from both camps to join hands and form a bond of friendship between the fighters.

In the triumph of socialism the workers now appear. Capitalism has been chased from the throne. Joyfully, they celebrate their wonderful work in solidarity. The figure of 'King Labour' is introduced, signalling the beginning of an ideal society without unemployment or slavery. The play concludes with a cantata dedicated to King Labour, after which the International is sung.

The audience was deeply involved in the performance, as they were positioned in the centre of the action. The participating organizations entered the performance space through various entrances and therefore had to pass through the audience, who were also encouraged to sing along with the socialist songs.

With regard to the staging, it is interesting to note that different stage levels were used to reflect the places occupied by the protagonists in capitalist society. At the highest level was the capitalist. Below him was the young labourer who rises up in protest, together with his young wife. And at the lowest level were the workers, working two by two at a huge factory wheel, symbolizing the oppression of the labouring poor.

Various reactions in the socialist press prove that *King Labour* was the highpoint of the May Day festivities. 'Thousands of spectators are still under the tremendous impression this workers' spectacle has made on them', wrote one.[24] Articles in *Vooruit* also make it clear that many others regretted not being able to witness the spectacle. For this reason, a second performance was reportedly under serious consideration. As a matter of fact, *King Labour* would indeed be performed again, namely at the Ghent velodrome in September 1932, before an audience of 6,000.

The Moral Education of Youth

One theatrical aspect of *King Labour* that was strongly accentuated in both the text and the staging, was the importance of youth. This refers not only to a crucial aspect of the content of interwar ideology (the 'rejuvenation' of society), but also to its method. Despite the ideological differences between movements such as socialism, communism and Catholic Action, there was one clear point of agreement among them: the explicit targeting of young people. Within this educational-moral project, choral drama and mass spectacle could function as building blocks in a new ethos. Crucial to the modernist Catholic theatre movement, and to 'socialism as a cultural movement' (to borrow the title of De Man's 1928 book), was the consideration of an experimental artistic practice from an ethical perspective.

The consideration of an artistic practice as *ethical* is precisely what lies at the heart of almost every socio-theatrical phenomenon. Not coincidentally, both socialist and Catholic essays from the 1920s frequently state that man's artistic activities are a reflection of his existence as a moral being. In the case of Catholicism, Lut Missinne has suggested that this idea was particularly strong in 'integrist' circles such as Charles Maurras's *Action Française* and his followers in France and Belgium.[25]

Examples also abound on the theatrical stage, however. In an article published in *De Standaard* in 1927, Jan Bernaerts, a prominent figure in Catholic theatre who ran both the *Algemeene Tooneelboekerij* (General Theatre Library, ATB) and its periodical *Tooneelgids* (Theatre Guide), was an unwavering protester against the establishment of a national umbrella organization that would group amateur associations of all inspirations (Catholic, liberal and socialist). Such an organization may be useful in terms of 'material interests', he wrote, but certainly not for 'the moral, i.e., the artistic interests'! To make his point even clearer, Bernaerts adds a quotation from the encyclical *Quas Primas*

24 *Vooruit*, 1 May 1932.
25 Missinne, *Kunst en leven*.

(1925) in which Pius XI had instituted the Feast of Christ the King in the hope of renewed participation of the faithful, directly aimed at reducing increasing secularism: 'Christ's Kingship includes all expressions and proportions of man, as an individual and as a social being'.[26]

This is a remarkably broad notion of a moral attitude, which brings the artistic practice within the ethos. Even more remarkable, though, is that such a view was not unique to the Catholic movement. Socialist leaders of the 1920s, such as Hendrik De Man, were broadening the objectives of the labour movement with cultural programmes. In that development, too, the topic of moral education was of great importance.

> Everywhere it is becoming increasingly clear that the fulfilment of the most immediate daily needs makes it necessary, alongside the transfer of knowledge, to complete cultural assignments in the broadest sense, in particular in the sense of moral education. We cannot wait for socialism to form socialist people. Without a core of socialist people, who show the way to others, socialism can certainly not be realized.[27]

The Catholic Movement in Flanders

The Modernization of Catholicism

The examples of Catholic socio-theatrical events from the Netherlands, discussed above, demonstrated how the Church responded to the growing popularity of socialist organizations by stimulating the creation of similar Catholic groups. The encyclical *Ubi Arcano Dei Consilio* ratified these ambitions in 1922 as the call for 'Catholic Action'.

Youth movements, assisted by chaplains, were widely deployed to counter the popularity of socialism among young workers. Catholic Action found one of the most outspoken and active promoters of its cause in the figure of Belgian priest Joseph Cardijn. From his 'unionized youth' movement

Jeunesse Syndicale (Young Trade Unionists), founded in 1919, the successful Young Christian Workers quickly emerged. Their members were labelled *Jocistes* in French-speaking Belgium (*Jeunesse Ouvrière Chrétienne*, JOC) and *Kajotters* in Flanders (*Kristene Arbeiders Jeugd*, KAJ).

The KAJ's foremost task was to encourage the Catholic unionization of young factory workers. To that end, they provided a Catholic version of Scouting-type activities, but additionally required that members closely monitor the local work force. It was evidently an attempt to copy the socialist youth movements' cultural projects, too. Catholic Action's program had already necessitated a strong revaluation of theatrical expressions of popular piety, such as processions and passion plays. In *Ubi Arcano Dei Consilio*, Pius XI had written:

> We refer to the various organizations of young people which have helped to develop such ardent and true love for the Holy Eucharist and such tender devotion for the Blessed Virgin, virtues which have made certain their faith, their purity, and their union one with another: to the solemn celebrations held in honour of the Blessed Sacrament, at which the Divine Prince of Peace is honoured through truly royal triumphal processions.[28]

Young Catholic theatre artists, such as Lode Geysen in Flanders, were enthusiastic about the modernization project, and saw its theatrical potential. In his 1934 booklet *Spreekkoren* (Speech Choirs), published at the height of the choral theatre movement in Flanders, Geysen raved about a possible renaissance of popular piety:

> We are witnessing a revival of many old established religious customs and ceremonies. Processions are being revived. Processions are increasingly lustrous and full of character. They are not only becoming more educational, but also more combative. The litanies should be taken up again. Thousands will join in the streets to beg

26 Bernaerts, "A.K.V.T. en 'het Nationaal Tooneelverbond'".
27 De Man, *Het sosialisme als kultuurbeweging*, 45.
28 Pius XI, *Ubi Arcano Dei Consilio*, 53.

God for help in the struggle against their human weaknesses. Excellent, these processions! Including those taking place on the land, where the fields are devoted to God! Where the sea is blessed! Where the Holy Blood is shown to the people [...].

Where are our big Catholic events now?! Imagine a day dedicated to the Kingdom of Christ. Processions pass through the streets, speech choirs reach out to the audience (perhaps next time they will also join in). The parade, with its slogans, pageant wagons, groups and speech choirs, clearly articulates the meaning of Christ in our lives, i.e., in the state, in the family, at work, in education. In the city's main square, finally, we experience a delightful tribute to the Kingdom of Christ.[29]

These traditional forms of popular piety would not only be intensified but also supplemented by new and modernist devotional events. Speech choirs and movement choirs, composed of amateurs, were trained by theatre and dance professionals so that they could participate in the mass events that celebrated the Catholic revival of the 1930s.

The largest and most notable events include the mass play by the KAJ at the Heysel Stadium in Brussels in 1935, directed by Lode Geysen; the Rerum Novarum play *Bevrijding* (Liberation, Antwerp, 1936) and Jozef Boon's *Credo!* at the Mechelen Catholic Congress (performed in the Heysel Stadium, Brussels, in 1936), which will be discussed below.

Modernist Catholic Theatre

As we have seen, Catholic Action may account for the religious and socio-political origins of these events, but we have said little to nothing about their artistic sources of inspiration. During the first decades of the twentieth century, a torrent of innovations in stage design, dramaturgy and acting had been introduced by the predominantly left-wing theatrical avant-garde, and these undoubtedly played a role.

Constructivist, Expressionist and Futurist artists had demanded that art conquer the public space, and let itself be conquered by the public space. To that end, they began to employ innovative dramatic texts that were composed by montage, and featured contemporary events. Popular theatre forms inspired new acting styles, such as Meyerhold's biomechanics, or the Futurists' provocative delivery.

In France and in Flanders, a movement for theatre reform was growing that strove to integrate modernist techniques in a traditionalist, Catholic framework. The *katholieke toneelrenouveau* (Catholic renewal of theatre), as it was soon baptized by the prominent Catholic journalist Jan Boon, focused on socio-theatrical phenomena and mass demonstrations, though not exclusively. Other key factors in this ideological and artistic movement were the amateur theatre, and a professional travelling troupe called the *Vlaams Volkstoneel* (Flemish Popular Theatre).[30]

That Catholic theatre was booming is evident from historical sources. In the press, the new movement was being well received. The Flemish Popular Theatre regularly attracted the attention of the influential Catholic newspaper *De Standaard*, in particular, that announced and discussed its productions in great detail.

There was also a strong organizational structure, the core of which was the *Katholieke Vlaamsche Tooneelcentrale* (Catholic Flemish Theatre Centre, KVTC). The Centre encompassed not only the Flemish Popular Theatre, but also the *Algemeene Tooneelboekerij* (General Theatre Library, ATB). The ATB's periodical *Tooneelgids* published recommendations on which plays to choose or avoid for Catholic stagings. Finally, the Centre also incorporated the *Algemeen Katholiek Verbond voor Tooneel* (General Catholic Theatre Federation of amateur groups, AKVT).

At that time, the Catholic theatre movement was looking for alternatives to the mainstream commercial theatrical forms,

29 Geysen, *Spreekkoren*, 47.
30 Boon, "De Tooneelrenaissance in Vlaanderen".

which would charge the medium of theatre with ideological content. Mass spectacle was an ideal solution, and not only because of the conspicuous novelty of the genre. It also transformed the chorus into the central structural element of the drama, and its stage designs were an innovation never seen before in Flanders.

Flemish innovations in staging were explicitly influenced by avant-garde stage design, especially (Russian) Constructivism, which is inextricably linked to the movement's origins. Many animators of choral drama in Flanders worked or had worked for the Flemish Popular Theatre, where, from 1925 onwards, formal experiments from abroad were regularly introduced by Dutch director Johan de Meester Jr. and set designer René Moulaert. Constructivist staging and stylized acting contributed to the staging of plays based on figures from Flemish folklore, such as *Tijl* (Anton Van de Velde, 1925). From the early 1920s, directors also began to experiment with larger groups of performers, even outside of the customary crowd scenes.

The search for an original way to stage the choral songs in tragedies by Sophocles and Vondel eventually led Renaat Verheyen and Lode Geysen to the production of autonomous choral plays. Geysen, along with teaching priests such as Jozef Boon and Gery Helderenberg, soon began to form small speech choirs with members of the KAJ and other Catholic youth movements. Next, a series of Catholic Action workshops were held to disseminate the newly developed method among Catholic teachers.

The group of Catholic choral drama directors who emerged from the Flemish Popular Theatre included both Verheyen and Geysen, but also Michel van Vlaenderen, who would direct Daan Boens' mass spectacle *King Labour* in 1932, according to the anti-realist premises that he valued so highly. Although this spectacle was commissioned by the socialist Multatuli Circle, the deeply religious and pro-Flemish director was also closely associated with the Flemish Popular Theatre.

These Catholic innovators were fully aware of the pronounced differences between their endeavours and conventional staging practices. A striking example of this awareness is the survey of choral drama that Geysen published in 1934, which begins with a brief biography of the author and closely examines the apparently offensive nature of his work:

> Directed, to the great dismay of the Flemish theatre community, *Gas* by Georg Kaiser. 150 actors. – No stage, just bare scaffolding and machinery. With intermezzos of acute contemporary relevance.[31]

Before we attempt to address the question of how such traditionalist and conservative theatre makers came to conceive of a renaissance of the ancient liturgical tradition in the form of mass spectacle, it may prove useful to give an overview of some of the most prominent early twentieth-century doctrines on the integration of drama and liturgy.

Theatre and the Return to Christianity

Soviet director Meyerhold was an ardent promoter of revolutionary mass spectacle, but he was also sharply aware that conservative society had since long been employing theatrical street actions for their own ends. Far from blind to the new impulses emanating from the proselytizing Catholic Action movement, he wrote in 1929:

> The Vatican has become a laboratory for research into the art of production. Of all theatre directors, the Pope is the most inventive, the most ingenious. Even now, as I sit checking this summary of my lecture, the newspaper contains a report of widespread anti-Semitic disturbances which have turned into an organized Jewish pogrom. But take note: 'On the eve of the disturbances in Lvov, organized Catholic processions took place' ... Now the Catholic Church has offered its hand to fascism. With their religious processions and their fascist rallies, these two organizations are unrivalled in their restoration of the traditional devices of street theatre.[32]

It was not only political parties and religious organizations who flirted with the social and dramatic potential of liturgy. A diverse range of contributors to modern drama were also caught up in the movement, perhaps the most caustic of whom was T.S. Eliot, who, in 'A Dialogue on Dramatic Poetry' (1928), wrote: 'The only dramatic satisfaction I find now is in a High Mass well performed'.[33] His experiments in liturgical drama would lead first to the pageant play *The Rock* (1934), and subsequently to *Murder in the Cathedral* (1935).

In the same vein, the French dramatist Paul Claudel came to reproach his modernist idol Arthur Rimbaud for attempting to approach Eternity through the senses, that is, through secular poetry. Being merely a 'poet without the power of the priest', in Claudel's eyes Rimbaud had failed to realize that only the unleavened bread of the Eucharist could be a material link to the eternal realm.[34]

Claudel's artistic conclusion was to introduce certain liturgical elements into the texture of his plays. He composed the final redemptive scene of *Partage de Midi* (1906), for instance, using litanical and confessional language (aptly entitled 'Mesa's Canticle').

In *Le Masque et l'encensoir* (The Mask and the Censer, 1921), Gaston Baty developed a similar line of thought into a historical essay on the origins of theatre. Religious ceremony, and most importantly medieval Catholic liturgy, was the true dramatic phenomenon, he claimed, because it had integrated all dramatic components – the spoken text and the non-verbal elements of spectacle – in a harmonious whole. Classicist drama had corrupted the dramatic harmony by privileging the spiritual and individualist dimension, i.e., the text, above the other elements.

31 Geysen, *Spreekkoren*, 5.
32 Braun, *Meyerhold on Theater*, 260.
33 Eliot, *Selected Essays*, 47.
34 Claudel, *La Messe là-bas*, 500-501.

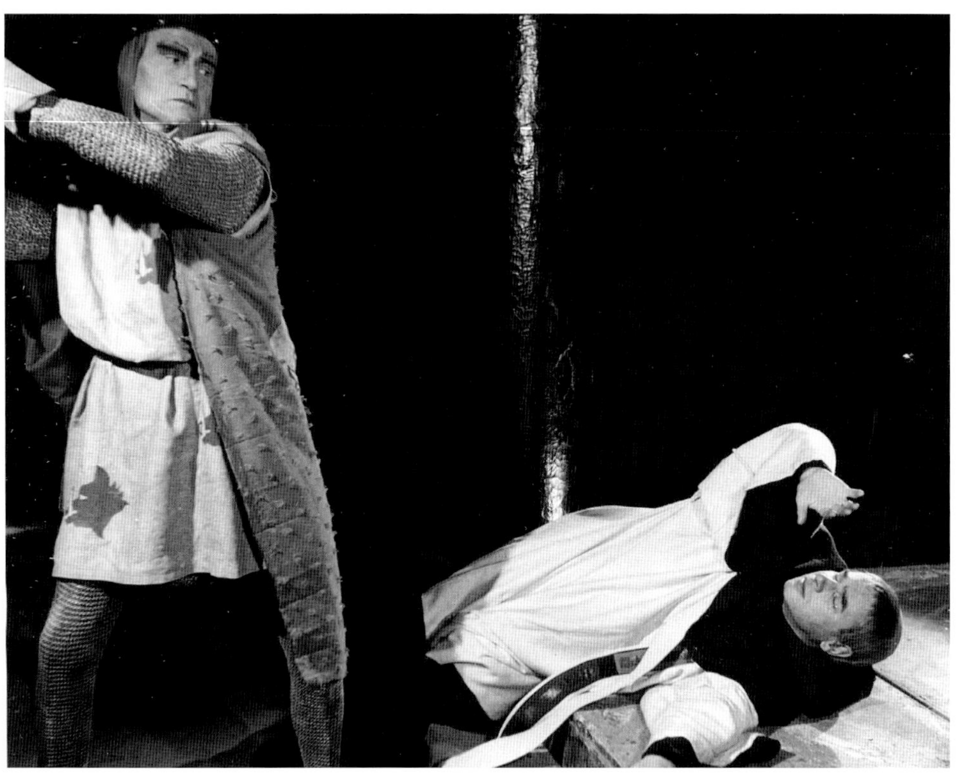

21. T.S. Eliot, Murder in the Cathedral, *London, 1935.*
[Leuven, KADOC-KU Leuven]

efficacy of ritual, it was unclear how this efficacy was to be understood or realized. Eliot and Claudel attempted to integrate a certain liturgical style in their drama, in their own distinct ways. For Baty, though, Catholic liturgy was the ultimate example of harmony between word and image. Others modernized and re-staged the medieval liturgical drama itself, such as Gustave Cohen and Henri Ghéon in France, or Herman Teirlinck and Herman van Overbeke in Flanders.

However great their admiration for the sacred efficacy of Mass, though, few modernists went so far as to strive for a genre that struck a true balance between religious practice and modern drama. They attempted to imbue existing Western theatre with the power of liturgy, but were reluctant to demand the creation of a new dramatic genre that would truly reinvent liturgy for the modern age. On the other hand, there were some who were certain that such a form could be created. Those who created it would be the ideologically organized masses of the twentieth century.

Flemish Polemics on the History of Choral Drama

It may prove useful at this point to contrast the views of Eliot, Claudel and Baty with those of the practitioners of modernist Catholic theatre in Flanders. Obviously, Flemish Catholic critics had good reasons for developing a coherent theory of choral drama: the phenomenon was brand new, and ought to be introduced quickly and convincingly among Catholic groups and theatre professionals alike, if the movement was to gather any momentum. As the first choral texts were beginning to appear in print, a series of theoretical manifestos was also being published by the same small but prolific body of writers (director Lode Geysen, writer-director Jozef Boon, and critics Aloïs de Maeyer and Herman de Vleeschauwer).

Promoters of choral drama knew very well that socio-theatrical phenomena were typically associated with socialist and com-

Baty attempted to rewrite Western theatrical history as a fluctuation between these two poles of theatre: the spiritual dimension of drama, which had dominated literary theatre since the Renaissance, and the material dimension of spectacle, which had resurfaced in such genres as commedia dell'arte, classical ballet, melodrama and pantomime. Only the distinctly Catholic and medieval formula of Mass – an ineffable divine mystery attired in the material splendour of liturgy – had succeeded in harmonizing the two poles.

For Baty, though, contemporary Catholic theatre did not necessarily imply an art form explicitly intended to edify or apostolize.

> The dramatic system of the Middle Ages does not require a religious topic at all. The same living and elastic form may serve a romantic intrigue or a historical event.[35]

Here we touch on the true problem that liturgy posed to modernist theatre practitioners. Convinced that theatre should break out of the autonomy of art and approach the

35 Baty, *Rideau baissé*, 87.

74

munist organizations. Yet they hoped it would be possible to appropriate the genre for the modernization of Catholicism. This resulted for example in their own version of the history of the genre, which Lode Geysen summarizes as follows:

> We have a choral movement of our own. It is not very old yet. It certainly emerged later than the German and Russian movements. I believe that it has grown into its current form without the performers having any knowledge of the foreign models.[36]

Subsequently, Geysen tried to show that the Catholic choral movement in Flanders was not just a carbon copy of the socialist practice, but had also drawn inspiration from choral experiments carried out by the Flemish Popular Theatre during the 1920s, and from liturgical antiphons. Other writers, too, emphasized the role of liturgy in their reflections on choral drama.

It is conspicuous that the Flemish theorists proposed a much more radical view of liturgical drama than the other modernists mentioned above, such as Eliot and Claudel. If we apply a classic definition of the avant-garde, such as that given by Peter Bürger in *Theorie der Avantgarde* (Theory of the Avant-garde, 1974), Catholic lay theatre ought to be called avant-garde.

According to Bürger's influential work – and numerous similar texts – the main project of the avant-garde was to reunite art with everyday life. In Bürger's concise words, the utopian aim of avant-garde artists could be described as 'the attempt to organize a new life praxis from a basis in art'.[37]

Catholic lay theatre literally strove to found a new, impassioned praxis of (Christian) life upon a basis of 'art', i.e., choral drama and mass spectacle. Boon surmised that recent developments in modern drama, and he was indeed thinking of choral drama, had led it to fuse with 'the chief drama – life – Catholic life with its Catholic tragedy'.[38] Geysen was echoing the Futurist definition of theatre when he asserted that, during choral plays, the action takes place in the auditorium:

> The spectator is a crucial element of choral drama, and must be targeted incessantly. [...] It is a confession of faith that petitions the audience. All doubt, all hesitation has to be overcome.[39]

Similarly, Geysen's conclusion that the lay player is not acting but actually playing himself is later echoed in Žižek's typically avant-gardist appraisal of *The Storming of the Winter Palace* as an aestheticization in which the people plays itself.

> [O]ne should perceive, in this minimal, purely formal, difference between the people and the roles they are playing, a unique case of 'real life' differentiated from art by nothing more than an invisible, formal gap.[40]

The Flemish nationalist critic De Vleeschauwer saw choral drama as a symptom of the contemporary era's inner need for liturgy. He insisted that 'from the art of choral drama, the liturgy of labour, freedom and humanity must grow'.[41]

'Socialism' – though De Vleeschauwer was probably thinking of national socialism – should be instrumental in this process. It should consciously cultivate the workers' need for 'irrational mythical and mystical forces'. De Vleeschauwer was clearly echoing such doctrines as Nietzsche's philosophy of 'vital lies', or the French sociologist Georges Sorel's discussion of the re-emergence of myth as a guiding force for modern social movements. In Germany, a similar train of thought would lead to the national socialist *Thingspiel*. This, indeed, is one of the possible outcomes of socio-theatricality, and also of the avant-garde: the use of mass theatrical art to refashion the structure of society.

Alongside choral drama's avant-garde radicality, a second important component of the Flemish essays was its history. This

36 Geysen, *Spreekkoren*, 11.
37 Bürger, *Theory of the Avant-garde*, 49.
38 Boon, *Spreekkoor en Massa-Tooneel*, 57.
39 Geysen, *Spreekkoren*, 41.
40 Žižek, "Heiner Müller out of Joint", 49.
41 De Vleeschauwer, "Het spreek- en bewegingskoor III", 172.

was a crucial topic indeed, since it was often the socialist or German promoters of choral drama who claimed to have invented it. Catholic theorists needed to prove, first, that choral drama had 'always been there' in the history of Western theatre and, secondly, that its modern revival had been equally due to their independent efforts.

As far as the first appearance of choral drama was concerned, all pointed to Greek tragedy and its reworkings in the early modern period. This aspect was not really stressed in the genealogical chain, however, since the choral songs of ancient tragedy seemed to have very little in common with their decidedly modernist efforts. Boon, Geysen and De Maeyer would instead underline that the versicles and responses of Mass were the true ancestors of modern choral drama, which was identically structured. This was in line with what Germany's main theorist of choral drama, Friedrich Karl Roedemeyer, had himself acknowledged.

A third remarkable point concerns the question of spontaneity. Although Boon and Geysen, both prolific producers of choral dramas, repeatedly complained that there were not enough suitable texts available, they also asserted that a true choral drama could only originate from a group's sense of solidarity and community. 'Choral plays [...] can only be staged when the text contains the thought and will of the performers.'[42]

This is interesting when discussed in relation to the subject of gesture. Boon and De Maeyer warned that accompanying gestures, rather than being truly animated, could easily turn into mechanical gymnastics when all performers were instructed to carry out the same movements. Producers therefore had to be attentive to any gestures that arose spontaneously out of the group itself, in response to its sense of community or to the choral play that was being performed.

The importance of spontaneity, in combination with the first idea - that of the avant-garde construction of a new life praxis and therefore a new community – indicates a problem that is central to socio-theatrical events. How spontaneous really was the collective life of the groups constituting the ubiquitous 'community' that was worshipped during the interwar period? A final quotation from De Vleeschauwer acutely shows how the tension of this question was alive just under the surface of choral drama discourse.

> Modern choral drama is the art of the masses. It is the art that the humanity of the future will use to combat that of yesterday and of today. It is an orchestra of human voices, graded and differentiated like organ pipes. It is a living organ, the tones of which are not united by a mechanism or by the will of a single human, but by the collective will of all performers.[43]

The Praxis of Liturgical Drama

If the spontaneity of choral drama was inherently problematic, the question arises of whether the promoters of lay theatre were right to profess that it was so closely related to liturgy. Was 'liturgical drama' a convincing description? In order to answer that question, we will examine a selection of events from the late 1930s in more detail.

In his book *Spreekkoor en Massa-Tooneel* (Choral Drama and Mass Theatre, 1937), Jozef Boon reported on an untitled choral drama he had directed in the town of Diest with a group of 100 students, on the occasion of the feast of Saint Jan Berchmans, a seventeenth-century Jesuit priest who was the students' patron saint.

The event took place in the local marketplace, and Boon had intentionally placed his chorus on a raised podium so that it could 'dominate the market', i.e., the audience of 2,000 students that would respond to the speech choir.[44] The spectacle was framed against the imposing backdrop of Diest's Gothic church. The relics of Saint Jan Berchmans were displayed just outside the church portal, and the carillon played music specially composed by Arthur Meulemans, a frequent collaborator in Boon's mass plays.

What is particularly striking about the Diest mass spectacle is that Boon strove to

42 Geysen quoted in De Maeyer, "Hoe wordt het spreekkoor omschreven", 115.

43 De Vleeschauwer, "Het spreek- en bewegingskoor II", 91.

44 Boon, *Spreekkoor en Massa-Tooneel*, 79.

integrate his choral drama in the official church festivities devoted to Saint Jan Berchmans. The bishop and clerics who participated were explicitly described as 'being part of the choral drama'.[45] Indeed, the event ended with a huge open-air celebration of Mass. If one is to believe Boon himself, the event truly 'conquered' its audience.

> Immediately the masses were overwhelmed: they were dominated by the fact that carillon, music, church, city hall, flags, podium, and flags and crowd were united in a single body. No small role was played by the all-encompassing music that made everything one wave … [I]t had grown into a mass happening, especially because it was a part of reality, namely, because of the integration of the Holy Relics and because, lastly, while the choir was still opening out plastically and the musical finale was bursting open, the priest began the Blessed Sacrament. All of that was really part of the choral drama, including the blessing given by the bishop and the Blessed Sacrament being administered amidst the kneeling choristers.[46]

One year later, Boon directed what was probably the largest Catholic mass play of the 1930s. *Credo!* ('I believe') was staged in the Heysel Stadium (Brussels) at the Sixth Catholic Congress of Mechelen in 1936. The spectacle numbered hundreds of participants grouped in singing, speech and movement choirs. A gargantuan audience of 150,000 filled the stadium, which was usually reserved for sporting events.

In Boon's eyes, the huge crowd saying the *Confiteor* prayer at the beginning of confession was 'the most beautiful and ardent drama [...] that we could ever dream of'.[47] The effect must have been that of an immense industrial-scale celebration of the Eucharist.

Moreover, the whole event was broadcasted over the radio. At the exact moment when the spectators in the stadium said the Apostles' Creed (the 'I believe'), all the church bells of Belgium began to ring. Besides modernist plot elements, such as the highly symbolic and antagonistic struggle between the 'people of Babylon' and the 'choir of angels', this event, however, also featured many recognizable elements from traditional popular piety. Local Flemish devotional customs were incorporated in the show, including the Halle cult of the Holy Virgin Mary and the penitential procession of Veurne. Still, this awk-

45 Boon, *Spreekkoor en Massa-Tooneel*, 79.
46 Ibid.
47 Ibid., 86.

22. Jozef Boon, Jeugdlitanie tot den Heiligen Joannes Berchmans *(Litany to Sain Jan Berchmans), Diest, 1935. [Leuven, KADOC-KU Leuven]*

23. Jozef Boon, Credo! *(I Believe)*,
Brussels, 1936.
[Leuven, KADOC-KU Leuven]

78

ward copy-paste procedure simultaneously revealed the typically modernist naivety of its makers. The processions' context could impossibly be replicated in the stadium. Instead, the events were merely copied and pasted into the quite inappropriate context of a mass spectacle.

These two events clearly show that it was possible, to a certain degree, to create new devotional performances that had successfully come through a radical modernization – and a substantial increase in scale – of liturgy's traditional means. However, these large-scale successes were quite rare. Catholic choral drama proved to be short-lived. Its popularity waned dramatically at the end of the 1930s, and it did only reappear sporadically after the Second World War. Jozef Boon's *Holy Blood Play* (*Sanguis Christi*), for instance, had first been produced in 1938,

and was restaged after the war in 1947, 1952, 1957 and 1962.

To conclude this discussion of the modernist potential of liturgy, we refer to an interesting anecdote found in the writings of French critic Robert Brasillach. His book *Animateurs de théâtre* (Leaders of Theatre, 1936) features an interesting report on a French theatre group performing in Leuven (Belgium).

The 'Théophiliens', led by Sorbonne professor Gustave Cohen, were an amateur ensemble who had acquired a solid reputation producing ancient and medieval plays in modern garb. At the end of a performance in Leuven, somewhere between 1933 and 1936, the bishop in *Le Miracle de Théophile* addressed the audience with the customary invitation to chant 'Te Deum laudamus'. To his surprise, the call was answered. The audience rose and was led in prayer by an actual bishop who was present among the spectators.[48]

The Leuven anecdote provides the Catholic counterpart, as it were, to the famous Soviet story of when Leon Trotski attended *Earth Rampant* at the Meyerhold theatre in 1923, and suddenly appeared on stage to deliver a speech on the fifth anniversary of the founding of the Red Army. Since Sergei Tretyakov's play was explicitly concerned with the events of the Civil War, his address was a perfect complement to the event. 'After thunderous applause, the action on stage continued as though it had not been interrupted, and Trotsky returned to his seat.'[49]

At the Leuven event, too, a true community was brought into being through inherently artificial and modernist means. Such successes, however, were not easily replicated. Yet the modernist reinvention of liturgy through theatrical means had great potential during the interwar period. Its impassioned creators applied an avant-garde artistic strategy to a most traditionalist problem: how to revive the efficacy of religious ritual.

48 Brasillach, *Animateurs de théâtre*, 205-206.
49 Yuri Annenkov quoted in Leach, *Vsevolod Meyerhold*, 19.

Case Studies

The third and last part of this book collects six essays on specific episodes from the history of mass spectacle in Europe and the Low Countries in particular. The first two chapters treat of the origins of mass spectacle in the political and popular culture of the nineteenth century. Frank Peeters discusses mass theatre performances in the context of national festivities, which originated in the wake of the French Revolution and constituted a powerful propaganda tool for the budding European nation-states. Evelien Dejonckheere turns towards mass phenomena in popular culture, and zooms in on the Belgian performances of the two shows that were possibly the greatest and certainly the most famous expression of the nineteenth-century society of the spectacle, namely, the travelling circus of Barnum and Bailey and *Buffalo Bill's Wild West*.

The following three contributions deal with open-air and mass theatre during the interwar period. Ad van der Logt describes how Expressionist drama found its most visible expression in the Netherlands in two mass performances that explicitly took the interaction between humans and machines in the industrial age as their topic. Staf Vos turns towards the connections between the modern dance movement, on the one hand, and the mass theatre movement, on the other. In Flanders, the most notable figure in that regard was Lea Daan, who applied her Laban training to both socialist and Catholic movement choirs. Karel Vanhaesebrouck, finally, focuses on the open-air theatre of Herman van Overbeke and particularly the idealized image of medieval community art that was central to his vision.

The book concludes with a case study in post-war socio-theatricality. It may be evident from the rest of this book that mass theatre was highly popular during the 1920s and 1930s, yet afterwards failed to capture the imagination of the post-war generations. However, there were still some notable exceptions to the decline of socio-theatricality during the postwar period. Luk Van den Dries, in his contribution on the annual Pilgrimages of the Yser, focuses on the difficulties faced by Flemish nationalist groups struggling to actualize their message through socio-theatrical means in an era of increasing globalization.

National Feasts in the Long Nineteenth Century

Frank Peeters

The Le Chapelier Law of 14 June 1791, which prescribed how professional associations were to be organized according to the principles of the French Revolution, had tremendous consequences for French theatre, and by association, for much of European theatre. Chapelier had built on the decree of d'Allarde, which guaranteed freedom of enterprise.[1] His fellow revolutionary Mirabeau filed a supplementary proposal that specifically related to the theatre, and stipulated that every citizen should be allowed to open a public theatre where all genres could be shown.

This event broke the privilege of the Comédie-Française, which had borne the title of *Théâtre de la Nation* since 1789. The consequences are well known: *théâtromanie* (theatromania) ran high. One year later, more than two hundred new theatres had opened in Paris, centring around the Boulevard du Temple, which featured twenty-three playhouses spreading the new creed of melodrama.

It is certain that theatre was often a hazardous undertaking in revolutionary Paris, and few professions were as jeopardous as that of an actor. One moment they were hailed as the heralds of a new age, and the next they were falling into disgrace, labelled reactionaries, or worse, royalists. A notorious example is the arrest of almost the entire company of the Comédie-Française, on 3 and 4 September 1793, and the issue of death sentences to four of the actors. The story of their rescue at the hands of a third-rate actor called Charles-Hippolyte de la Buissière, who burnt the records incriminating his fellow actors and threw the remains into the Seine, reads like a picaresque novel.[2]

However threatening the theatre may appear to a given regime, it is at the same time an extremely effective tool in helping to disseminate a new doctrine among a large audience. This is undoubtedly true for theatre in the traditional sense, e.g., performances with heroic-historical themes and characters that give shape to the national past for a wide (and often illiterate) audience. Such performances may help to justify national history, explain it and, where necessary, reinvent it. But in order to have the maximum effect, the spectacle should be performed not in the playhouse but in public spaces, in the streets and squares of the city. Here, a nation can prove its legitimacy to the largest possible number of spectators.

The rest of this chapter will discuss a number of examples of such events from Belgium, the Netherlands and Switzerland. Chronologically speaking, the first of these spectacles were performed in France.

The Feasts of the Revolution

The most prominent theatrical activities in which the spirit of the Revolution and the Terror breathed were the great parades of the early 1790s – the *Fêtes de la Révolution*. The parades of 1793 and 1794 in particular were designed as *tableaux vivants* by the painter Jacques-Louis David, who aimed to pass on his enthusiasm for the Jacobin ideals to all citizens.

It is impossible to discuss the performing arts of the late eighteenth and early nineteenth centuries without referring to

1   Carlson, *The Theatre of the French Revolution*, 73-93; Brown, *Theater & Revolution*, 68-69; d'Estrée, *Le théâtre sous la Terreur*; Lunel, *Le Théâtre et la Révolution*.
2   Blanc, *Histoire de la Comédie-Française*, 440-442; Carlson, *The Theatre of the French Revolution*, 200-202.

2. Jean-Jacques Rousseau, Lettre
à d'Alembert sur les spectacles,
Amsterdam, 1758.
[Paris, Bibliothèque nationale de
France]

philosopher Jean-Jacques Rousseau. Famous, or rather infamous, among his work is his *Lettre à d'Alembert sur les spectacles* (Letter to d'Alembert on Theatre, 1758).

The immediate cause of Rousseau's anti-theatrical arguments is well known. It was the publication of the lemma 'Geneva' in Diderot and d'Alembert's *Encyclopédie*, in which d'Alembert advocated the creation of a theatre in Calvinist Geneva. In his long tract, Rousseau condemns all theatre being shown in Europe at that time as morally pernicious.

The only form of theatrical presentation that found grace in his eyes is described in Section 129. It will be quoted in some detail because it is precisely this section which made a deep impression on one of the protagonists of the French Revolution, the 'incorruptible' Maximilien de Robespierre. It is known that Robespierre was fanatical about the ascetic philosopher from Geneva, who would act as his ideological guide for

the rest of his life, and he had read Section 129 from the *Letter to d'Alembert* attentively:

> These great and proud entertainments, given under the sky before a whole nation, presented on all sides only combat, victories, prizes and objects capable of inspiring the Greeks with ardent emulation and of warming their hearts with sentiments of honour and glory. It is in the midst of this imposing array, fit to elevate one and stir the soul, that the actors, animated with the same zeal, according to their talents, the honours rendered to the conquerors of the games, often the first men of the nation.[3]

In his speech on national festivals, the famous *Fêtes* of the Revolution, Robespierre starts from Rousseau's ideas, but takes them one step further: 'Man is the greatest object found in nature, and the most magnificent of spectacles is that of a great people assembled.'[4]

This, then, is precisely what would happen during the revolutionary *Fêtes*. Unlike customary theatrical events, where the audience was separated both spatially and functionally from the actors, the theatre of the Revolution and the Terror removed this barrier almost completely. Robespierre defined the people as an incarnation of virtue. It was the masses who took centre stage in the spectacles, and the familiar oppositions between theatrical illusion and reality, mask and face, and character and performer no longer applied.

The Feast of the Constitution (1793)

Apart from their immediate causes, which were usually related directly to a revolutionary event, the feasts had an essentially religious function. Rarely had this symbolic power been greater than during the Feast of the Constitution, also known as the *Fête de l'Unité et de l'Indivisibilité* (Feast of Unity and Indivisibility), on 10 August 1793. The painstakingly detailed mise-en-scène had been

3   Rousseau, *Letter to d'Alembert*, 308-309.
4   Brown, *Theater & Revolution*, 76.

3. Vue des six différentes stations de la fête de l'unité et de l'indivisibilité de la République, *engraving, 1793.*
[Paris, Bibliothèque nationale de France]

designed by painter Jacques-Louis David. He called on Parisians to rise before dawn and catch the first rays of the sun, symbolizing the light of truth that they had received from the Revolution. They were then expected at the site where the Bastille had once stood. Nearby was the colossal 'Fountain of Regeneration', with water flowing from the figure's breasts. As the crowd sang revolutionary songs and fired shots in the air, the chairman of the Convention held a cup under the jet of water and paid tribute to the Revolution by reciting an ode. Then, 86 elderly men from all departments followed his example and did the same.

A huge parade followed, which involved, according to some chroniclers, no fewer than 200,000 participants. For sixteen hours they would parade down the boulevards of Paris. On the Boulevard Poissonnière, actresses sat on cannons and impersonated the heroines of 1789. The procession passed a number of highly symbolic sites, where giant statues had been erected. It ended at the Champ-de-Mars, a vast parade ground in central Paris, where the first anniversary of the Revolution had been commemorated on 14 July 1790. In order to transform the parade ground into a huge amphitheatre, tens of thousands of Parisians had been enlisted to dig thousands of cubic meters of earth, accompanied by rhythmic drumming.

This *Fête de la Fédération au Champ-de-Mars* had begun one day earlier, on 13 July, in the Notre-Dame de Paris with a ceremony that was highly reminiscent of medieval Easter celebrations. The actors and musicians of the Comédie-Française, the Comédie Italienne, the Théâtre de Monsieur, the Opéra and numerous smaller (mime) companies sang songs and performed a stage play written especially for the occasion entitled *La Chute de la Bastille* (The Fall of the Bastille). As in earlier Easter celebrations, there was some dialogue between the soloists and the audience. The ceremony ended with a military song that was sung by all of the actors. Cannons were fired outside the cathedral, and finally the choir sang a passage from the Book of Judith. Never before had

4. Le jour de la fête célébrée en l'honneur de l'Etre Suprême le Décadi 20 Prairial, l'an 2e de la Republique Francaise, Vue du jardin national et des décorations, *etching, 1794.* [Paris, Bibliothèque nationale de France]

the Notre-Dame been the stage for such a spectacle.

As described above, the next day saw a seemingly endless procession of departmental deputies and army units through the boulevards, heading towards the Field of Mars. In the giant amphitheatre, 400,000 spectators were seated. At the head of the procession were the king and the chairman of the National Assembly, as well as ministers and departmental representatives. Three hundred priests in white cassocks and tricolour scarves opened the ceremony with a mass that was celebrated at an altar standing eight meters above the ground in the centre of the field. The highlight was the oath of allegiance to Louis XVI, sworn on the Constitution. The next day, Paris was the scene of numerous open-air festivities, but the Revolution also was celebrated in the theatres with plays written specially for the occasion.

A second and final example of revolutionary mass spectacle is the *Fête de l'Être Suprême* (Feast of the Cult of the Supreme Being), which took place on 20 Prairial of the Year II (8 June 1794). The Field of Mars

was once again the setting for this grandiose festival, which was held with the aim of launching a new state religion. As before, the production design had been entrusted to Jacques-Louis David. A large amphitheatre was constructed in the Tuileries. On the morning of 8 June, Parisians in all districts were awakened by the ringing of church bells, cannon fire and drums. When they arrived at the Tuileries, they were greeted by hundreds of actors who accompanied them to their places. It was noon when Robespierre made his entrance, wearing an extravagant costume and tricolour plumes on his hat. He would lead the ceremony, as the Convention had decided. Once the members of the Convention had taken their places, the actors sang a hymn, and Robespierre came forward and set fire to a large cardboard figure, which represented atheism. As the cardboard burned away, a white plaster statue emerged, symbolizing Wisdom.

The entire group then moved to the Champ-de-Mars. At the front of the parade were brass bands on horseback and one hundred drummers, followed by hundreds of men and women representing the twenty-four Revolutionary districts of Paris. Then came the 155 performers and artists from the capital, accompanied by 600 of their students, followed by the members of the Convention, headed by Robespierre.

The Champ-de-Mars had been transformed for the ceremony: on the side where the altar of the Fatherland had stood, a gigantic artificial hill called the Sublime Mountain had been constructed. The construction was so large that several thousand participants could take their places on it. It was decorated with caves, trees, rocks and artificial streams, and incense was burning all over it. Members of the Convention climbed to the top, followed by the actors and musicians, and 2,400 singers. Meanwhile, the masses stood on the ground below. Men and women were organized in separate groups, so they could alternate in singing revolutionary hymns.

The ritual began with the lighting of a flame on top of the mountain while the crowd chanted a hymn in honour of the Supreme Being. Taking into account the tens of thousands of participants, this was an unprecedented feat. Cannon fire and trumpets punctuated the end of each of the hymn's verses, and when it ended, mothers held up their children and young girls threw flowers over the heads of the crowd. Most theatres remained closed that night to let the actors recover from their performance at the festival, and also to prevent any attempt to imitate or parody the event.

The Feasts Revisited: Firmin Gémier

More than a century later, director Firmin Gémier took it upon himself to make open-air theatre into an experience by and for the people. Fortunately, his spectacles no longer involved the political fanaticism of the revolutionary era, but again the guidelines were provided by Rousseau's theatrical ideas. The infamous Feast of the Cult of the Supreme Being also functioned as an explicit benchmark for what theatre could mean to a nation.

It was the image of the Sublime Mountain, especially, that appealed to Gémier, because it was unique in its perfect representation of the symbiosis between the people and the arts: 'when art and the people merge like the sky and the sea [...] when emotions freely propagate themselves throughout the audience'.[5]

He uses the term *Fête* in its historical and revolutionary sense: 'Each *Fête* will be tantamount to one act of an immense play that will magnify the lives of the people and be enacted by the people themselves, in that majestic theatre whose stage is the soil of France'.[6]

This theatre would – in accordance with the views of Rousseau – be a *culte extérieur* (outdoor cult). By playing in open air, Gémier would juxtapose intellectual culture with physical culture, the individual with the masses. Such festivals are necessary, he claimed, because a people needs to give shape to its ideals.

After the First World War, he attempted to consolidate this theatre for the people by founding the National Popular Theatre (*Théâtre National Populaire*, 1920). In spite of all the outdoor cult ideals, however, the Parisian climate forced him to move his performances into the shelter of the Palais de Chaillot.

Closer to his ideal were the pre-war open-air productions in Lausanne (1903) and Geneva (1914). In 1903, French writer Romain Rolland invited Gémier to collaborate with Swiss composer and musical educator Jaques-Dalcroze in an open-air spectacle organized for the *Fête de Vaudois*, celebrating the hundredth anniversary of the canton of Vaud's membership of the Helvetic Confederation.

Like Jean-Jacques Rousseau, Gémier dreamed of a utopian society in which the community would have priority, rather than the individual. The best way to give theatrical shape to that society, he felt, was the popular

5 Brown, Theater *& Revolution*, 295.

6 Ibid., 295.

festival, or the mass spectacle. In 1903, this dream became reality. In an amphitheatre that could hold up to 2,400 performers (mostly inhabitants of Lausanne), the population of the canton was presented with precisely this form of community art on a huge stage built on the shores of Lake Geneva. The spectacle described the history of the canton since the Middle Ages, and reached a climax as the mass of spectators stood up and began to take part in the parade.

Gémier's reputation for directing such mass spectacles earned him an invitation to a similar rally in Geneva in June 1914, called the *Fête de Juin*.[7] Gémier would again work with Jaques-Dalcroze, who composed the show's music and choreography. Another Swiss artist, the famous architect and stage designer Adolphe Appia, was responsible for the scenic design. Switzerland had and has a long tradition of patriotic festivals – some federal, others cantonal – where folk music, dance and drama are combined to commemorate historical events.

The festival of 1914 was special in many ways, since it had been designed by three of the most prominent modernist artists. The event consisted of a theatrical play in four acts, and celebrated the inclusion of the Genevan Republic in the Helvetic Confederation a century earlier. A series of *tableaux vivants* were performed as part of a carefully orchestrated music and dance spectacle, which figured as a backdrop for the historical scenes being performed.

The entire event took place in a huge theatrical space that had been constructed on the shores of the lake especially for the occasion. Facing a stage of fifty meters wide sat an audience of 6,000 with a view of the lake and Mont Blanc in the distance. The *tableaux vivants* were performed by 200 of Dalcroze's students together with just as many extras, resulting in a eurhythmical mass spectacle, a synthesis of music, dance, theatre and song. Just as in the time of the French Revolution, the organizers were aiming for a sense of unity between performers and spectators, based on a common heritage, shared values and physical proximity.[8]

Staging the Great Moments of History

The French festivals found no match in (post-)revolutionary Europe in the late eighteenth and early nineteenth centuries, either in terms of intention, implementation or impact. Still, events in Belgium and the Netherlands, such as the Belgian Declaration of Independence (1830), the centenary of the end of Napoleonic domination (1913), and the coronation of Dutch Queen Wilhelmina (1898), provide examples of times when theatrical mass demonstrations were used as instruments for nation building.

In these cases, we cannot speak of 'mass spectacle' in the same sense as those encountered during the interwar period. They can more aptly be described as historical parades that evoked 'great moments' from the national past. These events were not held in sports stadiums or open-air theatres, but in the city's boulevards and squares, which functioned as a backdrop for such expressions of nationalism. Without exception, these were urban spectacles, in which the capital was often the symbolic location of choice. The capital city, where the head of state resided, was viewed as the ultimate incarnation of the nation and therefore the ideal location for commemorating national independence.

Other cities, however, were also eligible for the commemoration of specific moments. In Ghent, the third centenary of the Pacification was commemorated in 1876. In Kortrijk and Bruges, it was the Battle of the Golden Spurs. Finally, the city of Antwerp commemorated the man 'who taught his people to read', namely, Hendrik Conscience, in 1893, 1908, 1912 and 1938.[9] The return of the Prince of Orange to the Netherlands in 1813 was re-enacted one hundred years later in numerous Dutch seaside towns, and Eindhoven also organized a large festival of

7   Brown, Theater & Revolution, 286; Beacham, *Adolphe Appia*, 81-85.
8   Beacham, *Adolphe Appia*, 81-85.
9   For a discussion of the 1938 manifestation, see 'The Lion of Flanders in Antwerp, 9 July 1938' in chapter 1.

gymnastics where the masses of participating children performed rhythmical movements to the tones of the Dutch national anthem.[10]

To examine all of these events would far exceed the limitations of this chapter, so we will restrict the discussion to key examples of nineteenth-century public dramatization of the nation state.[11] In Belgium, the national celebrations held to mark the Declaration of Independence (1830) and the oath of allegiance of Belgium's first king, Leopold I, to the Belgian Constitution, are without doubt the most prominent examples. Also deserving of our attention, however, are commemorations of the mythical victory won over the French king at the Battle of the Golden Spurs (1302), and the homages paid to the 'writer of the fatherland', Hendrik Conscience, in 1893 and 1912. In the Netherlands, the most widely celebrated events were the festivities given on the occasion of Queen Wilhelmina's coronation (1898), and the commemoration of the Prince of Orange's return (1913).

Occasions that celebrated the anniversary of Belgian independence were ideal events for emphasizing national unity. Examples include the anniversaries of Leopold I's oath of allegiance; the great 'national' parades of 1848, celebrating the eighteenth anniversary of independence; and the parades of 1853, following the marriage of King Leopold II. Pageants were the most effective means for the government of shaping the myths of the national past.

The parade of 1856 is another excellent example. It was the main attraction of what were called the July Festivities, when the ascension to the throne of Belgium's first king on 21 July 1831 was commemorated. The theatrical forms *par excellence* were the *tableaux vivants* represented on pageant wagons. The parade consisted of two parts: one 'historic', and one 'allegorical' (nationalist or contemporary). In order to emphasize national unity, each of the nine Belgian provinces had provided one or more pageant wagons, on which amateur actors performed various *tableaux vivants*.

The highlight of the 1856 parade was the moment it passed through the Place des Palais, where the royal family watched from the balcony of the Royal Palace. Contemporaries such as Louis Hymans and Hendrik Conscience – who would later be the subject of a mass tribute himself – wrote of the enormous masses of people that had come to the capital on 23 July:

> The entirety of Belgium, united in the capital, watched them parading one after the other, to the enthusiastic cheers of a population of half a million souls.[12]

The various wagons, interspersed with groups of people in period costume, followed each other in chronological order, forming a kind of living story, and allowing the audience to gain an overview of this 'constructed' ideal past. Janssens notes that certain episodes of Belgian history were conspicuously absent from the spectacle:

> It was somewhat remarkable that the historic parade did not feature any scene from the Dutch Revolt of the sixteenth century, from the Brabant Revolution or from the Belgian Revolution. The evoca-

5. One of the floats of the province of Liège at the historical pageant in Brussels in 1856 to celebrate the 25th anniversary of Belgian independance. This float represented the Liège arms industry in a medieval setting. The engraving was published in H. Conscience, Beschryving der nationale jubelfeesten te Brussel *(Brussels, 1856). [Leuven, KU Leuven, Centrale bibliotheek: 4B6275]*

10 On the importance of gymnastics, and festivals of gymnastics, see Bank and Van Buuren, *1900*, 260-264. For a more complete overview of these events, see Ibid., 21-90; Janssens, *De Belgische natie viert*; Stynen, *Een geheugen in fragmenten*; Hooze, Tollebeek and Verschaffel, *Mise-en-scène*; Tollebeek et al., *België een parcours van herinnering*.

11 Anderson, *Imagined Communities*.

12 Hymans quoted in Janssens, *De Belgische natie viert*, 85.

tion of these episodes, which symbolized resistance to royal power, were not
deemed appropriate to the framework of
the 'monarchical' July Festivities.[13]

Besides the great procession, five triumphal
arches had been set up to welcome the king,
just as they had been for his entry into the
capital in July 1831. The events formed an
exuberant expression of the nation's recogni-
tion and gratitude towards the king, and the
engravings that illustrate them give a good
idea of the monumental theatrical performances taking place.[14]

That it was the organizers' intention to
create illusion and theatrical imagery is
evident from complaints received about the
staging of a later parade, in 1905. The festival committee knew that the urban setting
of earlier parades – the narrow streets of
old Brussels during the time of Leopold I –
complemented the historical evocation of the
spectacle very well. In contrast, the modern
look that the city had acquired after the
interventions of Leopold II, as he remodelled
it with broad boulevards in the style of Paris,
largely ruined the parade's illusion of homogeneity.

> Our streets and our boulevards are disap-
> pointing in this aspect: the small groups
> will be dwarfed by their surroundings, and
> in such large spaces, the decorative aspect
> will be reduced to zero.[15]

The number of pageant wagons was also
reduced for the 1905 parade, owing to the
tram power lines that had been installed
along the route. This time, the highlight of
the celebrations was not the historic parade
but a grand spectacle of knight jousting, a
re-enactment of the tournament that had
taken place in February 1452 in honour of
Charles the Bold. The premiere of the spectacle was reserved for the royal family and for
dignitaries, while two subsequent performances could be attended by the general public
if they were willing to purchase a ticket. This
was not to the liking of the audience, and

the press denounced the fact that the most
attractive spectacle of the festivities had been
reserved for the wealthy classes. Under pressure from the liberal press, the organizers
decided to put on a fourth performance free
of charge.

It was not only Belgium as a nation that
organized festivities as paragons of self-affirmation. Since the late nineteenth century,
the Flemish community had been strongly
attached to the symbolism of the Battle of
the Golden Spurs. A pageant was held in
Bruges on 29 August 1887, following the
inauguration of the statue of Jan Breydel
and Pieter de Coninck (the famous instigators of the Flemish protest against France),
but it was the city of Kortrijk in particular,
whose *Groeningekouter* had been the site
of the historical battle itself, that was the
central place of honour for this great event in
Flemish history.

In Kortrijk, numerous historical
parades took place that were typical of such
commemorations. The most theatrical of
these was scheduled for the festivities of
1902, entitled *Het groot vaderlandsch mimodrama van Groeninghe* (The Grand Patriotic
Mimodrama of Groeninghe). This 'drama',
mainly composed of *tableaux vivants*, had
been written by Gustaaf-Hendrik Flamen
and intended for performance before an
audience of 10,000 at the Groeningekouter.
Just as in the countless novels, songs and
poems about this event, the highpoint of
the spectacle was to be the scene in which a
number of Flemish warriors would eat some
of the Flemish earth, arousing their national
passions.[16] All of Kortrijk's inhabitants were
to be involved in the historical evocation.
Yet the mimodrama was never performed.
Officially, the performance was prevented by
technical problems, but it is more likely that
it was opposed by those who disapproved of
the anti-royalist and anti-French passages in
the text.

It was not until 1952 that a large-scale
theatrical event was performed in Kortrijk.
In July of that year, the Grand Place hosted
a mass spectacle written by Willem Putman

13 Janssens, *De Belgische natie viert*,
    86.
14 Ibid., 24 and 27.
15 Rouvez quoted in Janssens, *De
    Belgische natie viert*, 95.
16 Stynen, *Een geheugen in frag-
    menten*, 219.

and directed by Antoon Vander Plaetse. Most telling is the failure of a reprisal of this event, planned for 1962. Stynen concludes that 'the Kortrijk mass spectacle of 1952 ended a period of history'. The reasons for the failure included bad weather and the fact that Putman's *Guldensporenspel* (Golden Spurs Play) looked 'deplorably archaic and devoid of imagination' after the ten years that had passed. Also, though, there seemed to be a generally held view that the time had come to stop romanticizing the past.[17]

The situation in the Netherlands little resembled that of Belgium, and the euphoria of regaining independence after Napoleonic domination in 1813 was shared by all (except for a small number of Orangist circles). A century later, it was still the subject of numerous celebrations. Together with the coronation of Queen Wilhelmina on 6 September 1898, this event regularly provided a fine opportunity for a political spectacle.

What is remarkable about the coronation ceremony is that the festivities are very well documented: photographs were taken, and the entire event was even filmed. The film was then shown throughout the country and attracted great public attention as a particularly modern account of the ceremony. Two architects, Ed. Cuypers and Willem Kromhout, had been invited to decorate the capital in festive style for the occasion. Kromhout, in particular – who would later design the Hotel Américain in Amsterdam – had no wish to adhere to the traditional repertoire of triumphal arches executed in faux stone. He opted for a maritime theme, deemed especially appropriate as an expression of the Dutch national character. An example of this maritime theme is the Queen's being brought from the Royal Palace on Dam Square to the Nieuwe Kerk under a pergola of fishing nets. Similarly, in the evening, the festive lights decorating the city were intended to convey a 'Venetian' experience. Naturally, the festivities also included a historical and allegorical pageant. Museum Square had been chosen by the Orange dynasty as the setting in which it

would legitimate itself in front of the Dutch people. Extras taking part in the procession were members of (non-socialist) workers organizations and Orangist associations from Amsterdam.

Examples of festive events such as the celebrations of Belgian independence or the coronation of Queen Wilhelmina demonstrate adequately how mass culture had arisen and evolved during the long nineteenth century. In particular, they show how a political or ideological program could be transformed into an urban spectacle for a huge number of spectators, in which the representation of reality remained at all times subordinate to and determined by political discourse.

6. *The coronation of Queen Wilhelmina (Amsterdam, 1898). The Queen is brought to the Nieuwe Kerk under a pergola of fishing nets. [Amsterdam, Gemeentearchief]*

17 Stynen, *Een geheugen in fragmenten*, 131. See also the chapter 'The Pilgrimages of the Yser'.

BUFFALO
BILL'S
WILD
WEST
THE PARTINGTON ADVERTISING CIE
14, RUE LAFAYETTE, PARIS
171, STRAND LONDON, W. C.
DÉPOSÉ.
50 CENTIMES

Disciplined Freaks and Redskins

The Ghent Performances of the American Mass Spectacles *Barnum and Bailey* (1901) and *Buffalo Bill* (1906)

Evelien Jonckheere

This chapter will present two early-twentieth-century forerunners to the commercial mass cultural phenomena we know today under the form of music festivals and sporting events. The mass spectacle *Barnum and Bailey's The Greatest Show on Earth* was performed in Ghent on 9-11 November 1901. Five years later, *Buffalo Bill's Wild West and Congress of Rough Riders of the World* was shown on 20 and 21 September 1906.

Both shows were produced by the US company founded by Phineas Taylor Barnum, who was described by a local Ghent newspaper as 'an American who has achieved celebrity by showing all kinds of 'miracles' such as giants, dwarfs, etcetera, and by collecting exceptionally large menageries'.[1]

Like today's sporting events, these spectacles were characterized by massive ticket sales, large-scale publicity campaigns, daring entrepreneurship and big business. Mass spectacle is not easy to define, but may best be described as a theatrical production on an industrial scale that caters to exceptionally large audiences.[2]

After a brief description of the two shows, this chapter will focus on the issues of discipline and the spectacularization of reality. Both *The Greatest Show on Earth* and the *Wild West Show* were illustrations of the 'exhibitionary complex' that characterized modern visual culture from the late eighteenth century onwards, according to cultural historian Tony Bennett in *The Birth of the Museum* (1995).

According to Bennett, this 'complex' was one of the mechanisms used to spread self-regulation in modern society, whereby the ruling ideals of Western imperialism and capitalism became internalized. Mass spec-

tacles such as *Barnum and Bailey* and *Buffalo Bill* nicely illustrate this manipulative interplay of science, commerce and imperialism taking place in the early twentieth century. With the slogan 'seeing is believing', a society of the spectacle was created.[3]

In her study *Spectacular Realities* (1998), Vanessa Schwartz noted that in urban cultures such as that of fin-de-siècle Paris, reality was increasingly communicated through images. Both *Barnum and Bailey* and *Buffalo Bill* produced similar sensational images of reality, which prided themselves on their authenticity. Yet the disciplining power of 'spectacular reality' was not infallible, and reality regularly disproved the spectacular image, as the press reviews of the performances will illustrate.

Mass Spectacle

The size of the Barnum and Bailey circus that arrived in Ghent in November 1901 was unprecedented. It involved four trains, 67 wagons, 1,000 performers and staff, 170 horses, three troops of elephants and various wild animals, three arenas and two stages, twelve tents, including a hippodrome tent of nearly 14,000 square meter, and a separate menagerie. The hippodrome tent could seat 12,000 spectators, but some articles even reported that 50,000 spectators visited per day.[4] It was, after all, *The Greatest Show on Earth*.[5]

Buffalo Bill's arrival in 1906 was not far behind in size: five trains and fifty wagons, 800 artists and staff, 500 horses and, again, various sources that speak of between 12,000 and 20,000 spectators.[6]

1. *Programme of* Buffalo Bill's Wild West and Congress of Rough Riders of the World, *undated [c. 1902].* *[Ghent, UGent, Universiteitsbibliotheek, Collection of Ephemera]*

1 *Gazette van Gent,* 8 Nov. 1882.
2 Naremore and Brantlinger, *Modernity and Mass Culture*, 2.
3 Corbey, "Ethnographic Showcases, 1870-1930" , 360.
4 *La Flandre libérale*, 6 Oct. 1901 and *De Vooruit*, 13 Oct. 1901.
5 *La Flandre libérale*, 28 Oct. 1901; *Gazette van Gent*, 2 Nov. and 4 Nov. 1901.
6 Contrast *Gazette van Gent*, 8 Sept. 1906, *Bien Public*, 7 Sept. 1906 and *Bien Public*, 14 Sept. 1906, with *De Vooruit*, 22 Sept. 1906.

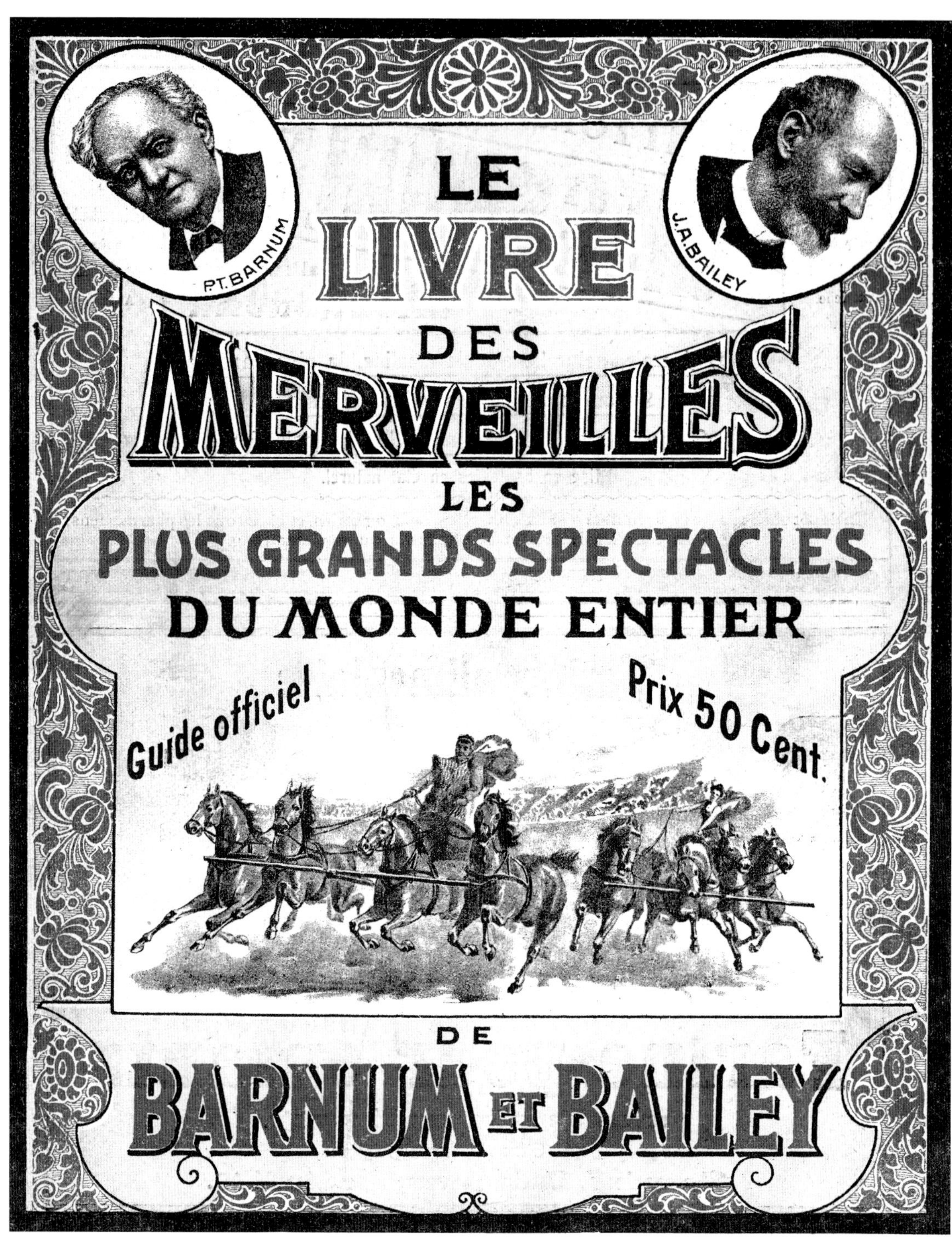

2. Programme of Barnum and Bailey's The Greatest Show on Earth, *undated [c. 1901].*
[Ghent, UGent, Universiteitsbibliotheek]

In order to engage a sufficiently large audience for a show of this size, a sophisticated publicity campaign was required. More than a month before the arrival of *The Greatest Show on Earth*, a white American car with gold lettering could be seen driving into town to awaken the public's curiosity.

Posters were put up all over the city, some of which measured up to 50 square meter, and thousands of promotional booklets were distributed.[7]

Newspapers regularly received reports with stories about the spectacle's origin and its previous travels, which were meant to

7   *Gazette van Gent*, 3 Oct. 1901.

94

3. Circus Barnum & Bailey.
Prunkwagen von 40 Pferden gezogen.
*Postcard of the advertising campaign for
Barnum and Bailey's, undated.*
[Collection Guy Puttevils]

4. Souvenir de Barnum et Bailey.
Déchargement des trains spéciaux de
Barnum & Bailey. *Postcard showing the
unloading of the Barnum and Bailey's
train, undated.*
[Collection Guy Puttevils]

kindle the readers' curiosity. For example,
a rumor was spread that Barnum and his
former competitor Bailey had decided to
tour together after the latter had set up
the following publicity stunt. Barnum had
wanted to purchase a baby elephant from the
lesser known circus of Bailey. No elephant
had ever been born in captivity in America
until then, and Barnum was offering 100,000
US dollars. Bailey turned him down, though,
and then began to advertise his show in the
following matter: 'come and see the elephant
that Barnum wanted, but could not buy'.
Barnum is said to have been so impressed by
this that he said to Bailey: 'I am a great king
of advertising, but you are still greater, and if
you want we will run our shows together as
Barnum and Bailey.'[8]

Despite the fact that P.T. Barnum had
already died by the time the shows came to
Ghent, his entrepreneurship was still widely
revered. In his autobiography, excerpts of
which were published in the newspaper
La Flandre libérale shortly before the show

8   *Gazette van Gent*, 3 Oct. 1901.

opened, he stressed that he was a 'self-made man' whose success had been down to his daring and his sense of business. A similar story was also run about William Frederick Cody, otherwise known as Buffalo Bill, who had also published an autobiography.[9]

In this way, both Barnum and Buffalo Bill had themselves become 'attractions' of their own shows. Their life stories, circulated through the press, were full of figures detailing their investments and profits. Neither did they hesitate to report the costs and profits of the Ghent spectacles in the newspapers: the daily food costs for the staff and menagerie of *The Greatest Show* reportedly amounted to 37,500 Belgian francs, while *Buffalo Bill* was reported as costing no less than 20,000 Belgian francs per show. Takings from the 1901 show amounted to 140,000 Belgian francs, according to *La Flandre libérale*. The *Bien Public* estimated the total capital of Barnum and Bailey Inc. to be as high as 50 million Belgian francs in 1906. Even the socialist newspaper *Vooruit* expressed its admiration for the company: 'The Barnum circus is living proof of the Americans' practical spirit and bold sense of business, and as such it commands our respect and admiration.'[10]

A Well-Disciplined Organization

Order and discipline were what the Barnum and Bailey organization was famous for in 1901. Even the show's program emphasized this aspect:

Those who visit the World's Greatest Fair Barnum and Bailey are particularly struck by three things: first, the gigantic nature of the enterprise, second, its splendid organization, and third, its indisputable superiority over everything that has ever been done or tried in the same genre. No organization has succeeded in managing the distribution of tickets, or the entering and seating of thousands of visitors, with an equally high degree of order and discipline.[11]

As the final song, the Belgian national anthem, was being sung at the end of the last show, the first workers would already be appearing, ready to dismantle the tent. Before all of the spectators had left the big marquee, almost all of the stands would have been dismantled, and most of the smaller tents would be lying on the ground. The entire menagerie was dismantled in less than twelve minutes, and in 52 minutes even the marquee had been loaded onto the trucks.[12]

The socialist newspaper *Vooruit* was quick to connect the systematic division of labour exemplified by the Barnum and Bailey show with a key social issue of that time, namely the factories' exploitation of workers.

The manner of assembling and dismantling the circus, the mode of travel and the lives of the staff, the marvellous discipline that reigns everywhere, all of these prove to us that the division of labour can perform miracles.[13]

The *Vooruit* journalists claimed that this kind of labour distribution was actually far from representing reality, since a large proportion of the population were not involved in real, well-organized labour. Moreover, they had noticed how quietly the work proceeded in the company of Barnum and Bailey. Each worker conducted his task calmly, without any shouting.

The strength of Barnum and Bailey's business, then, was felt to rely on the internalized sense of order that equipped the workers with the ideal psychological attitude for beginning their work. *La Flandre libérale* wrote that the miraculous order prevailing throughout the organization was enough to show that Mr Bailey 'had a knowledge of human psychology equally profound as his knowledge of running a business'.[14]

In his 1975 study *Discipline and Punish*, Michel Foucault described how social practices from the end of the eighteenth century onwards increasingly exercised power through processes of internalization rather than force. While in the past

9 *La Flandre libérale*, 20 Oct. 1901, referring to the autobiography entitled *The Life of P.T. Barnum, including his golden rules for money-making* (1888), translated by Jehan Soudan.

10 *La Flandre libérale*, 6 Oct. 1901; *Gazette van Gent*, 20 Sept. 1906; *La Flandre libérale*, 12 Nov. 1901; *Bien Public*, 21 Sept. 1906; *De Vooruit*, 10 Nov. 1901.

11 Program of *Barnum and Bailey's Greatest Show on Earth*, Collection of Ephemera, Ghent University Library.

12 *La Flandre libérale*, 12 Nov. and 28 Oct. 1901; *Gazette van Gent*, 20 Sept. 1906.

13 *De Vooruit*, 10 Nov. 1901.

14 *La Flandre libérale*, 18 Oct. 1901.

5. Barnum & Bailey's greatest show on earth. Dakzeil van Groote tent halverwege opgeheschen. *Postcard showing the erection of the Barnum and Bailey's tents, c. 1906.*
[Collection Guy Puttevils]

the sovereign's power had been imposed on the people through violent punishments, the Enlightenment introduced new social technologies that manipulated individuals' conduct in more subtle ways.

Foucault cites as an example the modifications to the British prison system that were proposed by Jeremy Bentham. His Panopticon offered an effective structure of surveillance that would make it possible to guide the behaviour of a prisoner through self-regulation.[15]

Besides prison life, many other domains, such as education and health care, were to be affected by the introduction of new technologies. Furthermore, the increasing dependence on the centralized organization of time, e.g., by means of timetables in the railway station and the factory, would have a disciplining effect on people's behaviour.[16]

This disciplinary trend was also reflected in the work ethic and the organization of mass spectacles such as *Barnum and Bailey* and *Buffalo Bill*. Every show began at the precise moment the bell was sounded, and every show proceeded according to a strict program. Such techniques were necessary in order to control both the masses and the large numbers of performers.

The Exhibitionary Complex

From the end of the eighteenth century onwards, this form of self-regulation, guided by minor interventions, was absorbed into the broader context of 'rational recreation'.[17] This was leisure that aimed to 'reform the self', and may thus be seen as a form of surveillance that was intended to improve moral and mental health.

On the modern concept of recreation, Tony Bennett quotes the following passage from the *Treatise on the Police of the Metropolis*, published in 1795 by the Scottish magistrate Patrick Colquhoun:

Since recreation is necessary to Civilised Society, all Public Exhibitions should be rendered subservient to improvement of morals, and to the means of infusing into

15 Foucault, *Discipline and Punish*, 172.
16 Foster, *The Anti-Aesthetic*, 45.
17 Bailey, *Leisure and Class in Victorian England*.

18 Colquhoun, *A Treatise on the Police of the Metropolis*, London: Bye & Law, 1806, 347-348 in: Bennett, *The Birth of the Museum*, 18-19.

19 Bennett, *The Birth of the Museum*, 65-57.

20 Reiss, *The Showman and the Slave*.

21 This information is based on the pamphlet *Adelaïde la Tigrée* and other documents related to the Ghent fair of 1870 (*halfvastenfoor*), Collection of Ephemera, Ghent, Universiteitsbibliotheek.

the mind a love of the Constitution, and a reverence and respect for the Laws.[18]

The orderly sequences of both the *Barnum and Bailey* and *Buffalo Bill* spectacles had a similar structure to that of traditional circus programs from the late eighteenth century onwards. During the nineteenth century, the disciplinary trend increasingly affected not only the circus but the entire fairground environment, which meant that the tumultuous disorder and uncontrolled behaviour of its visitors was from this point on 're-created'.[19]

Foucault describes how the prison became a form of education rather than of punishment. In the same way, the tumultuous festival of the fairground was transformed into an orderly school, in which the spectacles also became more and more like 'lessons' rather than just cabinets of curiosity filled with grotesque bodies.

P.T. Barnum, who had been a showman originally, understood this evolution well and chose to introduce the spectacular phenomena he exhibited to academic discourse. Thus, in the 1830s, he frequently invited scientists to examine 'his' Joyce Heth, the woman who had reputedly educated George Washington as a boy and was said to be 161 years old.[20]

In Ghent, too, similar practices were not uncommon at that time. A notable example is the case of Adelaïde la Tigrée, who was examined by doctors at the fair of 1870. She was billed as a gracious and charming woman, whose entire body was covered with tiger-like markings of about 3 to 4 inches across. A medical report documenting the examination was signed by three Ghent professors, who confirmed the authenticity of the spots. As other documents also show, they had indeed been invited by showman Philippe to come to the Café de la Concorde on 24 March 1870, where they could investigate this 'miracle of nature'.[21]

Though popular, such practices cannot be described as 'surveillance practices' in the sense described above. Instead, they made use of an ancient tool, that of spectacle, to clarify the norms and orders of nature which were to be internalized. The above examples concern the normative power of science, used to classify people according to a certain

6. Barnum and Bailey Limited. Grösste Schaustellung der Erde. *Postcard showing images of several Barnum and Bailey's 'freaks', undated.* [Collection Guy Puttevils]

hierarchy, over which the healthy white Western male presided. Even so, according to Bennett, this show could also be considered a 'set of cultural technologies concerned to organize a voluntarily self-regulating citizenry'.[22]

Bennett noted that nineteenth-century phenomena, such as the museum, the department store, the world fair, the panorama and many others, used the 'exhibition' format to offer the viewer a clear picture of the cosmic order. Bennett described this nineteenth-century increase in exhibitionary techniques as an 'exhibitionary complex'. Like the disciplining techniques of surveillance, such as the Panopticon, the exhibitionary techniques belonged to the wider framework of the 'disciplinary society'. Modern exhibitionary practices offered 'a set of educative and civilizing agencies' which functioned as a permanent display of power and knowledge.[23]

The most famous among them were the world exhibitions organized by any self-respecting city in the second half of the nineteenth century. They were meant to illustrate the progress of Western civilization through systematic orderings. They claimed to be comprehensive, and to contain a certain 'encyclopaedic power' which enabled them to represent the macrocosm inside a microcosm.[24]

The mass spectacles of *Barnum and Bailey* and *Buffalo Bill* were also part of this exhibitionary complex. They were promoted as 'the greatest exhibition in the world', or as exhibitions with the purpose of 'instructing'.[25] They presented themselves as complete, with titles such as *The Greatest Show on Earth*, or programs priding themselves on the representation of distant lands and ancient times:

> This exposition is particularly interesting for the new generation, which has not yet travelled to these far away lands. It allows them to see different peoples in their national costumes before they disappear, before they belong only to painters and to history.[26]

In both spectacles' programs, a clearly structured order of relationships between things and between people is evident. This hierarchy was in line with the rhetoric of imperialism, which contrasted the Western body

22 Bennett, *The Birth of the Museum*, 63.
23 Ibid., 63-66.
24 Corbey, "Ethnographic Showcases", 340.
25 Programs of *Barnum and Bailey* and *Buffalo Bill*.
26 Program of *Buffalo Bill*.

7. Barnum and Bailey Limited. Grösste Schaustellung der Erde. *Postcard of Roman-styled chariot races in the Barnum and Bailey's circus, undated.* [Collection Guy Puttevils]

8. *Programme of* Buffalo Bill's Wild West, *undated [ca. 1902].*
[Ghent, UGent, Universiteitsbibliotheek,
Collection of Ephemera]

with the 'uncivilized' body, and therefore meant that the spectacles of the exhibitionary complex were forms of propaganda for Western imperialism.[27]

According to Margaret Malamud, the Roman re-enactments which were part of the Barnum and Bailey show can be read as an allegory of the imperial forces of the modern West.[28] The program described them as follows:

> Then came the chariot races, a re-enactment of the ancient races as they were at the Olympics in Greece and at the Circus Maximus and the Colosseum in Rome. These are all absolutely unforgettable scenes. The various competitions, which engage man's energy, the accuracy of his eyes and his intrepidity, constitute one of the most captivating and grandiose spectacles of the greatest show on Earth.[29]

Buffalo Bill also demonstrates Western superiority. When battles were re-enacted, it was always the Western side that was victorious, and the other side, such as the Native Americans, were invariably portrayed as wild and uncivilized. Once the barbarous enemy had submitted to the West, however, a bond of friendship could be established. In contrast to *The Greatest Show*, there was a strong emphasis on military discipline and nationalism in this spectacle. It is also striking that the external aspects of the show, such as its logistical organization, exhibited the same order, thereby illustrating the self-regulating power of the spectacle. The various ethnic groups that made up the company were clearly segregated. The Mexicans, Japanese and other groups almost always sat at separate tables during meals. Even outside of the show, the Native Americans were completely sequestered within closed tents.[30]

The exhibition of 'freaks' or 'phenomena' in Barnum's *Greatest Show on Earth* can be read as scientific propaganda for the normative body. Based on the popularization of biological science through Darwin, nature was approached hierarchically.[31]

These 'strange and bizarre human beings, which do not fall under ordinary physiological laws' were even placed in the same category as wild animals, in the case of *Barnum and Bailey*, since they were exhibited in the same tent.[32]

The spectacles of *Barnum and Bailey* or *Buffalo Bill* not only contributed to the self-regulation of the viewer, but also reinforced the position of Western man in the 'cosmic order'. Such exhibitions were prime examples of how the 'new technologies of vision' would spread the knowledge being articulated in new disciplines such as history, biology, art history and anthropology.[33]

The Society of the Spectacle

Technologies of vision, such as world fairs, museums, department stores and mass spectacles, demonstrate the abundance of visual spectacle that existed in the modern age. Schwartz describes how modern Western society in the nineteenth century was transformed into a spectacular reality, in which the new mass culture generated sensationalized versions of daily life.[34]

The mass spectacles *Barnum and Bailey* and *Buffalo Bill* are illustrative of this tendency. These shows also claimed to offer a sensational version of reality and its actors, and were able to seduce large numbers of visitors using well-organized publicity strategies. According to Schwartz, such sensational images and stories created a 'common culture' or 'mass culture' among the public, among whom the shows became a major topic of everyday conversation.[35]

> The big event has finally arrived. During the last few weeks, it has become a true obsession. The famous American circus was the subject of every conversation. In every street, we saw posters announcing the most extraordinary attractions. Never before, we believe, has such publicity been created in our city for any exhibition.[36]

27 Bennett, *The Birth of the Museum*, 67.

28 Malamud, "Roman Entertainments for the Masses in Turn-of-the-Century New York", 53.

29 Program of *Barnum and Bailey*.

30 *Gazette van Gent*, 20 Sept. 1906.

31 Tromp, *Victorian Freaks*, 2.

32 Program of *Barnum and Bailey*.

33 Corbey, "Ethnographic Showcases", 363.

34 Schwartz, *Spectacular Realities*, 4-5.

35 Ibid., 6.

36 *La Flandre libérale*, 9 Nov. 1901.

PROGRAMME

1.   Entrée des célébrités et groupes

Groupes d'Indiens **Arraphoes**.
Plenty Wolves (beaucoup de loups) leur chef.
Groupe de **Cow-Boys** (bouviers américains).
Jim Mitchell, leur chef.
Groupe d'Indiens **Brûlés**.
Short Bull (le taureau trapu), leur chef.
Groupe de la tribu indienne des **Cut Off**.
Kicking Bear (l'ours qui rue), leur chef.
Groupe de **Vaqueras mexicains**.
Senor **Antonio Esquival**, leur chef.
Groupe d'Indiens **Cheyennes**.
Lone Bull (le taureau solitaire), leur chef.
Groupe de **dames** du **Far West** américain.
Groupe d'Indiens **Sioux**.
Les **Boy Chiefs**, fils de chefs Sioux.
Drapeaux des nations amies.
John Nelson, le plus vieux coureur des bois d'Amérique.
Bone Necklace, chef indien âgé de 80 ans.
Groupe d'Indiens **Ogallala Sioux**
Black Heart (le cœur noir), leur chef.
Low-Neck (le cou trapu), chef.
Long-Wolf (le loup allongé), sorcier, ou l'homme aux médecines des Sioux.
" **Buffalo-Bill** „ (colonel W. F. Cody), chef des Eclaireurs de l'armée des Etats-Unis.

2.   Courses de chevaux

entre un Cow-Boy, un Mexicain et un Indien, tous montés sur chevaux hispano-mexicains.

3.   Miss Annie Oakley, célèbre tireuse

maniant les armes à feu avec une virtuosité et une adresse sans égales.

4.   Faits historiques de la vie de Buffalo-Bill

Le 17 juillet 1875, à War Bonnet-Creek, dans le Dakota, Buffalo-Bill défia en combat singulier et tua Yellow Hand (la main jaune) le chef des Sioux. Ce duel, en présence des troupes américaines et des Indiens, et entre les représentants de la race blanche et de la race rouge, eut pour l'Amérique la même valeur pittoresque que le combat des Horaces et des Curiaces.

5.   Ancienne poste par poneys

Ceci représente la manière dont les lettres et les dépêches étaient transportées à travers les Etats-Unis avant l'introduction des chemins de fer et des télégraphes. Le postillon devait changer de monture tous les 10 milles (16 kilomètres) et faire ses 50 milles (80 kilomètres) d'une traite.

6.   Attaque par les Indiens d'un convoi d'émigrants
et défense de celui-ci par les habitants des frontières.

L'attaque étant repoussée, cow-boys et dames américaines dansent à cheval la Bourrée Virginienne.

N. B. Ces wagons sont exactement ceux qui s'employaient il y a 35 ans.

7.   Le petit John Baker, le célèbre tireur

Exercice d'adresse avec le fusil.

8.   Exercices à cheval

Ramasser à terre, en plein galop, des objets tombés. Lancement des lassos, indiquant la manière de capturer les chevaux et le bétail. Exécution d'exercices à cheval.

On y montera les buck-jumpers, les chevaux les plus rétifs et les plus intraitables qui existent. Il est impossible de les dompter et ils jettent à terre tout cavalier qui les enfourche.

9.   Tir au pistolet et au revolver

exécuté par C.-L. DALY.

10.   Courses entre dames américaines des forêts

11.   Attaque par les Indiens de la malle-poste de Deadwood

Ils sont repoussés par les cow-boys sous les ordres de Buffalo Bill.

N. B. Ceci est la véritable malle-poste que l'on appelait la vieille patache de Deadwood, célèbre par le nombre de personnes qui y ont perdu la vie. Elle roulait entre Deadwood et Cheyenne il y a quelque 18 ans. Deux présidents des Etats-Unis, quatre rois et d'autres princes qui assistaient au jubilé de la Reine d'Angleterre se sont fait trainer dans cette voiture, tant ils regardaient ce coche comme une rareté et historique. Elle relève encore l'intérêt de cette représentation.

12.   Courses entre enfants indiens, à cheval sans selle

13.   Façons de vivre des Indiens

Camp indien dans les prairies et courses à pied. Danses de caractère et sports.

14.   Colonel W. F. CODY (Buffalo-Bill)

Exercices de tir hors pair.

15.   Chasse au bison

telle qu'elle se pratique en Amérique. Le seul troupeau de bisons de pure race américaine et tel qu'il ne s'en trouve même plus dans les jardins zoologiques. Buffalo-Bill et les Indiens.

16.   Attaque par les Indiens

d'un village de frontière. Défense par les cow-boys sous les ordres de Buffalo-Bill.

Salut et départ

That sensationalized or 'spectacular' reality was often a simplistic caricature of real events. For example, the autobiographies of both P.T. Barnum and Buffalo Bill mixed real facts with fantastic tales of adventure. There are, for instance, strong doubts that Cody could really have been a member of the Pony Express postal service travelling through Native American territory in his younger years, although this scene was a permanent attraction of the Wild West Show.[37]

There was mutual interaction between Cody's sensational biography and that of the characters in Wild West stories in the US 'dime novels' or the European Aimard novels. The entire representation of the 'Wild West' therefore functioned as a kind of 'dream factory'. Reality was mixed with sensational stories in order to increase the sales of literature and spectacle.[38]

Creating dreams was the mechanism used by the new capitalist system to stimulate the consumption of goods and, simultaneously, to spread bourgeois Western values. Walter Benjamin wrote that the world fairs could be considered 'places of pilgrimage to the Fetish commodity'.[39]

The fact that major international corporations such as Barnum and Bailey, or Buffalo Bill's company, were responsible for these spectacles stimulated the suspicions of the European left, as early as the nineteenth century, that America was colonizing the rest of the world with a new kind of entertainment culture that was based not on high art but on the consumption of a standardized mass product which was aimed at the widest possible audience.[40]

This critique of mass culture came from theorists such as German sociologist Max Weber, Dutch historian Johan Huizinga, and German-Jewish exiles such as Max Horkheimer, Theodor Adorno, Leo Lowenthal, and Herbert Marcuse. The latter belonged to the 'Frankfurt School', who accused American radio, cinema and pulp magazines of causing the increasing 'disappearance of the inner life', the rise of the 'culture industry' and the development of a 'false consciousness' among the masses.[41]

Such thinkers inspired Guy Debord when he was writing his critique of the 'society of the spectacle', in which people were increasingly alienated from reality, and made into slaves of the capitalist consumer society.[42]

Only recently has this pessimistic evaluation of modern culture, in which an individual's free will is severely restricted by mass phenomena, been called into question, for instance by philosophers such as Jacques Rancière, who has criticized the dominance of the Foucauldian view on mass disciplining.[43]

That there were limits to the massification of the spectacle and the disciplining of the individual is apparent from a number of comments in the press about *Barnum and Bailey* and *Buffalo Bill*, which add a dissonant tone to the ubiquitous hymn to the greatness of the organization and its discipline.

As early as 1901, critics were beginning to complain that there were 'too many' attractions, and that it was impossible to see everything. The vastness of the 'hall', moreover, meant that the effect of the individual attractions was lost.[44]

Besides, the spectacle had nothing on show that was truly unseen, except for the sheer size and variety of it all, as may be learned from the following criticism:

> Before you enter the circus itself, there are a number of wondrous people on show: a man sticking needles into his body, one whose face is covered in hair like a dog, a girl with curly hair, a twenty-four-year-old who appears to be sixty-four, an electrical woman, a petrol drinker, a man breaking chains with the muscles of his chest, etc., besides some wild animals and elephants. All of this is remarkable, but not extraordinary. Most people who left the show were disappointed, and the idea that 1,000 spectators will come for each performance is questionable.[45]

The *Buffalo Bill* spectacle, too, seems not to have been entirely successful:

37 Springhall, *The Genesis of Mass Culture*, 109; program of *Buffalo Bill*.

38 Springhall, *The Genesis of Mass Culture*, 5 and 174-176; *Gazette van Gent*, 12 Sept. 1906.

39 Benjamin, "Paris: Capital of the Nineteenth Century", 167.

40 Springhall, *The Genesis of Mass Culture,* 5-6.

41 Jay, *The Dialectical Imagination*; Arato and Gebhardt, *The Essential Frankfurt School Reader*.

42 Debord, *La Société du spectacle*.

43 Rancière, *The Emancipated Spectator*.

44 *Gazette van Gent*, 9 Nov. 1901.

45 *De Vooruit*, 10 Nov. 1901.

In fact, except for the discipline, and except for some local American flavour, the Buffalo troupe offers nothing that has not already been seen in our ordinary circuses. Yet Buffalo, on his short trip to Belgium, has cashed in to the tune of about a million.[46]

Moreover, the *Buffalo Bill* spectacle was strikingly like *Barnum and Bailey*'s five years earlier. Some songs from the show were similar, and the wagons and the procedure also proved to be just the same. There does appear to have been a lower level of discipline in the second tour, however:

> The unloading of the heavy wagons happened in about the same fashion, but with less discipline and less coherence. After a very long row of carriages had arrived, a whole load of riders appeared, including Indians, Cossacks, Japanese and what have you, each in their peculiar costumes. These people indeed looked very poor and dirty, and were as indifferent as cattle. The whole thing actually looks dirty and worn out, and the interior of the seemingly splendid wagons is truly disgusting. Some coaches are real dustbins and the beds in which they sleep look much worse and much smaller than those on the emigrant ships.[47]

The lack of discipline is likely to have been due in part to the fact that Ghent was the last stop on a four-year European tour. Soon, the artists would take the boat back to America, where a well-deserved break awaited. Some of the horses that would not be taken back were sold after the show, and the Native Americans threw away their shields and belts, trampling them underfoot like rubbish.[48]

In this way, then, the press not only channelled publicity for the show, but also offered a critical response to what was happening behind the scenes.

As for the cost of a ticket for *Barnum and Bailey*, the newspaper *Vooruit* described the spectacle as 'truly expensive in the American style'. Tickets were not affordable for all of the city's households. Barnum could not sell all of the tickets for the five shows, and only the Sunday show was completely sold out. The majority of the city's inhabitants had to be content with the spectacle of the circus' arrival and its being put together and taken down, which perhaps explains why *Vooruit* – a workers' paper – treats this as the most conspicuous aspect of the event.[49]

Conclusion

Aside from any discussion of the value or danger of mass culture, *Barnum and Bailey* and *Buffalo Bill* may be considered pioneers of contemporary large-scale performance events such as rock concerts, festivals and sporting events. It was these American companies that first succeeded in creating serious investment in entertainment, disciplined organization, large-scale marketing and massive ticket sales. The evolution of commercial mass culture can also be considered a logical consequence of expansive urbanization and better worldwide transportation. Population growth, immigration and new capitalist structures therefore changed the scale of the entertainment industry.

Mass spectacles such as these demonstrated the potential power of order and discipline, through disciplining technologies related to the 'exhibitionary complex', and contributed in their way to the growing spectacularization of reality.

Critical press articles also demonstrated that they sometimes reached the limits of such order, however. The performances were not accessible to the entire public, for example, they induced a sense of disorientation, and the disciplined organization was not without flaws. The cracks in the order of mass spectacle highlighted the fragility of human beings' potential for disciplinization, and also revealed the boundaries of massification.

46 *Bien Public*, 21 Sept. 1906
47 *De Vooruit*, 21 Sept. 1906.
48 *Gazette van Gent*, 22 Sept. 1906.
49 *De Vooruit*, 10 and 12 Nov. 1901.

The Machine on Stage

Two Expressionist Mass Spectacles in the Netherlands

Ad van der Logt

Expressionist drama has never been very successful in the Netherlands. Between the wars, theatre received hardly any subsidies from the Dutch government, and even well-known directors such as William Royaards and Eduard Verkade were therefore forced to put on popular foreign plays which had a high chance of financial success in order to guarantee the survival of their companies. Moreover, the public was generally not receptive to experimental theatre with a Futurist, Dadaist or Surrealist slant.

The first Expressionist play performed in the Netherlands was *Vrijheid* (Freedom) by the German author Herbert Kranz, which premiered on 13 November 1921 in Haarlem, produced by *Het Schouwtooneel*. It was followed in 1923 by *Dat ben jij* (This Is You) by Friedrich Wolf, staged by *Het Nieuwe Tooneel*, but both performances were curiosities in the companies' repertoires.

These productions were mostly aimed at demonstrating a new artistic direction in the theatre, rather than at expressing a particular political tendency.[1] Only in *Gas I* by Georg Kaiser, performed in 1928 by the *Het Vereenigd Tooneel* (United Theatre) together with 250 members of the *Arbeiders Jeugd Centrale*, and directed by Albert van Dalsum, was the emphasis on the political content.

Van Dalsum was the only Dutch stage director who was a strong supporter of Expressionism. Despite his lecture on the topic in Arnhem on 13 July 1924, and his subsequent productions of *Gas I* and *D 16 MM* (both in 1928), his efforts were still little more than a voice crying in the wilderness. The call for innovation failed to gain much support among his colleagues in the professional Dutch theatre, mainly because of the disastrous economic and social developments that were taking place in the 1920s.

For Van Dalsum, theatre was the place to reveal the truth about his era. Together with August Defresne, with whom he founded *Het Oost-Nederlands Tooneel* (The East-Dutch Theatre), they regarded themselves as the chroniclers of their time, or as they put it: 'We play the living theatre of our time.'[2] That was why the theatre should receive its own place and a new function in a changing world. The theatre should be at the service of ideas, not of a general nature, as the famous actor and director Eduard Verkade had always emphasized, but specifically related to their own time, though this might be of a religious, philosophical or political nature.

In an Expressionist production, actors were required to let go of their customary acting styles, which were inevitably based on psychological realism. They had to employ their voices, gestures and facial expressions to portray something that transcended everyday reality. In Expressionist drama, actors spoke in a staccato-like way. Their movements and gestures had to be compelling and powerful, like those of a marionette. Stage design, which until then had tried to imitate reality, was now expected to represent the essence of the piece in a symbolic way, and be part and parcel of what was being performed.

Van Dalsum and Defresne did not succeed in their attempts to gain acceptance for Expressionist theatre in the Netherlands. The actors in their company were barely aware of what this form of modern drama was or could be. In Germany, where the

1   Van Gaal, "13 juli 1924: Albert van Dalsum houdt een voordracht in het Oolgaerthuis te Arnhem", 621.
2   De Leeuwe, "Dalsum, Albertus Wilhelmus van".

movement had originated, Expressionist drama had already passed its peak. However, Van Dalsum's two mass spectacle productions remain interesting case studies for both theatre history and cultural history.

Gas I by Georg Kaiser

Gas I (1918) was written as the second part of a trilogy that also included *Die Koralle* (The Coral, 1917) and *Gas II* (1920). In *Die Koralle,* the central protagonist is a labourer who, despite his unhappy childhood, works his way up to become a billionaire. Through this character, Kaiser examines the question of whether a happy life may be achieved through unscrupulous behaviour.

The billionaire's son is the protagonist of *Gas I.* Unlike his father, he is an idealistic socialist who shares the profits from the gasworks with his workers. During his daughter's wedding, however, the factory explodes. The owner refuses to rebuild the plant, since he has realized that modern technology is dangerous and inhumane. The workers must be retrained as farmers, so that they might live more freely and naturally. In the program brochure, Van Dalsum emphasizes Kaiser's intentions:

> Georg Kaiser says: but the product that you all create together, and which no one can oversee, is gas! It is an explosive and dangerous product, for it is produced with material means from a material spirit. There is no spiritual guidance, man has become a means ... The individual who would go against this inexorable system and come to claim the human would face certain death.[3]

The workers are not receptive to his message, however. They are degenerate, and have become part of the machines they operate day after day. Once again the billionaire's son warns them, but the people do not want to escape from alienation, since their sense of awareness has been dulled. Everyone goes back to his place and resumes work.

The billionaire's son eventually has to give up his resistance in the face of mounting pressure from his workers, who are led by an engineer (the embodiment of technocratic society) and from the capitalist factory managers ('the black men of labour') who are seeing their profits shrivel, and thirdly from the government, which intends to use the gas for war. Perhaps his own future son will realize his ideal. Since the problem is shifted to the next generation in this way, critics felt that *Gas I* did not succeed as a drama. They were of the opinion that Van Dalsum would have done better by combining *Gas I* and *Gas II.*

In *Gas II,* the gasworks have been rebuilt, and the son of the protagonist of *Gas I* (i.e., the original billionaire's grandson) is working among the workers. In the struggle between socialism and militarism – the war between Yellow and Blue has now erupted – he tries to convince the workers to strike. But while his grandfather had succeeded in protecting the people from themselves, he does not. At the end of the play, he commits suicide with a gas bullet and everything is destroyed: the day of the Last Judgement has arrived.

The dramatic conflict in *Gas I* takes place between the two main characters: the billionaire's son (played by Verkade) and the engineer (Van Dalsum). It is a struggle for working-class humanity, which functions in the context of this conflict, however, as a kind of sounding board. For today's audiences, Kaiser's drama seems not vivid enough, and his characters possess too little personality to truly captivate the audience. We might easily imagine that the gist of the text is better understood through reading it than by watching it in performance.

The critic of the *Nieuwe Rotterdamsche Courant* (5 March 1928) concluded that this play comes into its own as an oration rather than as a drama. Van Dalsum had attempted to compensate for the lack of dramatic tension between the main characters by enriching the production with considerable movement on the stage, along with

3 Quoted in Verkade-Cartier van Dissel, *Eduard Verkade en zijn strijd voor een nieuw toneel*, 436.

the impact of the explosion, and with the impressive crowd presence of the uniformed labourers.

Kaiser's drama was not possessed of the same relevance in 1928 that it had had when it was originally shown in 1919, just after the First World War. Many critics had the impression that the play had already been on Van Dalsum's list for a very long time, because it was a modern tragedy that was very different from the bourgeois realism generally appreciated by the Dutch theatre-going audience. Henrik Scholte, the critic of *De Groene Amsterdammer*, even accused Kaiser of having made a mistake:

> The billionaire's son, in his naive desire for a salvation colony, and the engineer, in his iron will to constantly increase gas production, continue to go from catastrophe to catastrophe, never backwards, never backwards to a lesser degree of motion. The play is therefore characterized by a duality of heroism, which means that it falls between two stools. Who is it really about? Both characters paraphrase the social conflict of formula and life in terms that have now only a distant resonance of those world orders which they wished to embody. The play has grown old very quickly.[4]

The critic sees Kaiser's Expressionism as the last spasm of humankind, which finds itself in crisis as it attempts to protect itself and its old-fashioned ideals from nihilism. According to Scholte, Van Dalsum would have been much better off in 1928 staging Bertolt Brecht's *Trommeln in der Nacht* (Drums in the Night, 1922), or Arnolt Bronnen's *Anarchie in Sillian* (Anarchy in Sillian, 1924).

The audience very much appreciated Wim Schumacher's set design, however. Critics even preferred its simplicity to the staging of the Berlin Volksbühne. The vast hall in the fourth act, especially, which featured two arches in a dimly lit space, as well as the stands and the sloping platform, were felt to have made a great impression.

One of the strongest scenes dramatically was when Van Dalsum and three other actors climbed into the stands one by one and addressed their heartfelt complaints directly to the audience.

Van Dalsum's company *Het Vereenigd Tooneel* was one of the leading Dutch companies of the mid 1920s, and held the exclusive right to play at the Amsterdam City Theatre for a considerable length of time. In the 1927-1928 season, the following plays were in repertory alongside *Gas I*: *L'Aiglon* (Rostand), *Mrs Warren's Profession* (Shaw), *A Servant of Two Masters* (Goldoni), *The Chinese Bungalow* (Osmond and Corbett), *John Marlay* (Dearden and Pertwee), *Nous ne sommes plus des enfants* (We Are Children No More, Léopold Marchand) and *The Game of Love and Chance* (Marivaux).

Strange as it may seem from today's perspective, the exalted Expressionist style and political content of *Gas I* were apparently not at odds with the distinctly traditional choices that made up the rest of the repertoire. The critic of *Het Algemeen Handelsblad* noted that this season's Amsterdam repertoires (including, therefore, that of *Het Vereenigd Tooneel*) presented no big surprises.[5]

Aside from the Constructivist-like set design, the most conspicuous elements of the production were the crowd scenes, which featured 250 members of the Young Workers' Centre. They represented the working masses, and were positioned on the sloping platform in the domed hall. Yet their actions made little impression, because they were disciplined, and therefore deemed too 'beautiful' for the tone of the play.

The only discordant element in the Expressionist framework was Verkade, who played the role of the billionaire's son. His idealism, according to the critics, did not come across as authentic because he could not appropriate the Expressionist style of acting. Moreover, he seemed not to know his lines well enough, which made him stress the wrong parts of the dialogue, and fall back on

4   *De Groene Amsterdammer*, 17 March 1928.

5   *Het Algemeen Handelsblad*, 17 June 1928.

2. Mannus Franken, D 16 MM.
[*Van den Boorn,* Mannus Franken]

the old-fashioned acting style he had used in his well-known interpretation of Hamlet.

Newspapers critics generally perceived the production as an interesting phenomenon. The main criticisms came mainly from the Catholic press, and, surprisingly, from socialist circles. The critic of the socialist newspaper *Het Volk* saw very little merit in the modern tragedy:

> Flat, plump nonsense, that is the content of this 'modern' play [...] Never has a more retarded and less imaginative mind written a utopian drama! [...] The first act, the only one of the five that was at all acceptable, was at least watchable, and the explosion was a good theatrical effect. The rest was a failure [...] A failure, which reached its saddest point in the fourth act, when the AJC took part in the crowd scenes.[6]

This criticism says a great deal about how contemporary socialists viewed art. A dramatic character who failed to achieve his ideal was apparently a disgrace to the stage.

Gas I was only performed six times and proved to be a financial disaster for Verkade and Verbeek's company. The two managers had agreed that the cost of stage design for a modern drama production should not exceed 600 florins. In this case, however, the sloping wooden floor alone cost ten times that budget.

D 16 MM by Mannus Franken

According to its author, Mannus Franken, the open-air mass spectacle *D 16 MM* was an attempt to capture the zeitgeist in theatrical form:

> There was a great catastrophe in the air – a fear that this Robot, this mechanized man, could turn into a Golem that would turn against the man who had conjured him. Thus arose the spectacle D 16 MM – blurry in its formulation, because the direction in which things developed became less and less clear; uncertain in its solution, because the time of the machine stormers was over, and one could not express

6   *Het Volk*, 5 March 1928.

anything else but a hope that man would not come out this fight too scathed.[7]

The play was Franken's reflection on the social, economic and political conditions of his time – a time of increasing industrialization and mechanization, which had transformed labour into production, seen consumption determine everyday life, and rationalized art.

The author of *D 16 MM*, Mannus Franken, had written the play to mark the 16th lustrum (or 80th anniversary) of the founding of the Delft Student Corps. It was performed twice in July 1928. The author was a playwright, translator and actor in the student theatre, and in 1927 he had been one of the founders of the Dutch Film League and of Amsterdam's avant-garde cinema *De Uitkijk*. Two years later, he collaborated with Joris Ivens on *Regen* (Rain) and *Branding* (Breakers), which are both regarded as key Constructivist films. In 1934 he became a pioneer of the documentary film, and his work in the Dutch East Indies in particular was regarded as an original contribution to the genre.

The performance of *D 16 MM* was one of the major contributions to the discussion on modernist architecture which was then taking place amongst students in Delft, which also included the International Course on New Architecture (December 1930). Such events were attended both by the traditional-thinking leader of the Delft School, Marinus Jan Granpré Moliere, and the main representatives of the 'new architecture' (including Walter Gropius, Marcel Breuer, Le Corbusier and Gerrit Rietveld). The staging and set design of Franken's play is testament to the impact that that discussion had.

D 16 MM fit in seamlessly with the debate on modern architecture taking place in the Delft School. It was also yet another attempt to develop a new community art, and in that sense, it belongs to the tradition of mass open-air spectacles staged by students from 1923 onwards. In the past, university lustrums had been celebrated with historic masquerades, a custom going back as far as the *Blijde Inkomsten* (Joyous Entries) organized by the Chambers of Rhetoric in the early modern period, which over the years

7   Van den Boorn, *Mannus Franken*, 12.

4. *Herman Teirlinck,* A-Z-spel *(A-Z Play), directed by Johan de Meester, Leiden, 1925.*

had degenerated into prestigious but costly spectacles.

The Delft students began the new trend in 1923 with *De torenbestormer* (The Tower Stormer, 1923) by Flemish writer Herman Teirlinck. Other student-organized mass spectacles followed in Groningen (1924), Leiden (1925) and Utrecht (1926).

Unlike those put on in the other university cities, the Delft spectacles could be called truly modernist at the levels of both content and staging. They were not just improved masquerades, as was the case with the mass student plays put on during the first two decades of the twentieth century. In content, the problem was truly contemporary and captivating: the extensive mechanization of man and of the human spirit. The design was reminiscent of the 'biomechanics' of Vsevolod Meyerhold, or of Alexander Tairov's theatrical productions. This modernist, industrial-style or Constructivist theatre was meant as a reaction to the naturalistic style used hitherto. It also modified the role of the audience: they should no longer sympathize with a fake sentimentalist version of reality, but realize that they have been assigned the task of reflecting on what has been shown.

The protest against mechanization in both *D 16 MM* and *Gas I* must have reminded contemporary spectators of books such as German politician Walther Rathenau's *Zur Mechanik des Geistes* (On the Mechanics of the Mind, 1913). In 1936, too, Walter Benjamin would examine how the mechanical evolution was being translated into the domain of the arts in his essay *Das Kunstwerk im Zeitalter seiner technischen Reproduzierbarkeit* (The Work of Art in the Age of Mechanical Reproduction). The tremendous impact that mechanization had in store, however, had already been proved by the comprehensive destruction of Europe that had taken place during the First World War.

The theme of man's mechanization was also evident in other cultural products, such as the films *Metropolis* by Fritz Lang (1927), *Philips Radio* by Joris Ivens (1931) and *Modern Times* by Charley Chaplin (1936), and the novels of Alfred Döblin and Maurits Dekker (such as the latter's *CR. 133* of 1926).

Franken's original idea was the image of man trapped within the modern movement of mechanization. Through discussions with Van Dalsum, the individual's struggle against the mechanization of his world shifted into an investigation of the roles that labour had played for the working masses throughout

the course of history. The problem of mechanized labour thus became the thematic foundation of the play. This problem was treated in three phases: firstly, 'work as craft' covers the period from the Fall of man to the Middle Ages; secondly, 'the mechanization of work' coincides with the Industrial Revolution, and is initially synonymous with great prosperity; and thirdly, at the beginning of the twentieth century, mechanization has reached a stage where technological developments have pushed man off his pedestal. The machine rules over mankind, and labour has become production, to which the mass of labourers must make their contribution. Exactly how this development can be reversed is not clear, but that changes may take place in the future is strongly implied in the play.

The architects responsible for the stage design, Piet Donk and J. Th. van Erp, incorporated a visual translation of these three phases. The decor consisted of three backdrops. A first, static backdrop represents the static primal form of life, the origin of everything. All groups have their origins here during the play and stay in contact with this background. A second, dynamic background represents the present: in the centre stands the machine. This background is all about movement. Unlike the static background, all is colourless here, and glass and iron are the main elements. The third backdrop suggests an undefinable future, best represented by a single-colour plane. The entirety of Donk and Van Erp's stage design actually consisted of three high wooden towers, a pyramid, a long tunnel-like construction and a large mechanical wheel nine meters in diameter.

A key idea in the play is the idea that God created labour as a punishment for man's original sin, but that this only refers to his sojourn on earth. His atonement prepares him for the real salvation that awaits after death. This idea is visualized in the first part of the play by a dome of light placed high up in the sky of the set, symbolizing the afterlife alongside huge choirs that praise God's eternal glory. In his remarks to the students, Franken said that this first part should not be a historical reconstruction with symbolic figures, but rather a visual symphony of recurring motifs, or a synthesis of images, as is common in film.[8]

Next, megaphones and music announce a new stage of labour. The transcendental perspective disappears as a group of workers begin to make a crown and another group builds a scaffold containing a church window. These symbols of Church and State are then lit more weakly, signalling the beginning of a new phase. Labour has become an economic problem and man is starving, until the wheel (the machine) is discovered. The actors climb upwards and succeed in setting the wheel in motion. They are the precursors of the machine age. Not everyone is equally enthusiastic, and some try to stop the wheel, but the machine becomes a monstrous Moloch. (This scene is obviously strongly reminiscent of Lang's *Metropolis*, which had come out the year

5. Walther Rathenau, Zur Mechanik des Geistes, *Berlin, 1922. [Antwerp, University of Antwerp, Universiteitsbibliotheek]*

8   Van den Boorn, *Mannus Franken*, 13.

before, and which uses the same term 'Moloch' to describe the horror of the industrial machine devouring the labourers.)

Three groups symbolize Intellect's conflict with Power and Property. The workers are forced into a tunnel, and are thus transformed into a blind, colourless mass. They all wear the same brown or blue overalls, and masks with no openings for eyes, ears or mouth. From two towers, which have been seized by the groups representing Property and Power, orders descend on the working people, who find no other refuge than in the entertainment offered by film and jazz in the towers. Once they are forced to work faster, Humankind revolts. This figure, which symbolizes the best in humankind, is then shot down by the masses but immediately resurrected. They adopt his thoughts, pull off their masks and climb the machine to reach the towers and move towards a better future, as the sky is again lit by bright lights. There, man and machine become a harmonious pair: the machine has become the means, and man has become the end.

The performance was staged with 300 students from the Delft Student Corps and the local high school, who constituted the crowd of upper and lower craftsmen. At one moment, the organizers were considering putting on a second production of the play using members from the Young Workers' Centre (AJC), and performing it for an audience of socialist workers in Rotterdam and The Hague.[9]

The production was choreographed by Abraham van der Vies and the music was composed by Leo Smit, conductor of the Rotterdam Philharmonic Society. The musical score also had to complement the concept of the production, of course, and it therefore had a kind of motor-rhythmic character. Its function was to fire up the performers, but the audience was apparently unimpressed.

Unlike most newspaper reporters, a number of professional theatre critics were rather negative about the show. Frits Lapidoth, a critic from the journal

Het Tooneel, saw in *D 16 MM* an imitation of contemporary Russian popular theatre (he was obviously thinking of mass spectacles such as Evreinov's *Storming of the Winter Palace*).

Most national and local newspapers, however, devoted considerable attention to this play, which was described as a fascinating modernist drama. The fact in itself that Delft students had addressed the problem of modern mechanization received critical acclaim: this initiative had shown that students were not shying away from their social responsibilities. Luc Willink of *Het Vaderland* wrote:

> What is performed is inwardly and outwardly so new, but also so important, that it should directly count as a manifestation representative of our epoch. [...] We were gripped by the masses in various forms, devoid of oaken splendour and oaken ornaments, but in their groupings always immediately understandable. No fancy costumes of the anniversary spectacles of the past, but overalls, no royally honoured hero, but a 'voice', no gold and purple in the stage design, but the fascinating, profound business of life itself.[10]

In general, it appears from the reviews and the audience response that the Delft open-air show was considered one of the first successful examples of community art, and the mass character of the play in particular was frequently emphasized in this regard.

Readers of reviews would have been able to get a clear pictures of the play's scope:

> Man is stuck between man and machine, a process in which man himself is lost, says director Albert van Dalsum. He realized that the representation of that conflict had to include the masses, and therefore expanded the play to include the general problem of labour, in order to reveal the deficiency commonly felt therein.[11]

The reviewers also provided a clear link between 1923's *The Tower Stormer* and the

9 Molema and Leemans, *Jan Albarda en De Groep van Delft*, 58.
10 *Het Vaderland*, 3 July 1928.
11 Ibid., 23 June 1928.

production of *D 16 MM* five years later. What was most surprising for them was that it was the Delft engineering students, commonly regarded as a reactionary milieu, who were developing a new theatrical art. The students had regarded the earlier initiative as a cultural scheme, which had only seemed more realistic once Herman Teirlinck, Dirk Coster and Johan de Meester Jr. had approached them with more definite plans, and when a group of students then made a commitment to realizing those plans. With *D 16 MM,* this trend had been continued.

Reviewers were quick to point out the similarities in theme and style between *Gas I* and *D 16 MM*. In their discussions, however, they make almost no mention of the intertextual relationship. Both the billionaire's son and the allegorical character that symbolizes Humankind are metaphorical representations of Christ. They both sacrifice themselves for a humanitarian ideal, but lose their respective struggles. Their words are not heard, and the working masses are initially only interested in greater material gain. The texts also provide other clues. When the workers in *Gas I*, for example, demand that the engineer be fired, the billionaire's son explains their action to the five 'black men of labour' with the words: 'No, they know not what they do', echoing the words of Christ when he is crucified at Golgotha ('Father, forgive them, for they know not what they do', Luke 23:34). For the billionaire's son, the explosion of the gas plant proves that the Last Judgement has arrived, along with a return to an agricultural society which represents a new paradisaical beginning. Ultimately though, no one will escape the Last Judgement, which follows in *Gas II*.

Conclusion

Although Expressionism has played a subordinate role in Dutch theatre history, it is striking that many national newspapers have given great attention to both of these productions. This is evident from the full-page previews, including pictures of the modernist stage set, in the case of *D 16 MM*, and from the extensive reviews. Apparently these performances were sufficiently newsworthy to inform the reading public of it.

Precisely these productions have been crucial in the theatre work of Van Dalsum, who had hoped to continue his Expressionist experiments with the East-Dutch Theatre company, established in 1929. Because his actors there were hardly aware of the Expressionist acting style, Van Dalsum and Defresne resorted to politically and morally engaged theatre. This form of 'witness theatre' (*getuigenistoneel*) would prove characteristic of their work in the 1950s. On the occasion of his Silver Jubilee, however, Van Dalsum was not only praised as a great actor, but also as an experimenter.[12]

12 *Het Vaderland*, 15 March 1935.

'Variations on a Cosmic Rhythm'

Collective Movement between Dance, Sport and Politics

Staf Vos

Between October 1930 and August 1931, the Flemish choreographer Lea Daan published several essays about dance in the progressive Catholic magazine *Opbouwen*. After reviewing the performances of amateur dance groups at the Antwerp World Fair, which had all been ballet-based, she wondered whether modern 'lay dance' featuring movement choirs, like those that had been introduced in Germany and the Netherlands, would not have been much more artistic.[1]

Several years earlier, Daan had been the first Belgian dancer and choreographer to become acquainted with the German modern dance movement through classes with famous German dance educators. She discovered a dance system that guaranteed the individual dancer's freedom, but also attached great importance to collective dance and expression.

In this contribution, I wish to map the influence of this new approach to group choreography in Flanders between the World Wars. Was dance taken seriously as a component of mass theatre? How was the relationship between movement and message conceptualized? Did the new models for dancing function independently of external values, or were they associated with clear ideological or political ambitions? To understand how dance could suddenly become considered to be of high artistic and ideological value in a country with no dance tradition, it is necessary to examine these practices from a broader (dance) historical perspective.

From Solo Presentation to Collective Experience

It was not a coincidence that Lea Daan identified ballet as the antithesis of modern dance. As early as the nineteenth century, ballet as presented in the opera houses and music halls was associated with moral and artistic decline. Ballet dancers were widely suspected of prostitution or at least of promiscuous behaviour, and at the same time a growing number of critics no longer considered their postures, gestures and movements artistically meaningful. Richard Wagner, in particular, charged ballet with consisting of superficial and outdated gestures accompanied by second-rate music. The composer, who died in 1883, did not recognize any aspect of his idealized vision of ancient Greek dance (as a spiritual expression of the body) in the ballet of his time.[2]

The American Isadora Duncan fulfilled this Wagnerian ideal around the turn of the century. She broke radically with the conventions of ballet by dancing in tunic and barefoot, with free and expressive gestures. Furthermore, she made a commitment to elements from the European intellectual tradition, by claiming to have reconstructed ancient Greek dances and by using first-class music from the classical concert repertoire. Her performances were sufficiently 'different' to be refreshing and progressive, yet sufficiently 'familiar' to encounter, at least in Belgium, little resistance.[3]

Duncan inspired numerous solo 'free dancers', who played the roles of 'high priestesses' of a new spirituality in ancient Greek, Spanish or oriental costumes. But Duncan also appreciated dance as activating a new

1   *Opbouwen,* 3 (1930-1931) 3, 83.
2   Vos, *Dans in België*, 15-32. Compare Wagner's statements in *Das Kunstwerk der Zukunft* (1849), *Oper und Drama* (1852), *Uber das Dirigieren* (1869), *Uber die Bestimmung der Oper* (1871) in Wagner, *Gesammelte Schriften*, vol. 10, vol. 11, 26, 74-75, 282-287; vol. 12, 304-305.
3   Duncan first came to Belgium in 1905. Vos, *Dans in België*, 45-70; Daly, *Done into Dance*; Naerebout, *Attractive Performances*, 54-71.

2. Félicien Rops, La Mort qui danse, *1865.*
[Namur, Province de Namur;
© Speltdoorn]

body culture. Private schools were established in Paris, Berlin and Saint Petersburg, which in turn inspired dancers in Brussels and Antwerp to found their own institutes. Compared with existing ballet training, these institutions had far greater moral and artistic prestige, and so they quickly became popular with (parents of) bourgeois children.

Émile Jaques-Dalcroze of Switzerland certainly played an equally important role in the development of this educational dimension. In 1904, his starting point was not dance but the pedagogy of music. He believed that music could be learnt better through movement. Soon both physicians and educators recognized the artistic and general benefits of the method. The French Catholic writer Paul Claudel even saw Jaques-Dalcroze's school in Hellerau as a 'laboratory for a new humanity'. Another commentator saw 'new possibilities for human evolution' that would lead them far away from the 'old civilization'. The

method indicated an opportunity 'to achieve intimate harmony between our instincts, our body and the spiritual'.[4]

The Dalcroze method, which was alternately described as 'rhythmic gymnastics', 'eurhythmics' or just simply 'Rhythm', was rather popular in *Lebensreform* circles, and this was no accident. This international (but especially German) movement was convinced that moral and cultural problems had physical causes, and could therefore be cured through individual body work. 'Working on yourself' was the central slogan. Dance here became a collective ritual of self-sanctification. It was thus part of a wider range of practices that were supposed to create a new human being in a new world. From vegetarianism to nudism, they attempted to use the body's own 'original' contact with nature to find recovery.[5]

For Dalcroze, the magic word in that process was 'rhythm'. In the nineteenth century, it was not only a musical term but also had spatial and biological connotations, and the latter in particular lent a certain vitalist significance. Rhythm came to signify life and pulsation, but was also restrictive: it was impossible to argue with rhythm. This ambiguity between liberation and discipline was at the core of Dalcrozian discourse. Moreover, the hierarchy between the individual and the collective was unclear. Students had to express their personalities and become aware of their individual 'natural' body rhythms, but eventually everything revolved around 'harmony' – between your own mind and body, and between the individual rhythms of society. The capitalization of the word 'Rhythm' even implied that it was a cosmic principle, a normative frequency with which all subordinate bodies should resonate.[6]

Many German commentators, however, found Jaques-Dalcroze's approach to exercise and 'rhythm' too rationalistic and quite subordinate to musical laws. An alternative was offered by the Austro-Hungarian Rudolf von Laban, who opened the *Schule für Kunst* in the *Lebensreform* colony of Monte Verità near Ascona, Switzerland, at around the

4 *Le Rythme*, June 1920, 1-6; Vos, 'Waanzin of kuur?', 105-126; Toepfer, *Empire of Ecstasy*, 15-20.

5 Peeters, *De beloften van het lichaam*, 9-25 and 343-351.

6 *Le Rythme*, Febr. 1924, 26-29 and Dec. 1921, 1-8.

same time. Laban extended the expressive range of the individual dancer much more systematically than had been possible in ballet or in the theories of Duncan and Jaques-Dalcroze. He did so by situating the dancer in an 'icosahedron': a twenty-sided self-built wire frame model. The dancer could then use all of its vertices to explore the different combinations of motions and their associated emotions. Those accompanying emotions were important. Modern dancers were supposed to maximize their expressiveness using simple movements. In a reference to painting, the dance style was later defined as 'Expressionist', but its contemporary name was *Ausdruckstanz* (expression dance). Unlike the ballet tradition and Jaques-Dalcroze's system, this kind of expression did not even need music, and hardly even a story. Laban was promoting a pure, autonomous dance.[7]

Simultaneously, Laban was choreographing a series of group rituals at Monte Verità that would shape his views on 'lay dance' for amateurs. In his movement choirs, Laban had originally not aimed for a militaristic parade where the guidelines for how to move were imposed on students by the authoritarian teacher, as nineteenth-century gymnastics dictated. Instead, everything was based on improvisation and play. Participants were allowed to take turns leading the group, by showing a movement that the others would follow. The movements could also result from the interaction between the subgroups.

Again, this movement choir did not have to be illustrative or narrative, but was concerned with physical fantasy alone, 'variations on the cosmic rhythm'. In its purest form the movement choir was strictly focused on the physical and spiritual experience of the dancers, and not on the spectacle value for the audience. This does not mean that Laban took complete leave of the art dance, however, and he and students such as Kurt Jooss brought regular dance performances to the theatre stage which had evolved from this new dance concept.[8] Such performances had a dramatic purpose and were

mostly choreographed by the leader, not improvised by the dancers.

In the dance schools that Laban founded in Germany during the interwar period, both female and male students were active, and this was remarkable because until then dance instruction had almost exclusively targeted women and children. On the ballet stage, male dancers had become a rarity during the course of the nineteenth century,

3. *Rudolf von Laban,* Agamemnons Tod *(movement choir). Photo published in* Opbouwen, *1930-1931, 11, 247.*

4. *Albrecht Knust,* Die Welle *(The Wave), a 'dance play' (Tanzspiel). Photo published in* Opbouwen, *1930-1931, 11, 247.*

7 Guilbert, *Danser avec le IIIe Reich*, 30-35.

8 Ibid., 50-66.

except in Russia. And in the Belgian 'free dance schools', established according to the principles of Dalcroze or Duncan, dance was primarily seen as a way of experiencing and interpreting an idyllic femininity, at least until the early 1920s. Male dancers, because of their supposed 'effeminacy', could hardly be seen as role models.[9]

There was great astonishment when Kurt Jooss, a student of Laban's, came to Brussels in 1933 with his show *Der grüne Tisch* (The Green Table). The choreography was not a dreamy evocation of an ideal world, but an indictment of political cynicism and the consequences in the real world. In addition, the athletic bodies of the dancers, both men and women, were highlighted much more emphatically than before: they were 'really athletic dances, and the men who perform in them are really good-looking men, very muscular, without fat'.[10]

The participation of energetic men and women as well as the setting of the story in the real world meant that a dance could now represent contemporary social groups and comment on existing social conditions. Flemish theatre directors began to take note of this from the early 1930s onward. Flemish and Dutch avant-garde directors such as Herman Teirlinck and Johan de Meester Jr. had already introduced dance scenes in their productions in the 1920s, but these had mostly been professional solo dances. It was not until the 1930s that the modern dance movement instigated by Laban made it possible to transform amateur dancing groups into the protagonists of a stage show.

Lea Daan and the Desire for an Organic Community

Lea Daan – pseudonym of Paula Gombert – had studied in Germany during the late 1920s with Albrecht Knust, Kurt Jooss and finally their teacher Laban himself. Back in Belgium, she aimed for a career as a performing dancer, but it was not easy. The traditional employers of dancers – the opera houses – were not open to modern dance, despite the more progressive period that the Antwerp Flemish Opera went through during the 1920s. Daan therefore began to focus on education, by establishing her own school. Besides the actual 'art dance' (*kunstdans*) for professional students, she also taught 'lay dance' (*lekendans*) to amateurs.

Most of the students were women, but the new approach eventually convinced a number of men to join. In a three-day course for adults in 1932, even more men than women took part (the group included a construction worker, but otherwise mainly middle-class professionals and students). Besides her educational activities, Daan founded a dance group with some professional students, with whom she also wanted to perform outside of the established theatre circuit.[11]

In order to recruit students and increase opportunities, Daan pushed herself forward as a speaker and writer for socialist, Catholic and Flemish nationalist associations and periodicals. She presented her courses in lay dance as an autonomous form of artistic entertainment. Yet she was still seeking additional ideological support for her project. Eventually, it was cultural criticism from Laban himself that would prove inspirational.

According to Laban, lay dance indeed proposed a way to counteract the disintegration of modern society, and to strengthen the cultural affinities of the participants. As a result of industrialization and technology, the ancient organic character of the *Gemeinschaft* had been lost, according to many nineteenth-century and twentieth-century observers. Previously, people had been in touch with subtle and multifaceted 'cosmic knowledge', whereas in Laban's view, now only the simplistic rhythms of factory work and the modern dance palaces remained.

Yet Laban believed he could provide an alternative to the crisis of collective movements in modern society. In the movement choirs he had designed, city dwellers could again explore cosmic space, enrich their spir-

9 Burt, *The Male Dancer*, 9-29.
10 *Le Peuple*, 22 Jan. 1933 and *Les Beaux-Arts*, 27 Jan. 1933.
11 Daan, *Danskunst, kursus n° 55 (Volksuniversiteit Herman van den Reeck, februari 1931)*, typescript in the Lea Daan Archive (ALD) at the Letterenhuis in Antwerp, box 3.

5. *Lea Daan and her students in 1938. Daan is giving instructions to a male student practicing in the 'icosahedron', a didactic tool developed by Laban. Jeanne Brabants (second from right) is mirroring his movements. [Antwerp, Letterenhuis, Archives Lea Daan]*

ituality, and feel that they were an integral part of a collective body.[12] Daan suggested that the 'era of the masses' had arrived once and for all. The challenge, however, to quote German theologian Paul Tillich, was to transform the masses of industrial civilization, where the individual feels alienated, into the 'organic masses, where the individual is recognized and feels that they are in the right place'.[13] Daan believed a new movement culture could contribute to the formation of this 'new organization of life'.[14]

Not all physical culture was good, according to Daan. In addition to individualization and industrialization, she also attacked sport. While sport offered a means of compensating for the limitations of physical space during the daily routine, in practice physical exercise was too heavily influenced by continuous attempts to achieve new records. In one of her lectures Daan even argued that sport had led to passivity and to a superficial inner life, while dancing preserved and developed a 'spiritual' aspect. Since the movements of dance, she said, are 'inspired by the domain of art, they contain the cultural values which

form human beings', and are an 'educational factor for the community'.

Another criticism of the worlds of sport and art was that the 'culture of the spectacle' partially negated the experience of the 'organic masses'. Instead of having participants who were equally active in a single celebration, a separation had arisen over the centuries between active performers and passive spectators, both in the arena and in the concert hall. The voyeuristic gaze moreover transformed the dancers into instigators of sensual temptation. Daan wanted a change of perspective from 'dance as presentation' to 'dance as experience'. It was the intention of the choral spectacle to fuse all participants together into 'one soul'.

Following Laban, Daan held that the movement element would ideally grow spontaneously and harmoniously from the dancers themselves. If the choreography was composed by a 'movement poet', the whole had to be conceived 'in vivid sympathy' with the experiences of the lay choir. Such 'lay dance leaders' had to know how to behave 'as an equal among equals'.

12 Guilbert, *Danser avec le IIIe Reich*, 30-35.
13 Compare Tillich, *Masse und Geist*, 51.
14 The following paragraphs draw on the articles published by Daan in *Opbouwen*, 2 (1930-1931), 11, 248 and 5, 137 and in *Vrouwenfront*, 1 (1934-1935) 8, 9-10, and on typescripts of lectures in Letterenhuis, ALD, boxes 7 and 12.

How did Daan then interpret her own role as a professional artist in relation to those 'organic masses'? She herself was the leader of a professional dance troupe with whom she performed regularly in front of a 'passive audience' until as late as 1956 (with the exception of the war years). Moreover, from 1932 onwards she was frequently engaged to choreograph lay dance performances for political organizations where the expression of the individual personalities of the participants was no longer thought to be so important. The theory of 'representing one's own experiences' suited improvisations at a dance school, but in order to convince the masses of a political message, a carefully orchestrated spectacle was apparently still needed.

Red Movement Choirs

In Germany, Labanian movement choirs were swiftly appropriated by the political domain, and because the movement choir now had to illustrate a pre-established and politically biased storyline, its original conception as a playful and improvised practice disappeared. The dance notation system that Laban had designed was now an instrument for the choreographer-director to control and discipline the dancers.

This system was further refined by a student and confidant of Laban, Martin Gleisner, who introduced movement choirs to the German Socialist Party. In 1931 he spent eight months preparing the choral drama *Rotes Lied* (Red Song), during which he sent directions in 'labanotation' to various local departments. As a consequence, only a single dress rehearsal with all participants was needed to finish the production. In this case, the choreographer – especially a politically motivated artist such as Gleisner – aimed to dominate the space with a 'message' instead of merely exploring it.[15]

This became very clear during the closing ceremony of the Third Workers' Olympics, held in Antwerp in 1937. The sporting

events (which looked increasingly like those of the regular, individualistic, 'bourgeois' Olympics), Gleisner's movement choir *Aan ons de toekomst* (The Future Belongs to Us), and the singing of *La Marseillaise* and the *International* all outlined the contours of socialist ideology very clearly. A French journalist concluded: 'While watching this great spectacle by a crowd with noble and lofty feelings, how can you still doubt the future of democracy?'[16]

The expansion and politicization of the movement choirs in leftist circles, which had a marked preference for monumental and even mechanical aesthetics, would also be fatal for the personal initiative of the dancer. Nevertheless, the spectacle made a most 'democratic' impression on the spectators.

Previously, Belgian socialist leaders had engaged Lea Daan for smaller-scale speech and movement choirs. The *Belgische Werklieden Partij* (Belgian Socialist Workers' Party, BWP) was convinced of the effectiveness of this form of expression by Hendrik De Man, who had been a professor of Social Psychology at the University of Frankfurt until 1933. He had become fascinated by the

15   Guilbert, *Danser avec le IIIe Reich*, 55-58.

16   Box, *De derde Arbeidersolympiade*, 153-164 and Eichberg, 'Das Fest der Bewegung'.

120

effect of mass demonstrations on the psychology of the individual, and had written a socialist *Festspiel* himself, entitled *Wir* (We). The script featured movement choirs, an orchestra, film projections and speech choirs, and aimed to overcome the gulf between actors and spectators 'in an almost religious way'. *We* was performed on 1 May 1932 in a banqueting hall in Frankfurt and included 2,000 performers.

De Man also managed to convince a number of key figures in the Belgian socialist youth movement of the value of this new combination of propaganda and entertainment. With members of the Antwerp branch of the *Arbeidersjeugd* (Young Workers), Gust De Muynck rehearsed *De moderne Prometheus* (Modern Prometheus), a choral drama by the Dutch revolutionary poet Henriette Roland Holst. Daan was asked to work on the choreography of the production. It was performed twice in 1932 and again in 1936. In 1933, Daan also choreographed the movements for the Antwerp Young Workers' performance of the speech choir *Wij* (We). Despite the title, this is unlikely to have been the same play as De Man's text. In any case, the word 'we' was prominent in the titles and texts of speech choirs from all political ideologies. As a collective exclamation it was a powerful marker of community awareness.[17]

Lea Daan's students were also meritorious in this area. Jenny Laroche was a physical education teacher at the Antwerp Municipal Normal School for Girls. In the park, the students practiced movement choirs such as *Prayer* or *Melopee* (Melopoeia), inspired by Paul van Ostaijen's poem. At a school celebration in 1937, politically engaged scenes such as *Slaves* and *Resurrection* were performed by a mixed group of girls and boys. The concept of the curved bodies crocheted together in *Slaves* had been copied by Laroche from the movement choir *The Wave* by Knust.[18]

As the daughter of socialist leader Gustaaf Laroche, social topics were inevitably close to her heart. Laroche proved this in 1936 with the movement choir *Mens en Machine* (Man

7. Still from the movement choir Mensch en Machine *(Man and Machine), choreographed by Jenny Laroche and (probably) Martin Gleisner.*
[Private collection]

and Machine), which she realized with pupils from the Normal School, probably with Gleisner's help. His role is explained by the fact that he was a politically active German Jew who had emigrated to the Netherlands after the Nazi takeover. He regularly worked for the socialist youth movement and, so it seems, occasionally crossed the border to Belgium.

The most remarkable thing about *Man and Machine* is that it was filmed, and that the recording has been preserved. According to American historian Karl Toepfer, the film technique used for this recording was remarkable. The camera was very close to the dancers and captured them from unusual angles. The effect of such a film was very different from that of observing a live event, in which the spectator usually observed the performers from a considerable distance. According to Toepfer, the frog perspective provided a heroically styled staging of the bodies, yet also allowed the viewer to experience the workers' oppression.[19]

The silent film was indeed a propagandist tool. The text plates between the images made the distinction between factory work, where 'hands are still necessary', and work which was dominated by 'automatons'. As the machines start pumping at an accelerated speed, more and more images of unemployed people were shown. The intertitles then read: 'The situation is represented synthetically by a movement choir'. Three rows of four women each, dressed in sackcloth, move in the fashion of pumping machines,

17 See the testimony by Bert Van Kerkhoven in Avermaete, *Lea Daan*, 64 and 'Activiteit Lea Daan', typoscript, Letterenhuis, ALD, box 9. Compare with Blockmans, 'Beziel tot hooger leven!', 203-204.

18 Vos, 'Interview with Jeanne Brabants', Antwerp, 10 June 2009.

19 Toepfer, *Empire of Ecstasy*, 305-306. Toepfer incorrectly claims that Gleisner collaborated with Daan for this film.

20 *Tooneelgids*, 1 April 1933, 98-99 and Geysen, 'Het spreekkoor'.

8. Movement instructions for the KAJ mass spectacle De Nieuwe Jeugd *(The New Youth), 1935, published in KAJ, July 1935. The corresponding exclamations are specified below the images.*
[Leuven, KADOC-KU Leuven]

while women in a black robes with contorted faces and hands express the suffering of the female labourers. Encircled by the machines, the women revolt, but finally succumb. The film ends with a motionless monument of entwined bodies. Close-ups of contorted faces, a clenched fist and a pleading hand again reinforced the message.

Catholic Movement Choirs

In Catholic circles, the movement choir was introduced by theatre directors who were not primarily interested in dance, but in the possibilities provided by the chorus on the stage. The idea was not immediately accepted, though. In the Catholic theatre periodical *Tooneelgids*, for example, B. Gruwez argued that the field of dance should not be ventured into, and that movements should be used sparingly. In a previous edition of the same magazine, however, Lode Geysen had expressed his great admiration for the German way of not just reciting but 'performing' a poem.

Geysen wrote about his own experiments in composing a movement choir to the text of Henry Longfellow's *The Song of Hiawatha*, in the Dutch translation by Guido Gezelle. The story was generally recited in an expressive fashion by a single actor, while Geysen's group 'played' the emotions of each passage, punctuated with exclamations. Geysen also mentioned the successful performance of *The Modern Prometheus* by Lea Daan and Gust De Muynck.[20] Only in 1938, however,

would Daan devote two full articles to movement choirs in the pages of *Tooneelgids*.[21]

Several Catholic schools and organizations wished to complement their speech choirs and mass plays with movement choirs in the 1930s. Usually, the task of coaching and choreographing these groups was given to the same group of stage directors, including Geysen. Was this simply because too few specialist choreographers educated in Laban's system were available? Or were the exclusively female choreographers working in Belgium not considered up to the task without the help of male directors?

The use of speech choirs was especially popular with the *Kristene Arbeiders Jeugd* (Young Christian Workers, KAJ), an organization founded by Father Joseph Cardijn as a Christian alternative to the socialist youth movement. Geysen was hired in 1932 to direct the choral drama *Wij* (We) by Jesuit priest J. Bogaerts, performed by the KAJ department of Wilrijk (Antwerp). Very soon the scale of these events was spectacularly enlarged. In 1935 Geysen directed the mass spectacle *De nieuwe jeugd* (The New Youth) to celebrate the tenth anniversary of the KAJ. The performance involved a speech choir with 1,560 participants, besides 2,000 flag bearers and 1,000 marching singers, in front of an audience of 70,000 to 80,000 spectators.[22]

Physical movements played a more than emblematic role in these events. The organizers themselves stated that the content of the text was no longer of chief importance, but rather the sound, the passion, the unity and the powerful gestures of the performers. The press were recruited to help organize a dress rehearsal over the radio. Since Geysen, unlike Gleisner, was not proficient in Laban's notation system and certainly had no network of well-trained teachers at his disposal, the movements of the chorus were restricted to simple arm movements and leg positions. Pictures of these postures were distributed along with the accompanying songs and exclamations through the KAJ magazine. The performers were supposed to have this

document at hand during the national radio rehearsal.[23]

Does this mean there was no role to play for Lea Daan on the Catholic side of things during the interwar years? She did indeed give performances for Catholic organizations throughout the country with her own dance group. This gradually led to choreographing assignments, too, such as that for a movement choir near Antwerp, and the movement direction of the open-air play *Beatrice* for Leuven University students.

In 1938 Daan was given responsibility for a large-scale group choreography, though only in the role of assistant director to the male Ast Fonteyne. The spectacle took place in the Ghent Velodrome on the occasion of the fiftieth anniversary of the founding of the *Algemeen Christelijk Vakverbond* (Confederation of Christian Trade Unions, ACV). A group of 110 men and women – Daan had explicitly asked for women – constituted the movement choir that danced and performed the action. A singing choir and a speech choir recited or sang the lyrics. Separating the speech choir from the movement choir was hailed as innovative, which suggests that movement choirs were not frequently given such leading roles in Belgium. The film re-

9. *KAJ mass spectacle* De Nieuwe Jeugd *(The New Youth), 1935, Heysel Stadium, Brussels.*
[Leuven, KADOC-KU Leuven]

21 *Tooneelgids*, 25 (1938) 1, 6 and 25 (1938) 4, 41-42.

22 Geysen, 'Het spreekkoor'.

23 Thomé, 'Les chœurs parlés'.

cordings made during the event were supplemented with previously shot close-ups of the
movement choir. This led to the remarkable
documentary feature *De christelijke vakvere-
niging* (1938), most probably the work of
Charles Dekeukeleire, who had been a key
pioneer of Belgian 'pure cinema' in the preceding decade before he turned to the documentary genre.[24]

The ACV mass spectacle proved successful. Even the usually sober music critic
Denijs Dille stated that, unlike other spectacles, this mass play had been able to reach
the 'critical point' where 'the masses start to
live [...] so much so that they totally forget
their passive state as spectators or listeners
and submit to the action with all its mighty
burgeoning exaltation'.[25] Daan seemed to
have no qualms about putting her persuasive
choreographic powers to use in an indictment of the Catholic God (in *Modern Prometheus*, for instance) at one moment, and in
an attack on socialist and anarchist militants
(in the ACV spectacle) at the next. Still, some
components of the spectacle were appropriate to both the Belgian Socialist Party and
the Catholic Confederation, such as the
'dance of capital', the 'slave dance', 'rebellion'
and 'unity'.[26]

The use of dance in mass spectacle was
not limited to trade union issues. A colleague

of Lea Daan's, Elsa Darciel (pseudonym of
Elza Dewette), would use her choreography
in 1939 for a more liturgical event. In a Catholic secondary school for girls in Kortrijk, a
10-day mass spectacle involving 1,500 performers was performed, entitled *Vredesoffer*
(Peace Sacrifice). A two-level stage set was
used to represent scenes from the Old Testament and the New Testament, on the lower
and the upper level respectively. Additionally, two smaller choruses, choreographed
by Darciel, depicted the significance of the
Holy Mass in an abstract way. Afterwards
the bishop is said to have thanked her with
the words, 'You have made it possible for
the audience to rediscover something from
religion through art'. Dancing was used to
demonstrate the symbolic aspect of religion,
at exactly those points where conventional
drama was felt to be inadequate. Belief, symbolism and physical experience were seamlessly fused.

Conclusion

The presence of dance in mass spectacles
during the interwar period in Flanders was
a result of changing attitudes towards the
body. While nineteenth-century gymnastics
promoted physical training for men – and

24 Saerens, 'Het Wendepunkt', 112-
    117; *De christelijke vakbeweging*
    and postcard from Ast Fonteyne
    to Lea Daan, s.d., Letterenhuis,
    ALD, Correspondence of 1932-
    1941.
25 *Nieuw Vlaanderen*, 27 Aug. 1938.
26 ACV, *Verslag over de jubelviering
    van 7 Oogst 1938.*

later for women too – as a way of saving the nation, the turn of the century saw the rise of the idea that dancing could increase health and fitness. The teaching of dance gradually acquired more prestige as an educational project. Under the influence of German innovators, it became a collective experience for both sexes instead of a presentation performed by individual women. The physical truth of the dance could represent the shared truth of the community, which made dance attractive for political propagandists. Language, as a medium of traditional propaganda, took a backseat in favour of the massive and dynamic physical image, which was able to convey a spiritual message. In that context, careful reasoning and argumentation were less important than swaying to the 'cosmic rhythm'.

Specialized choreographers such as Lea Daan certainly played a role in spreading these ideas in Flanders, by means of lectures, publications and performances with her group, but especially through her pedagogical work as a guest choreographer in youth groups, for both Catholic and socialist organizations. The exact choreographic vocabulary of Daan and her Flemish colleagues still needs to be studied, but preferred themes seem to have been those of oppression, liberation and praise.

Daan apparently took a similar approach to the use of movement choirs for political ends to that of Laban himself. Laban directed several socialist celebrations for German municipalities, but insisted that he himself, as well as his movement choirs, were politically neutral.[27] From 1933 onwards, this self-proclaimed 'neutrality' implied a certain bowing to the ideology of the Nazi regime. Moreover, while Jooss and Gleisner fled the country, Laban's statements and actions during the 1930s clearly evidenced his endorsement of the *völkische Gesinnung*, racist views associated with the reinterpretation of 'modern dance' as *Deutscher Tanz*. He definitively lost the label of political neutrality when he prepared a contribution to the cultural programme for Hitler's Olympics in 1936. After-

wards, however, he fell out of favour with the Nazi regime, and joined Jooss in England.[28]

In Flanders, things would not go so far. Taking everything into consideration, the presence of professionally trained choreographers in the Flemish political mass demonstrations was rather modest. Male directors tended to believe that they could handle matters themselves, with the notable exception of Fonteyne.[29] Furthermore, as far as we know, Lea Daan never cooperated with fascist or radical right-wing groups, except for one presentation and gymnastics lesson in 1937. She fell out with the socialists after the war, though they had previously worked together very closely.

Had Lea Daan shown any enthusiasm about the rise of fascism? It seems unlikely. She did not perform during the war years, and there can be no question of any real collaboration with the occupying forces. In socialist circles, she was nevertheless discredited, and her student Jeanne Brabants would take her place. Brabants would later commit herself to the professionalization of ballet in Flanders, but she also choreographed a number of socialist events. Lea Daan, on the other hand, took up a new role as permanent assistant to Ast Fonteyne, thereby acting as Brabants' counterpart in Catholic organizations and in schools. The choreographies served little direct political purpose, but were intended to deepen the religious feelings of the participants and the spectators, in addition to developing their sense of community. In doing so, they indirectly supported the continuing importance of Catholicism as a political power in post-war Belgium. Up until the early 1960s, several Flemish cities continued to host events featuring danced *tableaux*, such as processions, school celebrations and open-air spectacles, given in honour of the Virgin Mary or of a local saint.

27 Guilbert, *Danser avec le IIIe Reich*, 171-180.
28 Ibid., 171-180, 221-230 and 299-340.
29 On mass manifestations in general, see Dumont, 'Fenomenologie van de massamanifestaties in België in de jaren dertig', 145-226.

Herman van Overbeke and the Open-Air Theatre in Ghent

Between Scenic Innovation and Medieval Traditionalism

Karel Vanhaesebrouck

Few people living in Ghent know that there is an open-air theatre concealed in Citadel Park. It is rather well hidden. In the northern corner of the park, near where Charles de Kerchove Avenue crosses King Leopold II Avenue, there is a shell-shaped, natural space, hidden in the greenery. The theatre is no longer used, and has become somewhat neglected and overgrown. It is now a hotspot for anonymous sexual rendezvous, but it was once the official 'green theatre' of Ghent's *Koninklijke Nederlandse Schouwburg* (Royal Dutch Theatre, KNS).

It played this role only briefly, at the beginning of the Second World War, when it functioned as the KNS's summer stage during the period of Staf Bruggen's management. Herman van Overbeke was in charge of the general management of the 'green theatre', though this was referred to as *kunst-leiding* ('artistic direction') on the posters. And that was no coincidence: Van Overbeke was *the* specialist in open-air theatre in Flanders at that time.

Much of his work involved attempts to reconcile his militant Christian background with his preference for modernist forms. With this artistic perspective in mind, he directed a number of open-air or mass spectacles, mostly on location, during the interwar period. He made frequent use of historical town centres, and in 1930, for instance, he put on *Het Lam Godsspel* (The Lamb of God Play) in front of Sint-Baafs Cathedral in Ghent, on the occasion of the Belgian centenary celebrations.

In this mass spectacle he used the medieval inner city of Ghent as a museal setting. The way in which he incorporated the setting dramatically is a good example of how the Middle Ages were culturally represented during the interwar period and of how this imagining was part of a broader *réveil* in which medieval theatricality played a central role. This article will focus on two landmarks in Van Overbeke's career: *The Lamb of God Play* in 1930, and his brief adventure with the Ghent open-air theatre. In both cases we look at the theatrical-historical roots of his theatrical practice outside the official *stadsschouwburg* (municipal theatre) and investigate how these two examples represent a 'community', or rather, an idea of communality.

Mass Spectacle in Flanders

Through his preference for large, open-air spectacles involving considerable numbers of participants, Van Overbeke associated himself with what was a highly popular practice, especially in the interwar period: the mass spectacle. It functioned as a form of *community art*, a theatrical regime in which the formation of a sense of community takes centre stage. This community was most often represented as a homogeneous entity. As is explained more extensively elsewhere in this book, mass spectacles were very popular in Flanders, and almost every socio-political group was appropriating the genre. The mass spectacle therefore functioned within socialist, Catholic and nationalist contexts, always with the intention of representing the community's homogeneity and of finding an adequate mode of representation that would also be accessible to those outside of the community. The mass spectacle was used

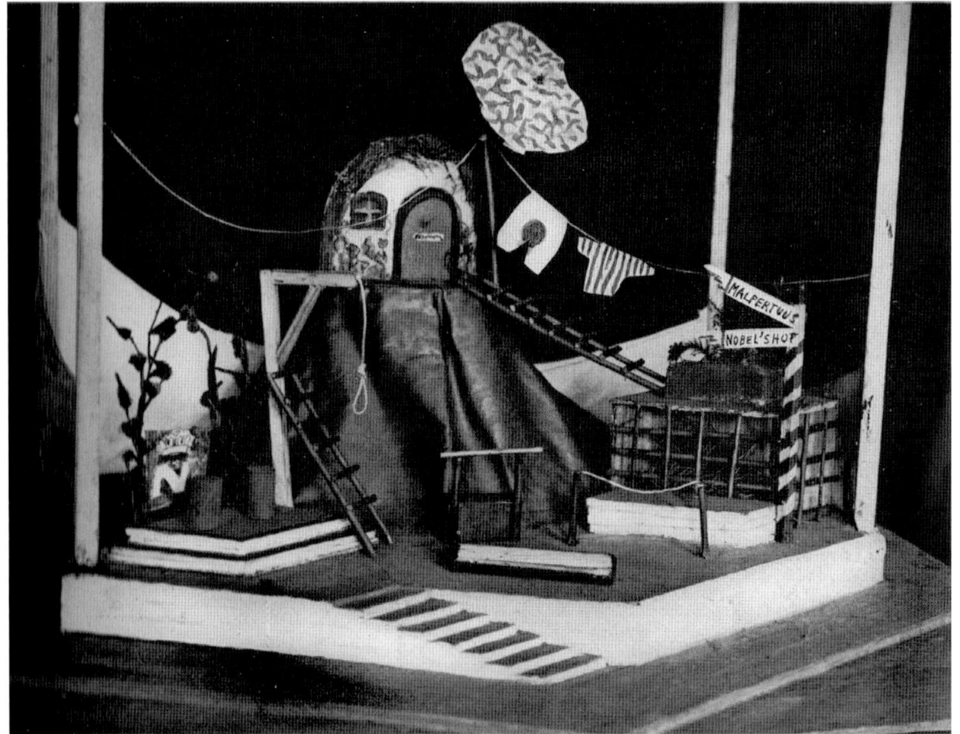

2. Paul de Mont, Reynaert de Vos, *directed by J. De Meester, VVT, 1923. The set was designed by De Meester and R. Moulaert.*
[Leuven, KADOC-KU Leuven]

3. Joost van den Vondel, Lucifer, *directed by J. De Meester, VVT, 1927. The set was designed by R. Moulaert.*
[Leuven, KADOC-KU Leuven]

At the intersection of these two antipodes was a preference for outspoken anti-realism (and thus an aversion to the bourgeois realism of the official playhouses).

The Catholic mass spectacles developed by Herman van Overbeke also strove for a symbiosis between avant-garde formal principles and Catholic content, hoping to arrive at a sort of 'retheatricalization of the liturgy'.[1] Its purpose was to temporarily immerse the spectators in a shared liturgical moment and to unsettle their familiar experiences of reality for a short while. In this literally extraordinary moment, the faithful were supposed to feel part of a community. The structuring principle in this process was chorality;[2] the crowd onstage would move as a choir through a series of consecutive motions. Abstraction, symbolism and rituality were central in a juxtaposition of performative moments, which would at first appear to be entirely devoid of hierarchical arrangement.

The Sint-Baafs Play

As an author and director, Van Overbeke aspired to connect his Catholic inspiration with contemporary modernist views on mise-en-scène, for example, in his production of Cyriel Verschaeve's *Judas.* In the *Nieuwe Encyclopedie van de Vlaamse Beweging* (New Encyclopaedia of the Flemish Movement), he is appropriately described as 'a traditionalist with modern views'.[3] He continually emphasized Catholicism's function as the backbone of a homogeneous Flemish identity, a conviction that was also at the root of his involvement in the *Algemeen Katholiek Verbond voor Tooneel* (General Catholic Theatre Federation of amateur groups, AKVT), founded in 1924. In an interview published in *Tooneelgids* in July 1930, just before the Sint-Baafs spectacle, he describes himself as 'a modernist who loves tradition because of the tiny bit of tradition he is allowed to know, but who loves tradition all the more as he learns more and more about it'.[4] This modernism, he states in the same

in this way as an instrument within various ideological contexts.

Catholic mass spectacle was closely linked to the ambitions of Catholic Action, and several artists – with the *Vlaamse Volkstoneel* (Flemish Popular Theatre, VVT) as their main vehicle – were hard at work searching for an adequate symbiosis between Catholicism and avant-garde art.

interview, by definition rejects any form of bourgeois taste:

> [T]he modernist records a 'modern' moment of the artistic life of his time, which will be part of tomorrow's tradition. The bourgeois, on the other hand, loves yesterday's forms, not because he recognizes the tradition in them, but because he is used to them and because the habit has given him a certain sense of security, whereas new appearances are beyond his comprehension.[5]

At the same time, Van Overbeke explicitly links his anti-bourgeois starting point to the negative reactions open-air play often receives:

> I told you this [...] because certain bourgeois heroes put on a doubtful face as soon as open-air theatre is mentioned, because of the rain, and because, among others, my new attempt has already immediately been classified among [...] the medieval-style plays.[6]

It is no coincidence that Van Overbeke refers to the Middle Ages in this interview, and contrasts theatre from that period with the bourgeois preference for harmless realism. Moreover, in his work as a director, he frequently reverts to medieval theatre culture as a source of inspiration. In his own writing and in interviews he glorifies the unified medieval culture in which life, art and religion were one and art was 'at the service of a higher ideal'.[7] For Van Overbeke, the Middle Ages – not their historical reality, but, as we will see later, the role they played in the cultural imagination of the time – represented the perfect intersection of his 'militant Christian convictions' with his admiration for the Expressionist formal experiments he carried out with the vvt, for example in the work of Johan de Meester.[8]

Van Overbeke brought these elements together in his *Lamb of God Play*, which was performed in front of Sint-Baafs Cathedral in 1930. It was inevitably a large-scale spectacle, deploying all possible technical resources:

> Indeed, until recently we have not had at our disposal the means of enabling, economically and artistically, an audience of thousands to witness the performance of hundreds of actors, singers and musicians near a cathedral or any other major building in the open air, and we therefore feel that such a setting is part of the entire dramatic practice of creating 'depth' and 'meaning'.[9]

The surroundings thus become an immediate part of the staging, and the historical location creates an association with the medieval spectacle culture Van Overbeke considered to be a community art, in which citizens stage themselves as a homogeneous entity, within the spectacular visual regime of medieval theatre. In addition to the integration of the architectural surroundings as a fully-fledged theatrical element, the production made use of the carillon as a musical instrument: the performance was accompanied by music of the municipal carillonist Dierick.

The full list of collaborators is quite impressive and is indicative of the large-scale theatrical dimensions of this event. Buyle wrote an oratory text, Hansen of the Antwerp conservatory composed the music, De Gezelle directed the drama, theatre groups 'Fonteyne' and 'Mariën-Theeren' provided around 200 amateur performers, and the Maria group performed the Lamb of God tableau under De Wilde's direction. According to Van Overbeke's records, even the military orchestra and searchlights from the civil aviation authority were involved.[10]

It was the use of lighting and the movements of the crowd that together formed the backbone of the open-air spectacle. These elements were intended to produce the grand 'choral' effect. In achieving this, the production explicitly distanced itself from the illusionism of the bourgeois theatre. It was not the creation of a coherent illusion that was of central importance, but the submergence of the open-air spectacle's audience in a shared ritual moment.

Sophisticated use of lights in the public space enabled the director to focus the audi-

1 Crombez and Hoet, 'Cerebraal doorgevoerde tendenskunst', 232.
2 Triau, 'Choralités diffractées'.
3 Florquin and Verschaffel, 'Overbeke, Herman van', 2365.
4 De Ronde, 'Het Lam-Godsspel te Gent', 2.
5 Ibid.
6 Ibid.
7 Florquin and Verschaffel, 'Overbeke, Herman van', 2365.
8 Peeters, '22 augustus 1909. Openluchtvoorstelling van *Philoktetes* door de Vlaamsche Vereeniging voor Tooneel- en Voordrachtkunst te Sint-Martens-Latem', 572.
9 De Ronde, 'Het Lam-Godsspel te Gent', 2.
10 Ibid., 3.

4. Poster of the Lamb of God Play, *Ghent, 1930.*
[Leuven, KADOC-KU Leuven: KCC 708]

ence's attention and, at the same time, make the audience aware of its own size. In that period many authors referred to the Russian socio-theatrical events as a source of inspiration, such as *The Storming of the Winter Palace* discussed in the first part this book.

> A revelation in this area was the performance of a play from the Russian revolution in a vast marketplace with the collaboration of the soldiers and the searchlights of the Soviet army; thus it became possible: 1) to set a big crowd into motion, and 2) to create 'holes of light' in that crowd and in the surrounding setting with searchlights, precisely where the full attention of the spectators was needed.[11]

Apart from Soviet mass spectacle, two other examples are quoted as sources of inspiration. The first of these is *Jedermann* by Hugo van Hofmannstahl, directed by Max Reinhardt and performed annually from 1920 onwards on the steps of Salzburg Cathedral.[12] The second is the *A-Z-spel* (A-Z Play), a night spectacle performed on platforms floating on the Zoeterwoudse Singel, which Herman Teirlinck and Johan de Meester produced together on the occasion of the 70th lustrum of the University of Leiden.[13]

Dupont emphasizes that the term 'open-air spectacle' does not refer to the end product but to the process itself, a process in which the text becomes a peripheral element and the surroundings themselves become the central framework of the process:

> An 'open-air spectacle' only deserves to be called that when it has been built and re-built in proportion, and with the elements of the open-air surroundings (country-side, village view, townscape or monument), so that the open-air atmosphere, the massive movement, the size of the action and the monumental character that frames the 'play' all convey a very special impression, which cannot be achieved in an enclosed space.[14]

11 Dupont, 'Herman van Overbeke en het openluchtspel', 479.
12 Dozy, 'Openluchtspel te Salzburg'.
13 Van Schoor, 'Teirlinck en de Russen', 105-106.

An open-air play aims at monumentality, and 'direction' refers first of all to the theatrical organization of a crowd in phased movements. At that moment, the same crowd becomes a sort of theatrical choir speaking with one strong communal voice. Those movements are integrated in a hyperbolic mode of representation (e.g. accompanied by the sophisticated lighting of the medieval city centre) which may attract a new audience while maintaining the interest of those already present. The dramatic text is thus made subordinate to the total effect that is intended. As early as 1924, Van Overbeke formulated this integrated view of mise-en-scène as follows:

> Ten years ago – in Flanders at least and almost everywhere else – one not only faithfully, but slavishly followed the stage directions in the text, which the author had inserted. Nowadays the director has greater freedom with the text and with so many other things … and his imagination should be given its due in the spectacle.[15]

It is precisely this integration that is central to Van Overbeke's work, as he invariably searches for a theatrical symbiosis of light, space and crowd, in order to generate the maximum visual effect. The Sint-Baafs play was also one of those 'grandiosely arranged historical and religious evocations, in which text and dramatic action were subordinate to visual effect'.[16] Moreover, from his Catholic perspective, the mass play seemed to be the ideal means of realizing a shared religiosity.

14 Dupont, 'Herman van Overbeke en het openluchtspel', 480.
15 Van Overbeke, 'Kantteekeningen bij de expressionistische insceneering van Verschaeve's *Judas*', 195.
16 Peeters, '22 augustus 1909. Openluchtvoorstelling van *Philoktetes* door de Vlaamsche Vereeniging voor Tooneel- en Voordrachtkunst te Sint-Martens-Latem', 573.

5. *Poster of* Beatrijs, *directed by H. van Overbeke, Knokke, 1932. [Leuven, KADOC-KU Leuven: KCC 917]*

In a review of his production of *Beatrijs*, Karel Van de Woestijne describes this religious impact:

> It would therefore not be legitimate to call this new achievement of Van Overbeke's a theatrical event. It was instead a purely religious manifestation of very high artistry, from which an appeal emanated that we can best compare with the impression that all liturgical ceremonies leave on the faithful spectator.[17]

Van Overbeke also conceived of his Sint-Baafs play as a shared liturgical moment, in which the monumentality of the historical town centre, emphasized by clever lighting, functioned as a perfect set. This historical setting would transport the spectator to an imagined medieval past that was symbolic of a time in which community, religion and society were intertwined. It is no coincidence that Van Overbeke repeatedly referred to that period in his open-air spectacles.

The Middle Ages as a Construction of the Imagination

The similarities between this kind of open-air play and the historical practices of the medieval theatre (notably the mystery plays) are obvious. Both take place in a public space, aim to provoke spectacular surprise and use similar staging. The city space is integrated in a theatrical ritual in which a community stages itself. Both medieval theatre and open-air spectacles such as the Sint-Baafs play were public events that functioned according to a topographical logic, where the setting of the action played a crucially significant role and the attention of the spectator was led from one spot to another, by light and music for example.

That medieval theatricality was referenced is by no means coincidental, as it was part of a broader cultural fascination manifested emphatically in the interwar period. This fascination was a direct carry-over from the nineteenth-century romanticization of the typical medieval past, and in it, historical inner cities were no longer meaningless relics from the past – boring stone heaps that were freely built over – but symbols of an (imagined) national past. This kind of romanticism injected the historical inner city with a past and an identity. The medieval heritage of Europe was revalued, the cityscape was renovated, or, in other words: towns had their own pasts repaired.

The work of the Ghent photographer Edmond Sacré elaborately documents this radical transformation.[18] Indeed, at the end of the nineteenth and the beginning of the twentieth century, Ghent underwent a thorough transformation in which the revaluation of the medieval heritage was central. In the centre of Ghent, rows of houses were pulled down to form new squares and to restore the theatrical monumentality to the historical buildings. Sacré's photographs show how the modernization of Ghent ran parallel with the restoration of an imagined medieval past, which was intended to function as a historical oasis in the modernized city centre.

The highpoint of this transformation came in 1913 when the renovated Gravensteen castle was opened to the public on the occasion of the world exhibition. This revaluation of the medieval inner city was carried out in the style of Eugène Viollet-le-Duc who was renowned in France for his restorations of medieval churches and other buildings that had been severely damaged during the iconoclastic fury of the French Revolution. The first purpose of a renovation, Viollet-le-Duc states, is not to reconstruct a historical reality, but to establish a correlation between the new version of the building and an idealized past.

According to this logic, then, a renovation adapts the historical reality to the cultural imagination of the present. Something is restored that has never actually taken place, as Viollet-le-Duc puts it:

> to restore a building is not to maintain, to repair or to rebuild it, but it is to restore

17 Van de Woestijne, 'Tooneel in Vlaanderen', 426.

18 Notteboom and Lauwaert, *Edmond Sacré.*

it to a complete state that may very well
never have existed at any given time.[19]

This imagined historical past forms the
metaphorical backdrop for Herman van
Overbeke's Sint-Baafs play: thanks to the
clever lighting of the newly renovated city,
the spectator is immersed in a 'restored' experience of the medieval inner city.

The emphasis on this medieval city architecture was part of a more general cultural
imagining in which both medieval architecture and theatre were employed in constructing a shared historical past during the interwar period. Within that imagination, medieval theatre functioned as a form of community art, as an allegorical practice in which
the actors symbolized their community.
Van Overbeke, too, seems to have participated in this medieval theatrical practice with
the forms of mass theatricality he embedded
in medieval settings. With his Sint-Baafs play
he associated himself with the contemporary
nostalgia for a unified medieval culture in
which art, life and liturgy were bound up
with one another.

In its fascination with medieval forms of
theatricality, Van Overbeke's work is in line
with other theatrical practices common during the interwar period. The popular company Les Théophiliens, for example, under
the leadership of medievalist Gustave Cohen
(who had worked at the Sorbonne),
presented modernized 're-enactments' of
medieval plays. In these performances,
which were also staged in Belgium, Cohen
investigated the specific medieval theatricality of the visual experience's taking priority
over the handling of the text.[20] French author Henri Ghéon whose work was introduced in Flanders by Prosper Thuysbaert,
also acted as a pioneer in the revaluation of
medieval theatre. Herman Teirlinck translated epic dramatic texts from Middle Dutch.
All of these were part of a broader cultural
climate in which the medieval performative
culture became linked to modernist views
on directing, partly inspired by Russian mass
spectacles.

Two crucial elements were used by
Van Overbeke to revive the renovated medieval city centre in his Sint-Baafs play: lighting and sound. The theatrical lighting of the
Ghent town centre was first undertaken in
1913 on the occasion of the world exhibition. Spotlights were used to 'free' the monu-
ments, to detach the medieval relics from the
fabric of the city and thus develop them into

19 Viollet-le-Duc, *Dictionnaire rai-
    sonné de l'architecture française*,
    vol. 8.
20 Cohen, 'Expériences théophi-
    liens'; Id., 'Les Théophiliens'.

133

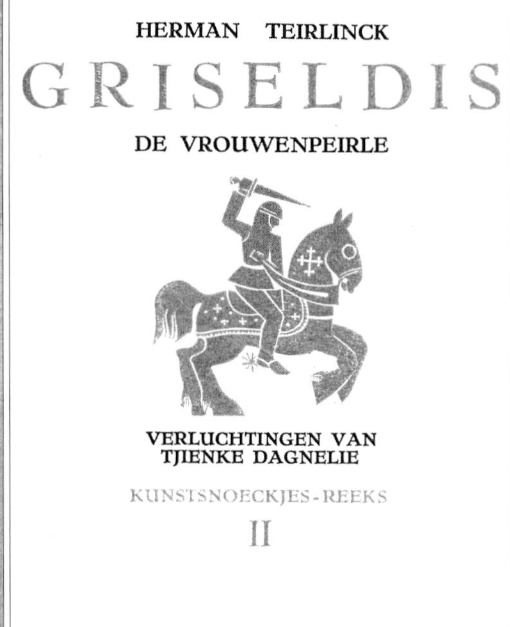

7. Covers of 'medieval' plays by
H. Ghéon (1923), H. van Overbeke
(1930) and H. Teirlinck (1942).
[Leuven, KADOC-KU Leuven
and Leuven, KU Leuven, Centrale
bibliotheek]

open-air museum pieces. This theatricalization of the inner city was made possible, among other things, by the advent of electrical lighting. Lamps were able to turn a visit to the city centre into a museal experience which submerged the spectator, in the spirit of Viollet-le-Duc, in a historical experience that had never actually been real.[21] That effect was further magnified when in 1930, on the occasion of Belgium's centenary, the towers of Ghent were also lit and the theatrical experience of the inner city was maximized. Picture postcards entitled 'Illumination de la Belgique entière' (Illumination of all of Belgium)[22] are testament to the magic of this nocturnal cityscape, which Van Overbeke exploited fully in his Sint-Baafs play.

In addition to lighting, he consciously used the city carillon to add an aural element to his spectacle. Under the influence of romanticism, the carillon had gained a new role. While in the seventeenth and eighteenth centuries, especially, the carillon had functioned as a sort of local radio, it lost this role in the romantic period and became, as Rombouts describes it, 'a non-musical symbol' or 'a resounding witness of a glorious

past or [...] a musical relic that inspired nostalgic feelings, just like architectural ruins'.[23]

Again, it is no coincidence that this preoccupation with the carillon happened in the 1920s, nor that Van Overbeke made use of this nostalgic symbol. Rajesh Heynickx points to '[t]he deep transformations (the rise of technology, internationalization and secularization) that characterized the 1920s'. In his opinion, these had generated 'a fundamental uncertainty among Catholics about their own social position'.[24] It was no accident that the carillon attained an important place within Catholicism as a symbol, as it was an important part of the cultural policy imposed by Catholic Action.[25] Aesthetically, this preoccupation with the Middle Ages was translated into a neo-Gothic imagination at the intersection of traditionalism with modernity. This particular symbiosis can also be found in the Sint-Baafs play, a spectacle in which Van Overbeke demonstrates his militant Catholicism through a large-scale open-air performance, while attempting to link his preference for an imagined medieval universe to his modernist poetic views. Here too is the nineteenth-century myth of

21 Van Dijk and De Rynck, *Belichte stad.*
22 Stadsarchief Gent.
23 Rombouts, 'Klok en beiaard', 18.
24 Heynickx, 'Van cultuurproduct naar productcultuur', 128.
25 Ibid., 133.

a unified medieval culture called into play. Starting from their Catholic ideal of *Bildung*, the adherents of Catholic Action were searching for an antidote to the abundance of impulses that confronted modern man with himself; they found this antidote in a return to a shared historical past and thus to a collective consciousness.

The Green Theatre in Citadel Park

It is perhaps unsurprising, then, that Herman van Overbeke was ultimately appointed to act as 'art director' for the Ghent Open-Air Theatre in 1940. In the meantime, he had become renowned as a specialist in performances on location and in the open air. Still, this was also a new development for him: while his earlier work, including the Sint-Baafs play, aimed at integrating theatre in cityscapes, he had now been assigned a specific space for staging plays. From this point on, he seems to have distanced himself from the medieval imagination and the related theatrical regime. The provision of the open-air theatre in Citadel Park meant that he found himself working in production conditions similar to those of ancient tragedy, but also to those of the *Thingspiel*, the only substantial contribution of national socialism to German theatrical history.

At first, open-air theatres were a Dutch phenomenon. In the first quarter of the twentieth century, open-air theatres were built in various places, among which Oisterwijk (1915), Valkenburg (1916), Oosterwolde (1918) and Amsterdam (1925).[26] Flanders followed somewhat reluctantly. In the 1920s, the Antwerp KNS company used the open-air theatre in Valkenburg during the summer. That way the actors, who were only contracted as members of the ensemble for seven months, could make ends meet finan-

26 Alexander and Van der Krogt, 'Openluchttheaters in Nederland'.

8. *Unknown performance from the interbellum period in the Open-Air Theatre in Oisterwijk.*
[Alexander and Van der Krogt, Openluchttheaters in Nederland*]*

9. *The Groentheater or Théâtre de Verdure (Green Theatre) in Brussels. [© Lien Robberechts, 2013]*

27 Arcadis, *Opmaak van een survey en waardering voor het Citadelpark in Gent*, 48.

cially. The *Groentheater* or *Théâtre de Verdure* (Green Theatre) was eventually built in the Ossegempark in Brussels in the 1930s. Ghent's own open-air theatre in Citadel Park was opened in 1940. It took until 1953 for the first real large-scale open-air theatre to open in Belgium: the *Rivierenhof* in Deurne. In order to justify the initiatives, the link between community and nature was always emphasized. The open-air theatre was meant to bring the community back to its cultic origins, as it were, far from the city culture of the playhouse.

Throughout its history, Citadel Park in Ghent has undergone a number of metamorphoses. Time and again new plans were made, building on and improving the previous plans. In its present state the park is a heterogeneous mixture, with elements from various historical periods alongside and sometimes on top of one another. The biggest change came in 1913, on the occasion of the world fair: a centenary palace was built, thematic gardens were laid out and an area of 130 hectare was cleared for the exhibition itself. The result was a varied architectural jumble:

> Next to the traditional pavilions of cities and (sometimes seemingly) exotic countries and the nostalgic Oud Vlaenderen (Old Flanders) there are imposing and vast exhibition halls, all in all a motley mix of historicizing and more progressive architecture.[27]

Baroque, classicism, art nouveau, art deco, neo-renaissance, new realism: all were represented. An aqua slide and a 'scenic railway' were added to this diversity. On the occasion of the centenary in 1930 the park underwent a second metamorphosis: the flower show palace was rebuilt, and the northern rose garden and the court of honour were laid out. In 1940 a 'green theatre' (after the French *théâtre de verdure*) was added to this architectural tangle in the northern corner of the park. Van Overbeke drew the original designs, but it would be architect Bontinck and garden architect

Bourgeois who eventually produced the final plans, which also included a dressing cubicle and a booth for the prompter. The theatre, nick-named 'the Shell', could accommodate more than 1,300 spectators. Unfortunately, as mentioned above, the theatre has today fallen into disuse and ruin.

As 'artistic director', Herman van Overbeke was in control of the artistic management of the open-air theatre and its programming. On 2 and 3 August 1940 a Dutch version of *Les Fourberies de Scapin* (Molière) was staged in 'the Shell'. Staf Bruggen, director of the KNS in Ghent, directed this play in collaboration with the Royal City Opera's *corps de ballet*. A year later, on 26 and 27 July 1941, Michel van Vlaenderen, who would take over the management of the KNS from Staf Bruggen after the Second World War, directed Vondel's *Jozef in Dothan* (Joseph in Dothan).[28] The posters for these two performances show that the weather conditions caused quite a few complications, and that an alternative location may have been necessary. Both posters expressly state that 'in case of bad weather the performance will be given in the *Koninklijke Nederlandsche Schouwburg* (Royal Dutch Theatre), with half an hour's delay for the matinee and an hour's delay for the evening performance'.

10. Posters of two performances in the Open-Air Theatre in Ghent, 1941. [Ghent, Stadsarchief]

28 Vanhaesebrouck, 'Geen rijker kroon dan eigen schoon?'

Aside from *Joseph in Dothan*, Michel van Vlaenderen also directed *Reis naar 't Paradijs* (The Scholar Bound for Paradise) by Hans Sachs, *Jonkvrouw de la Seiglière* (Mademoiselle de la Seiglière) by Jules Sandeau and *Mirandolina* by Goldoni, while Herman van Overbeke staged *Kaatje Van Heilbronn* by Heinrich von Kleist (Käthchen of Heilbronn).

Staf Bruggen not only directed *De Schelmenstreken van Scapin* by Molière (Scapin's Deceits), but also presented *Krelis Louwen* by Pieter Langendijk.[29] The entire enterprise turned out to be a financial disaster, however. The Belgian weather thwarted the organization, and the acoustics of 'the Shell' appear to have been far from excellent. The war circumstances, too, did not help matters. After only two summers, the initiative wound down prematurely.

This adventure may only be of peripheral importance as a specific, theatrical-historical episode. The more interesting question concerns the theatrical context in which an initiative such as this open-air theatre could be realized. Without suggesting that there is a causal relationship between the two phenomena (that relation can be found in the reception *post factum* rather than at the level of artistic intention), the concept of the Ghent Open-Air Theatre is reminiscent of the *Thingspiele*, the official national socialist theatrical practice.

Thingspiele were performed in *Thingstätte*, or amphitheatres in the open air, quite a number of which were built in the 1930s (such as the Heidelberger *Thingstatte* or the *Thingsplatz* in Ordensburg Vogelsang, for example). The etymology of the word refers to 'Thing', a meeting place where members of old-Germanic communities entered into consultation with one another. The *Thingspiele* can therefore be related to a determined mystification of the old-Germanic roots of the German people, as they were a conscious attempt to activate a kind of shared cultic mythology.

The designers of such theatrical spaces purposefully used the natural surroundings such as ruins, impressive landscapes, hills, etc. In other words, the sublime monumentality of nature was central and should have brought the spectator into a sort of premodern rapture. The *Thingspiel* focused on the staging of a communal experience – the spectator was intended to recognize that he or she was a member of a homogeneous and militant (national socialist) *Gemeinschaft*. 'The German should no longer consider himself a private person or an isolated individual, but a part of the people's community', Wilhelm von Schramm wrote in 1934.[30]

Historically speaking, the *Thingspiele* were attempting to imitate ancient Greek theatre practice. Both had an exceptional, cultic status, both used codified modes of

29 Van Schoor, *Een huis voor Vlaanderen*, 205.
30 Von Schramm, *Neubau des deutschen Theaters*, 39 (quoted in Niven, 'The Birth of Nazi Drama?', 56).

12. Goethe, Oer-Faust (Ur-Faust), *Brussels, 1942.*
[Leuven, KU Leuven, Centrale bibliotheek]

we do know that Niessen visited Flanders several times during the Second World War (notably as guest director for a production of the *Ur-Faust* at the Antwerp KNS in 1941).[32] The programming of the Ghent Open-Air Theatre must have been a difficult balancing act, in which Van Overbeke would have been required to respect the occupiers' tastes while not treating his public with contempt by bowing all too emphatically to those tastes.

Above all, what this initiative shows is how the anti-realistic disposition of open-air theatre had ultimately become part of bourgeois leisure culture. It was no longer a place where the community represented itself, in all its democratic dissent, such as in the ancient tragedies, or as a homogeneous entity, such as in the *Thingspiel.* It had become a place where bourgeois spectators could consecrate their own theatrical past, in unison with their bourgeois tastes and even within the setting of a leisure park. But above all, Herman van Overbeke's open-air theatre functioned as an interesting arena in which various elements of the cultural-historical imagination of the interwar period could meet, both ideologically and aesthetically.

representation (there is little or no stage setting) and both utilized emphatic gesture and rhetoric. The *Thingspiele* referred to classical performances in their outspoken anti-realism: they were theatrical rituals that were meant to represent a homogeneous community. Carl Niessen, the founder of the official doctrine of the *Thingspiel,* made the connection to ancient Greece explicitly:

> Now, however, the meeting hall and the theatre have again become identical, just as in ancient Greece, and space has a role to play once more.[31]

A *Thingspiel* was in the first place a *Gesamtkunstwerk* that was to form a unity with the site of the performance. In other words, according to Niessen, the *Thingspiel* removed the fourth wall and involved the spectator once again in the theatrical event.

There is no concrete historical evidence to indicate a clear link between the *Thingspiel* and the open-air theatre in Ghent, even if

31 Niessen quoted in Wulf, *Theater und Film im Dritten Reich,* 166.
32 De Gruyter, *Boekje open,* 122.

NO MORE WAR

The Pilgrimages of the Yser (1948-1970)

Luk Van den Dries

It may be evident from the rest of this book that mass theatre was highly popular during the 1920s and 1930s, yet afterwards failed to capture the imagination of the post-war generations. Contributing factors were the distrust of mass movements and collectivism, which had been so important to interwar politics and art, and the rise of individualism in the consumer society. In the Flemish context, the construction of the open-air theatre Rivierenhof in Deurne (Antwerp) may function as a case in point.[1] Although the plans for constructing an open-air theatre in this location went back as far as the early 1920s, it was only effectively realized in 1953. The *Rivierenhof* theatre, which was and is the largest of its kind in Belgium, may truly be called an anachronistic building, for the ideal of community art, which had been so central to the discussions around its construction, belonged firmly in the interwar period. After merely one decade of intensive use, both public attendance and the number of productions shrank dramatically.

However, there were still some notable exceptions to the decline of socio-theatricality during the post-war period. The year 1948 saw the breathing of new life into the yearly *IJzerbedevaart* (Pilgrimage of the Yser), a mass event held at the river Yser in the Belgian city Diksmuide, which had arisen in the interwar period as a tribute to the fallen Flemish soldiers of World War I. Subsequently, the event would gain an important symbolic function as part of the Flemish movement. Initiated as a ceremony of pilgrimage and remembrance, the mass event quickly acquired a dimension of political awareness and empowerment.[2] It was a clear manifestation of Flemish combative-ness against the French supremacy in the Belgian state.

The focus of this chapter, however, is not the concrete political significance of the Yser happening. Instead, we examine the ways in which the masses of participants were sensitized to the Flemish cause through the use of theatrical devices. Obviously, the theatrical choices were not made independently of the political content, but our focus lies less on the content of the Flemish emancipatory process, and more on the empowering of the masses that gathered every year around the *IJzertoren* (Yser Tower) in Diksmuide. The main thesis of this chapter is that although the pilgrimage has been modernized and professionalized from 1948 to 1970, the romantic and Catholic core of this event remained untouched.

As Gita Deneckere has noted, 'the manifestation was introduced into the repertoire in Western European countries during the nineteenth century as an eminently bourgeois form of collective action'.[3] She borrows the theatrical metaphor 'repertoire', here used to describe the public manifestation, from the American sociologist and historian Charles Tilly. He had described

> the basic rules or scripts according to which ordinary people in the course of time have manifested their presence on the public stage. Their repertoire is, just like that of a theater company, bound to a specific period, and determined by concrete historical circumstances.[4]

Deneckere therefore concludes, rightfully, that manifestations are a form of political theatre, and are meant to be observed in

1. Pilgrimage of the Yser, 39th edition, 1966.
[Antwerp, ADVN]

1   Crombez and Vanhoeck, 'De bouw van het Openluchttheater Rivierenhof te Deurne (1953)'.
2   On the origins and the development of the Pilgrimage of the Yser, see De Lentdecker, 'IJzer-bedevaart' and Beck, 'IJzerbe-devaart'.
3   Deneckere, 'De macht van de straat', 26.
4   Ibid., 25.

some way by the Other. 'A manifestation is aimed at manifesting a problem, i.e., at making it manifest outside of the circle of those directly concerned with the problem.'[5]

The Pilgrimage of the Yser is clearly such a form of public manifestation. Other pro-Flemish examples include the *Guldensporenviering* (Commemoration of the Battle of the Golden Spurs, 11 July) and the *Vlaams Nationaal Zangfeest* (Flemish National Song Festival). It was conceived as both a pilgrimage, in which the union of a group of like-minded people would be professed and strengthened, and as a memorial ceremony for the fallen. Moreover, it was used as a platform for voicing specific political complaints and demands regarding the unequal treatment of Flemings and Walloons in Belgium.

This multiple identity of the Yser Pilgrimage form the basis of a script that has hardly changed since 1948. A traditional Yser Pilgrimage begins with a celebration of the Eucharist, after which a speech is given on behalf of the youth.[6] Next, a representative of the *Verbond van Vlaamse Oud-Strijders* (Association of Flemish War Veterans, VOS)

speaks. The central part of the ceremony is the floral tribute, which takes place around the symbols of the Yser Tower.

Finally, the chairman of the Yser Pilgrimage Committee gives a speech. All then pledge their allegiance to Flanders and sing the Flemish anthem (the Flemish Lion). The speeches are usually interspersed with flag parades and flag-dancing performances, and with choirs and spectators singing songs from the traditional Flemish repertoire.

The Yser Tower had been conceived as a place for commemorating a number of intensely symbolic memories from World War I: the tombstones of a number of soldiers who had fallen at the Yser Front, the gun-damaged crucifix of Nieuwpoort, and the stone in Merkem bearing the red-painted slogan, 'Here our blood, when our right?' Other symbols of the Yser Pilgrimage included the *Heldenhuldekruis* (Hero Tribute Cross), a kind of tombstone symbol designed by Joe English and bearing the characters AVV-VVK (*Alles voor Vlaanderen-Vlaanderen voor Kristus*, 'All for Flanders, Flanders

5   Deneckere, 'De macht van de straat', 27.

6   The Eucharist was initially celebrated in the marketplace of Diksmuide, after which the Pilgrimage moved to the Yser fields. Later, the Eucharist also came to be held in the proximity of the Yser monument.

for Christ') alongside the image of the mythical 'bluefoot' bird.[7]

The key element is the sacrificial death of the fallen soldiers, romanticized not only in the memorial moment, but also as an incentive to contemporary Flemish people to convert the historical sacrifice into renewed militancy. Sufficiently eloquent in this regard is the verse by Flemish poet and chaplain Cyriel Verschaeve, which is affixed to the tower: 'Here lie their bodies as seeds in the sand / Hope for the harvest, O Flemish land'.

The Pilgrimage of the Yser is essentially an event of thoroughly romanticized 'memory work' (analogous to Freud's *Trauerarbeit*, or 'mourning work'), based on anecdotes about some of the fallen soldiers, around which an ingenious symbolic ritual was constructed. It is a very personalized cult of martyrdom that strongly appeals to emotions such as pity, anger, pride and hope. The Pilgrimage of the Yser thus functions as a direct offshoot of the 'Front Movement', a protest movement that quickly grew popular during and after the First World War among Flemish officers and soldiers in the Belgian army,

7   *Blauwvoet*, a Flemish word for the Northern Gannet, was used in the opening lines of a famous poem by the nineteenth-century poet Albrecht Rodenbach.

5. *Pilgrimage of the Yser, 29th edition, 1956. The official flag of the Pilgrimage.* [Antwerp, ADVN]

6. *Pilgrimage of the Yser, 31st edition, 1958. A float symbolising the bloodshed of the First World War ('Here our blood').* [Antwerp, ADVN]

8   Balduck, *Diksmuide, onze trots en onze schande*, 26; Verdoodt, 'Allen daarheen!', 17.

9   Benvindo and Peeters, *Scherven van de oorlog*, 92.

10 De Lentdecker, 'IJzerbedevaart', 705.

based on their feelings of frustration and resentment that French was the only language of command (which itself functioned as the 'founding myth' of the nationalist Flemish movement).

The ingenious mix of the rhetorical repetition of these emotive strategies in the speech portions of the event, along with theatrical techniques such as the spatial design, mass singing, speech choirs, flag parades and floral tributes, and the almost religious veneration of certain Flemish relics, preserved in 'Flanders' mausoleum', guarantees a massive annual turnout at this event.[8]

Mass Singing and Speeches

From the end of the 1930s onwards, the Yser Pilgrimage became appropriated by national socialist politicians, after the Committee began collaborating with the pro-German *Vlaamsch Nationaal Verbond* (Flemish National Association, VNV) and eventually also with the Nazi occupiers. After the war, this led pro-Belgian groups to blow up the monument twice, once in 1945 and again in 1946. Of the great monument to the 'Flemish-national memorial community',[9] only a pile of rubble remained.

However, the harsh punishments meted out to Flemish people who had collaborated with the Nazi occupiers (the 'Repression' of the post-war years), together with the double dynamite attack, would quickly reignite the dormant sense of injustice that had always been the driving force behind the mass meetings at the Yser.

It was therefore little wonder that soon after the war, the Committee was reorganized in order to re-launch the annual Yser Pilgrimages. The war Pilgrimages were simply edited out of the official records, and the numbering of the events started again from the final pre-war Pilgrimage of 1939. The question of whether this caesura changed something in the theatrical strategies of the Pilgrimage is central to the rest of my argument.

One might argue that the top level of the organization responsible for the Yser Pilgrimage had been thoroughly renewed after the war. The Yser Pilgrimage Committee was now headed by a new chairman, Jan-Frans Franssen, and a new executive, Edward Clottens, chairman of the Association of Flemish Veterans (VOS), who would, behind the scenes, re-design the new series of Pilgrimages.[10] The composition of the General Assembly and of the Board of Governors, the association's central administrative bodies, had also changed.

What had not changed, however, was that the central co-ordination of the association remained in the hands of Clemens

De Landtsheer, who had been the secretary of the association and its driving force since 1921. It was De Landtsheer who had been behind the building of the Yser Tower, the promotion of the event, and the practical realization of the program.[11]

Another element of continuity between the pre-war and the post-war events was that Juliaan Platteau had stayed in place as a member of the team that designed and directed the mass events. During World War I, Platteau had been a member of the *Fronttooneel* (Front Theatre), a company formed by the Belgian government to provide some distraction to the war-worn soldiers of the trenches. After the war, he was an actor with the *Vlaams Volkstoneel* and a speaker at numerous Pilgrimages. Other protagonists of the pre-war Yser Pilgrimages that stayed in place were Sam De Vriendt, a painter and a good friend of Joe English (one of the most prominent martyrs commemorated at each Pilgrimage), and Lode Van Kerkhoven, the association's propaganda leader, who was also an active member of the *Davidsfonds* and the Cultural Association of the *Noordstarfonds*. After the war they were responsible for simply continuing the pre-war scenarios of the Yser Pilgrimage, with the same ingredients, the same mixture of nostalgia and hope, and the same theatrical processes.

Occasionally, an original proposal was put forward, such as the invitation extended to director and dramatist Anton Van de Velde to write the text and design the production for a mass spectacle in 1949, a proposal that was later rejected at the general assembly of the Yser Pilgrimage Committee.[12] At most, small modifications were made, for instance, with regard to how the oath to Flanders should be performed.[13] Generally speaking, however, the traditional scenario was followed to the letter, composed of speeches and singing, theatrical interventions that accompanied the floral tribute, directed by M. Vandeputte, and flag parades. Even the religious celebration preceding the event was carried out according to a strict pattern:

Regarding the <u>Holy Mass</u>, we will investigate whether the Messa brevis can again be sung by the masses, and if a <u>people's speech choir</u> can again be included, along with short answers for the masses.[14]

7. Pilgrimage of the Yser, 25th edition, 1952. A float with members of the Boerenjeugdbond (*Farmers' Youth League,* BJB).
[Antwerp, ADVN]

Plans for the construction of a new Yser Tower were obviously a welcome motif in the theatrical amplification of communal feelings and the hopeful desire for a better future. It was hoped that the building of a new tower would prompt a monumental reconstruction of the symbolic power of the past, confirming the personality cult that had been laid down in the sculptures, and a restoration of the hero worship that had taken place before the war. During the General Committee Meeting of 14 June 1952, for example, it was decided that the ceremonial laying of the first stone of the new Yser Tower would be incorporated in the 25th Pilgrimage:

The first stone was to be solemnly brought forward from the rubble, then passed through the masses in the direction of the new foundations, together with fragments of the Hero Tribute tombstones and of the ruined tower, accompanied by miners, longshoremen, clerks, etc., and preceded by the fourteen small Pilgrimage flags

11 On the role of Clemens De Landtsheer: Van de Winkel and Biltereyst, *Filmen voor Vlaanderen*; Durnez, 'Clemens De Landtsheer'; Coppieters, 'Clemens De Landtsheer'.
12 'Verslag Algemene comitévergadering 24 december 1949', ADVN 1255/2/4.
13 'Verslag algemene comitévergadering van 15 april 1950', ADVN Y 122/1.
14 'Verslag van de algemene vergadering van 22 oktober 1949', ADVN Y 122/1, emphasis in original document.

borne by ensigns on foot. The director will see to the appropriate arrangements.[15]

This staging followed the proven procedure for the procession through the crowd, just as the 'symbolic Flemish fallen soldiers' had been laid to rest during the 13th Pilgrimage in 1932.[16] The same process was used again in 1955, with the slogan 'Bring forward stones', when huge trucks loaded with tons of bricks were driven past the audience decorated with large banners reading: 'Stones for the Yser Tower'.[17] These were powerful images, that provided a kind of theatrical motor to the event. The construction of the Tower, in its various phases, would remain an important propagandist tool in the process of theatricalizing the Yser Pilgrimage.

The Problem of Youth

A more important problem, meanwhile, was the question of how the young could be mobilized. With every Pilgrimage of the Yser, a significant distance was opening up between the original symbolic events (connected to World War I) and the present, and younger members therefore had to be increasingly sensitized towards participation in the event. Again a pre-war formula provided the solution. On the eve of the Yser Pilgrimage, it had been customary to set up a youth camp offering certain activities in the spirit of the Pilgrimage. In 1952, the performance of an open-air play by Ferdinand Vercnocke was proposed, since he was an author who specialized in pro-Flemish poetry, mass plays and choral drama.[18] The committee was enthusiastic about the proposal:

> Before the war there was indeed discussion about organizing a kind of <u>Yser play</u> on <u>Saturday evening</u> on the steps of the tower, because then too we had the same problems of bonfires, separate groups, etc. [...] Remember the living images of Ganda in the marketplace, which were much appreciated despite their flaws! I believe that

we have here what we seek: <u>a series of images from the Yser Tragedy</u>, put forward tangibly so that young people are struck by a short series of images, teaching them a lesson <u>they will never forget</u>.[19]

Vercnocke wrote *De IJzersage* (The Yser Saga), a play in which all of the symbols and myths of the war events surrounding the Yser were re-translated for this new audience. It is a romantic ode, intended as a memorial to and a continuation of the symbolic struggle. In eleven 'images', the history of the Front Movement is outlined. It is also a kind of educational project in which new generations are made familiar with the symbols and the history of the Yser Tower. The members of the Yser Pilgrimage Committee were immediately enthused by the play: 'It is the epic of the Yser tragedy, written especially for the young. It is the mysticism of the Flemish Yser happening captured in a dozen scenes of poignant tragedy.' Or: 'These are synthetic and very evocative images. If the concise text is properly recited, and well supported by appropriate music and lighting, it may have a huge propagandistic influence on receptive youths.'[20] Almost no one of the Committee had any critical remarks to make about the play, with the exception of Aloïs De Maeyer:

> It would be good if Mr Vercnocke were to review his text well. Romance is healthy, but romantic scholastic recital is wrong. Maybe he could – especially at the beginning – prune a few of the replies in that sense [...]. It could turn into a litany.[21]

Interestingly, the direction of this open-air spectacle was entrusted to Remi Van Duyn, who would play a prominent role in the renewal and professionalization of the Yser happening ten years later. In his production of *The Yser Saga*, resources were immediately put to use on a grand scale. Actors from local amateur theatre groups were recruited, dancers for the choreographic depiction were engaged from *De Uilenspiegels* in Kortrijk, musical support was offered by the

15 'Verslag van de algemene comitévergadering 14 juni 1952', ADVN Y 120/1.

16 *De symbolen van de IJzertragedie*, 16.

17 'Overeenkomst met de firma Florizoone, Steenbakker 'Nieuwpoort & Extensions'', ADVN 124/3/15.

18 During the war, Vercnocke had also been an active member of the pro-German movement *De Vlag* (*Duits-Vlaamse Arbeidsgemeenschap*, German-Flemish Labour Community), and had collaborated on the pro-German radio station *Zender Brussel*.

19 'Brief aan de programmacommissie, 9 juni 1952', ADVN Y 49/2, emphasis in original document.

20 'De IJzertoren, 4e Mededeling voor de XXVIe IJzerbedevaart (1953)', ADVN Y 49/2; Letter from Remi Sterkens / VOS, 8 Dec. 1952, ADVN Y 49/2.

21 Letter from A. De Maeyer, 24 June 1953, ADVN Y 49/2.

Veremans choir, and Van Duyn also enrolled 20 students for the core *tableaux*, 6 men to represent the Yser scenes, 40 people for the procession, and 2 altar boys.

Three years later, in 1956, the propaganda play was performed again, with the intention of instructing the young, in a slightly revised version and with a new production design by Remi Van Duyn, who would pay closer attention to the indications of the author, particularly the advice that the play ought to

> continue in the spirit of the Pilgrimage, i.e., here the <u>people themselves</u> should participate. [...] The play should be reminiscent of an actual pilgrimage. The <u>spectators</u> should be involved in the spectacle, so they do not sit as though in a theatre.[22]

This dynamic concept of an audience, who are not only to be addressed but also activated and engaged in the action, would be one of the main objectives of the Yser Pilgrimage reform. Remi Van Duyn had already applied this principle during the production of Vercnocke's *Yser Saga*, but he would apply it again to the mass event of the Pilgrimage itself ten years later.

Whether young people were actually able to relate to Vercnocke and Van Duyn's romantic imagery is difficult to say. Their active contribution to the organization continued to be limited to a variety of small tasks during the event, such as the selling of badges or the formation of a security staff. But youth organizations were also approached for precisely the most dramatic elements of the event, such as the floral tribute, the parade of flags and all sorts of flag-dancing performances. The floral tribute consisted of a long parade in which flower arrangements gifted by countless organizations and towns were placed at the foot of the monument. In 1961, for instance, the parade involved 480 flower girls from various youth organizations.[23]

A good example of the prominent involvement of youth organizations is the 1951 enlisting of the *Boerenjeugdbond* (Farmers' Youth League, BJB), as described below:

8. Pilgrimage of the Yser, 34th edition, 1961. 'Theban trompeteers' announce the start of the festivities. [Antwerp, ADVN]

At the next Yser Pilgrimage, the Floral Tribute and the Flag Parade will form the highpoints of the event. During this part of the program, the stake of the new Yser Tower will be ceremonially driven into the ground. The Production Committee for the Pilgrimage is planning a performance involving 50 riders on horseback in a Flag Parade. In order to realize this plan, we appeal to the members of the BJB's equestrian division.[24]

Ten years later, in 1961, the Yser Pilgrimage took as its theme 'Flemings Be as One'. The program included a parade in which the youth organizations portrayed different social classes.[25] For the same Pilgrimage, a flag-dancing spectacle was staged, involving various groups of dancers.[26]

The youth clubs can therefore be seen as an indispensable part of the Yser Pilgrimage Committee's theatrical strategy. Their participation, often in uniform, in group formation or as a mass, ensured the symbols associated with each Pilgrimage were given shape theatrically. The formal choices have remained relatively old-fashioned. The repertoire obviously stems from the pre-war period and follows the tried and tested procedures of floral tributes, parades and flag-dancing. Those

22 Vercnocke, 'Nota bij de 'IJzersage' en de opvoering van 1953', ADVN Y 49/3, emphasis in original document.

23 'Jeugdkomitee voor de IJzerbedevaart. Verslag van de vergadering van 24 juni 1961', ADVN Y 8/2.

24 Letter from Lode van Kerkhoven, 19 June 1951, ADVN.

25 'Jeugdkomitee voor de IJzerbedevaart. Verslag van de vergadering van 24 juni 1961', ADVN Y 8/2.

26 '16 flag-dancers from Limburg for representing the struggle of the lions against the attackers, 4 flag-dancers in black uniform carrying black flags or flags in bold colours with long fringes, 12 lion flag bearers wearing BJB flag-dancer uniforms; an additional 15 dancers from West Flanders will be asked to join', 'Jeugdkomitee voor de IJzerbedevaart. Verslag van de vergadering van 24 juni 1961', ADVN Y 8/2.

ingredients are never contested during the deliberations of the production committee, or by the higher councils of the organization. Only a few critics are occasionally disturbed by poor implementation of the basic concept.

A Cumbersome Flagship

Behind the scenes, however, new formulas for designing the Yser Pilgrimage are being developed. A single document survives from the late 1950s that already mentions the term 'renewal', albeit still very cautiously.[27] This innovation should be situated in the period following the departure of secretary Clemens De Landtsheer in 1960, and his replacement by Rik De Ghein, when a general attempt to rejuvenate the Pilgrimage Committee and amend the articles of the association was launched.[28]

For the realization of this renewal, the Committee approached a number of directors who were familiar with open-air theatre and mass spectacle. Thus, in 1959 Antoon Vander Plaetse, a former actor with the Flemish Popular Theatre who had achieved renown as a reciter of poems by Flemish poets such as Stijn Streuvels, Albrecht Rodenbach and Cyriel Verschaeve, was asked to advise in the process of renewal. Like many of his generation, he combined teaching in secondary schools with acting and directing assignments, recitals and other activities.[29] His productions of large open-air spectacles such as the *Guldensporenspel* (Golden Spurs Play, 1952) by Willem Putman in Kortrijk and the *Rodenbachspel* (Rodenbach Play, 1956) by André Demedts in Roeselare had already received quite some attention. Additionally, he was familiar with directing parades such as the Rodenbach parade in Roeselare and the *Reinaert de Vos* parade in Hulst.

As far as the Committee members were concerned, Vander Plaetse was the ideal person to help re-think the Pilgrimage, on the basis of his extensive professional knowledge of mass spectacle. At the same time he was still someone who sympathized with the old romantic Flemish values (as will be clear from the brief life sketch given above). At the meeting of the directing committee on 9 January 1959, he outlined the innovative concept in broad terms. It was:

to transform the Pilgrimage into a sort of Play that includes the following main parts: History, Yser Saga, Youth Future. The imagination of the masses would be addressed by groups and figures. Songs, speeches, flags and floral tributes would all have a place, but framed within the play. Mr Vander Plaetse will commit his plans to paper for the next Committee meeting, including an estimate of the costs. This latter point concerns the renting of costumes, wigs, etc.[30]

On 10 February 1959 he elaborated on his plan. His proposal sounded like the script for a romantic and propagandist play, similar to Vercnocke's *Yser Saga*, and bore the motto: 'more combativeness and more youth'. I quote extensively from his proposal:

After the Mass: trumpets. Fifty girls with wreaths and flowers appear on the steps of the new tower. Fifty boys with streamers take their places on the first floor of the new tower.

Wilt thou now come forward: Rodenbach and 200 students with Bluefoot Flags appear at the left and right of the new tower. Through the Pax-gate enter fifty WWI soldiers, joined together and pulling a carriage shaped like a cannon, upon which rests a block of blue limestone bearing the slogan 'Here our blood, when our right!' + blown up Yser Tower. They are surrounded by 20 symbolic figures: intellect, finance, army, economy, capital, Fransquillonism, bourgeoisie, etc. They carry whips and drive the troop forward.

Goodbye my brother: from the Pax-gate appear Joe English, Deprez, Van Raemdonck, Derudder, De Boninge, Kusters, Van der Linden. They wear their personal symbol and lion flags. They are

27 A remarkable point on the agenda of the 19 March 1959 meeting is 'Production design of the 32nd Yser Pilgrimage. Renovation of the Pilgrimage'. The meeting, however, is later postponed and this agenda point has disappeared by the time it is actually held. ADVN 553/4.

28 Van de Winkel and Biltereyst, *Filmen voor Vlaanderen*, 74.

29 An overview is given in *Huldeboek Antoon Vander Plaetse 60 jaar*.

30 'Verslag van de vergadering van de regie- en kunstcommissie 7 januari 1959', ADVN Y 8/2.

148

surrounded by 50 Flemish mothers who carry pieces of concrete and violated tombstones.

We are ready: from the new tower appear all the youth organizations of Flanders + 10 members in uniform. They go in the direction of the Pax-gate.[31]

Apparently not everyone was convinced of the desirability of converting the Yser Pilgrimage into some sort of romantic agitprop theatre, because from the minutes of the production and art committee's meeting of 4 March 1959 we learn that 'the Ant. Vander Plaetse proposal is only partially appropriate' and was therefore rejected *de facto*.[32]

Another name that appears during the discussions of the Yser Pilgrimage Committee is that of Remi Lens. He is first mentioned in a discussion following the 1961 Pilgrimage.[33] Remi Lens, priest, poet and artist, was especially active as a director of processions. It was he, for instance, who had revived the Holy Blood procession in Hoogstraten. In 1962 he would draft a memorandum for the production committee in which his plans for a redesign of the Yser Pilgrimage are explained.

Again, the event is clearly re-theatricalized, albeit with less symbolic and romantic bombast. For example, for the floral tribute he proposes installing a walkway 1.5m high between the new tower (still under construction) and the ruins of the old tower. This walkway would be lined on both sides by 'standing garland-bearers, who take their places in advance in the way of a parade, so that the flower parade (dynamic) goes through a lane of garlands (static)'.[34]

Furthermore, he proposes releasing 30 seagulls during the singing of the Blauwvoet song. Lens also planned to place 'many men (warriors)' on the highest platform of the tower under construction, holding long lances of 6-7m decorated with flags. 'I do not think it will even be necessary to costume these men. In any case, the intention is that the tower, as it were, puts up its spikes at the

end. These figures can be positioned there in advance, so that they appear by surprise.'[35]

Some of Lens' suggestions would indeed be realized later, such as the releasing of the birds and the construction of a scaffolding footbridge that was meant to increase the visibility of the events on stage. They came about in a very slow process of development in which the element of spectacle was slowly winning over the long speeches and the rhetorical bombardment. Every time Yser Pilgrimages of the late 1950s were discussed after the event, the same things were reported: the speeches are too long, and the audience's attention wanes, so there must be fewer speakers and shorter speeches. As compensation for the loss of text, the introduction of additional theatrical elements was suggested.

Gradually, the Committee realized that re-theatricalizing the Yser Pilgrimage required professional help. Between intention and implementation, however, was a rather large gap. It was difficult to set the flagship of the Flemish Movement into motion. The Yser Pilgrimage Organization was an unwieldy colossus, and fresh ideas from individual members had to pass through various committees, councils and meetings, finally coming out of that process beaten up so thoroughly that they hardly ever saw the daylight of the Diksmuide meadow.

Renewal

It was therefore also necessary to reorganize the internal structure. This was done from the early 1960s onwards, when the working process that had been used as a template for decades was held up and examined against the light. All levels of the organization were critically examined. The organization looked at itself in the mirror, so to speak, and concluded:

In principle we all heartily agree, and have done for years, that innovation is needed in the Pilgrimage and rejuvenation

31 'Bijlage bij het Verslag van de Regie- en Kunstcommissie van 7 januari 1959', ADVN 124/3/15.

32 'Uitnodiging Regie- en Kunstcommissie van 2 januari 1959', ADVN Y 553/4.

33 'Beschouwingen na de 34e bedevaart. Verslag van de vergadering van 14/10/61', ADVN Y 8/1/2.

34 Lens, 'Nota voor de regiecommissie' (1962?), ADVN Y 553/4.

35 Ibid.

9. *Pilgrimage of the Yser, 41st edition, 1968.*
[Antwerp, ADVN]

36 'Nota 'Vernieuwing'' (1965?), ADVN Y 16/2.

37 Ibid.

38 Hein Nackaerts notes in a letter: 'the answers from the masses with specific slogans [...] It seems to me that this belongs to the pre-war period. The young are no longer used to that. Besides, it strikes me as unnatural. It is also an enormous effort to make that mass speech choir succeed each time.' 23 May 1963, ADVN Y 554/4.

39 'Verslag van de Kommissie 'Vernieuwing Bedevaart' op woensdag 22 december 1965', ADVN Y 554/4.

is needed in the Committee. At regular intervals we repeat this with much conviction. In practice, however, very little or nothing has changed. Sometimes we do not dare to change, and are not always very consistent.[36]

It was important for the whole of the organization to make a firm commitment to rejuvenating the Pilgrimage Committee, which still largely consisted of members of the World War I veterans' generation. People under the age of forty were now actively sought out. The same spirit of innovation was also applied to the most visible part of the organization, the Pilgrimage of the Yser itself, where the memorandum notes that the duration of the event should be drastically shortened, some speeches replaced with a symbolic hap-

pening, and 'the global direction put into the hands of a professional director'.[37]

Certain pre-war ingredients, such as the use of mass reciting, also came under discussion.[38] Thus, a new Pilgrimage formula was developed in which more space was given to spectacle and less to rhetoric, and which was better suited to the changing world. It was decided that the motto *Nooit meer oorlog* ('No more war') should be brought to the forefront, that the languages of the world should resound during the happening, that the binding texts ought to be shorter and that they should be recited by both male and female speakers.[39]

The idea of innovation, which had lain dormant for years, met with a different social context in the 1960s than before. Now the gap between generations and values became the important issue of the day. The Pilgrimage Committee, after a thorough examination of conscience and repeated appeals from within their own ranks, realized that the tribute to the soldiers at the Yser front and the emancipation of the Flemish community should be re-conceptualized to reflect the changed relations within society. To this end, a number of remarkable and radical initiatives were introduced during the mid-1960s.

In particular, a very democratic instrument – a survey – was used to gauge the opinions and wishes of the youth associations, which had always constituted a crucial element in the continuity of the event. The results of the survey paint a picture of a more progressive youth, with many reservations about the way in which the event's content was being presented at the Pilgrimage: 'In addition to the protest aspect, the liberal attitudes of the Flemings themselves should be more strongly accentuated, and the audience's attention should be directed to the need for revolutionary commitment.' In terms of form, they felt it should be 'less folkloric (for example, costumes of Theban trumpeters); in a more contemporary style (language, symbolism, etc.).'. Lastly, the delicate point of the oath of Flanders is touched upon. Here, the survey results state that 'any phrasing of the oath that reminds the audience of the past had better be avoided'.[40]

A second important step taken at the beginning of the 1960s was the move towards a larger degree of pluralism. The Yser Pilgrimage had always been an event that took place within a wholly Catholic frame of reference. Catholic imagery was evident in the symbolism of sacrifice and resurrection, the cult of suffering and redemption, and the idea of the martyrs of the people. The entire idea of a mass pilgrimage to the crypt of a holy monument is itself founded on Catholic practices and beliefs. This was also confirmed in the custom of opening the event with a celebration of the Eucharist.

In 1962, the non-Catholic community in Flanders was cautiously approached with the intention of 'revising the content, the scenario and the program of the Pilgrimage in order to take non-Catholic Flemings into account'.[41] It would still take some time before the Pilgrimage Committee itself also became more pluralistic, and before the Eucharist was effectively separated from the actual event, but from the early 1960s onwards, Flemish cohesion was being deemed more important than the element of faith.

A third crucial step was that of professionalism, which had long and repeatedly been called for.[42] The final breakthrough occurred in October 1964:

> Now we must already think of the next Yser Pilgrimage, and the inauguration of the tower. A skilled director, who understands the meaning of the Yser Pilgrimage and is one of us (for example R. Van Duyn), would have to be involved in the production design. In advance, however, a budget needs to be drafted in order to see if an appeal to such a director is appropriate to our financial capabilities.[43]

The two conditions mentioned in this passage of the report reveal the inner workings of the organization: firstly, artistic budgets were always severely limited, and contributions to the Flemish cause that cost little were actively sought out; secondly, it was crucial that people were recruited from the organization's own ranks, though it was not always clear what this meant exactly. In any case, Remi Van Duyn was a loyal friend of the Yser Pilgrimage, having directed the *Yser Saga* in 1953 and 1956, and he was a proud Fleming. Following an induction period consisting of the 1965 Pilgrimage, he was appointed director for the period 1966-1972.

New-style Pilgrimage

Remi Van Duyn (pseudonym of Remi Ponjaert) belonged, along with Anton Vander Plaetse and Ast Fonteyne, to the generation of theatre makers who were used to operating outside of the mainstream theatre world.[44] They performed as reciters of poetry, taught eloquence and speech training, and directed school theatre productions and open-air plays. Precisely because of their wide-ranging contact with various generations of students, however, and because of their experience in producing all kinds of theatrical events in public (school plays, pageants, parades, demonstrations, mass spectacles), they in fact contributed a vast amount to the public image of theatre during the interwar period and the period that followed.

It was undoubtedly his open-air mass spectacles that brought Van Duyn into the limelight, much more so than the amateur groups in which he was also active. In 1955 he directed the *Godelievespel* (Godelieve Play) in Gistel, followed by *Gudrun* in Roeselare in 1956, and the *Heilig Bloedspel* (Play of the Holy Blood) in Bruges in 1962. He was also the director of the annual Flemish National Song Festival.

From 1966 onwards, Remi Van Duyn brought a new style to the Pilgrimage in which theatricality appears to have been a crucial element. He sought out spectacular theatrical effects. For the Eucharist dialogue, he asked the Order of Discalced Carmelites for chasubles; he appealed to the mime actors of the Hoste Sabattini to form symbolic groups of performers; the choreography was

40 'Verslag van Vlaams Verbond der Katholieke Scouts', 10 April 1965, ADVN Y 16/2.

41 'Verslag Raad van beheer', 14 April 1962, ADVN Y 60/2.

42 'Verslag algemene vergadering', 20 Oct. 1962, ADVN Y 67; 'Verslag algemene vergadering', 30 March 1963, ADVN Y 67.

43 'Verslag van de Raad van beheer', 10 Oct. 1964, ADVN 16/2.

44 Anthonissen, 'Alles is detail', 239.

10. *Pilgrimage of the Yser, 40th edition, 1967.*
[Antwerp, ADVN]

led by Monica Steens and her dance group Dansa Ritmica; and in the same atmosphere of feminization, the faithful old reciter Hein Nackaerts was replaced by Marga Neirynck.

Besides these straightforward means of introducing more professionalism in the crowd scenes, he also aimed for a greater activation of the audience, who should not merely listen but also be moved by the visual and musical spectacle. Together with lyricist Anton van Wilderode, he created a narrative of songs, ballads, masked theatre, poetry, rhythmic movement and especially images: evocations of collective memories and illustrations of themes, at which Dansa Ritmica excelled, or enlargements of photographs and drawings. Furthermore, an 88 meter long walkway was built between the old ruins and the new tower, providing much greater visibility of the event. The following year he even planned to have three planes fly over which would scatter petals over the mass audience. These were indeed the years of flower power and internationalization. Remi Van Duyn noticed this too, albeit in his own Flemish nationalist way. For the 1967 Pilgrimage he asked Caritas Catholica to place a group of 30-40 boys and girls from foreign countries at his disposal:

> The Pilgrimage this year will take place under the motto WORLD PEACE. We would like to make this clear symbolically using a performance involving boys and girls from Vietnam, Israel, China, India, Japan, Congo, etc. (especially from the yellow and black races). So we need the widest possible range of types and races of people.[45]

The Minister of Tourism, Jan Piers, was asked to write a letter of recommendation to the International Air Transport Association, in order to expand the international floral tribute with a number of air hostesses from the most diverse airlines. 'The intention is to lend an international, touristic character to our peace rally.' Again, he gives priority to hostesses of 'especially the yellow and the black races'.[46]

The newspaper *De Standaard*, which sympathized with the initiative, praised the new theatrical concept: 'At the 1969 Yser Pilgrim-

45 Letter from Remi Van Duyn, 7 June 1967, ADVN Y 554/4. It is no accident that Van Duyn expressly asks for members of yellow and black races, since these are the main colours of the Flemish flag.

46 Letter from Remi Van Duyn, 7 June 1967, ADVN Y 554/4.

age, various political themes were expressed through intelligently produced spectacle, and connected with one other.'[47] And in the even more sympathetic reports written by the Yser Pilgrimage Committee itself we find:

> While Pilgrimages to date have focused for a very large if not predominant part on the various speeches and messages, the official 'words' have now taken more of a back seat. This Pilgrimage was primarily a very moving spectacle in which the masses, thanks to the masterful text and evocative production design, were engaged so intensely that they became co-performers. Diksmuide heard this time not the calls and beliefs of a series of famous or less famous persons, but the unanimous testimony of the huge masses themselves.[48]

The interventions of Remi Van Duyn were mainly aimed at touching a mass audience emotionally, in order to strengthen their sense of unity and togetherness, which according to Dumont is a typical ingredient of commemorative events.[49] In this way, the masses themselves also found their place in the whole, and experienced the feeling of being an active part of the event: 'The mass spectacle becomes a kind of theatrical performance, in which the distinction between actors and spectators fades, and the masses perform their own symbolic role as masses.'[50]

The innovations of Remi Van Duyn are certainly visible in the spectacular use of space, in visual representation and in rhythmic evocation. I hesitate, however, to use the expression: 'in modern garb'. He continues to focus on romantic symbols such as the flower, the cross and the flag. The personality cult of the symbolically sacrificed soldiers remains in place, albeit portrayed using more contemporary visual resources. The essential narrative of the Yser Pilgrimage has thus been left untouched; in fact, it has been visually intensified. It is exactly this that explains the success of Van Duyn's and Van Wilderode's interventions. They let a warm wind blow over the fields of Diksmuide, and nobody cares where it originated.

47 'Knipsel in archief IJzerbedevaart, *De Standaard*, 1969', ADVN Y 8/1/6.
48 Pilgrimage report of 1966, quoted in Beck, 'De IJzerbedevaarten', 167.
49 Dumont quoted in Deneckere, 'De macht van de straat', 28-29.
50 Ibid., 29.

ABBREVIATIONS

ACV: *Algemeen Christelijk Vakverbond* (Confederation of Christian Trade Unions)
ADVN: *Archief, Documentatie- en Onderzoekscentrum voor het Vlaams-nationalisme* (Archive, Documentary and Research Centre for Flemish Nationalism)
AJ: *Arbeidersjeugdverbond* (Young Workers' Association)
AJC: *Arbeiders Jeugd Centrale* (Young Workers' Centre)
AKVT: *Algemeen Katholiek Verbond voor Tooneel* (General Catholic Theatre Federation of Amateur Groups)
ALD: Lea Daan Archive
ATB: *Algemeene Tooneelboekerij* (General Theatre Library)
ATBH: *Arbeiders Theater Bond Holland* (Holland Workers' Theatre League)
BWP: *Belgische Werklieden Partij* (Belgian Socialist Workers' Party)
CJB: *Communistische Jeugdbond* (Communist Youth League)
IVAO: *Instituut voor Arbeidersontwikkeling* (Institute for the Development of Workers)
JOC: *Jeunesse Ouvrière Chrétienne* (Young Christian Workers)
KAJ: *Kristene Arbeiders Jeugd* (Young Christian Workers)
KNS: *Koninklijke Nederlandse Schouwburg* (Royal Dutch Theatre)
KVTC: *Katholieke Vlaamsche Tooneelcentrale* (Catholic Flemish Theatre Centre)
NSB: *Nationaal-socialistische Beweging* (National Socialist Movement)
NVV: *Nederlands Verbond van Vakverenigingen* (Dutch Federation of Trade Unions)
OSP: *Onafhankelijke Socialistische Partij* (Independent Socialist Party)
SDAP: *Sociaal Democratische Arbeiderspartij* (Social Democratic Labour Party)
VARA: *Vereeniging van Arbeiders Radio Amateurs* (Association of Worker Radio Amateurs)
VNV: *Vlaamsch Nationaal Verbond* (Flemish National Association)
VOS: *Verbond van Vlaamsche Oud-Strijders* (Association of Flemish War Veterans)
VVSU: *Vereeniging van Vrienden van de Sovjet Unie* (Association of Friends of the Soviet Union)
VVT: *Vlaams Volkstoneel* (Flemish Popular Theatre)
WA: *Weerbaarheidsafdeling* (NSB's militia)

BIBLIOGRAPHY

ACV (Algemeen Christelijk Vakverbond van België). *Verslag over de jubelviering van 7 Oogst 1938 en over het XIIIde Congres gehouden op 21, 22 en 23 Juli 1938.* Brussels, 1938.

Alexander, Eric and Van der Krogt, Nico. "Openluchttheaters in Nederland" in: Bob Logger et al., eds. *Theaters in Nederland sinds de zeventiende eeuw.* Amsterdam: Theater Instituut Nederland & Stichting OISTAT-Nederland, 2007.

Alexander, Eric and Van der Krogt, Nico. *Openluchttheaters in Nederland: Vermaak onder heldere hemel.* Zutphen: Walburg Pers, 2011.

Anderson, Benedict. *Imagined Communities: Reflections on the Origin and Spread of Nationalism.* London: Verso, 1983.

Annales Parlementaires de Belgique. Chambre des Représentants. - Belgische Kamer van Volksvertegenwoordigers. Parlementaire Handelingen. 1937-1938. Brussels: Moniteur belge, 1938.

Anthonissen, Peter. "'Alles is detail'. Ast Fonteyne als regisseur in en buiten het onderwijs" in: Peter Anthonissen et al., eds. *Ast Fonteyne, 1906-1991. Een kwestie van stijl.* Leuven: KADOC, 1999, 197-253.

Arato, Andrew and Gebhardt, Eike, eds. *The Essential Frankfurt School Reader.* New York: The Continuum Publishing Company, 2005.

Arbeidersontwikkeling. Rapport uitgebracht door de commissie ingesteld door SDAP en NVV. Amsterdam, 1924.

Arcadis. *Opmaak van een survey en waardering voor het Citadelpark in Gent. Eindrapport.* (Unpublished report commissioned by the Ghent City Authorities.) Deurne: 2011.

Avermaete, Roger. *Lea Daan. Huldealbum door haar vrienden uitgegeven ter gelegenheid van haar zeventigste verjaardag.* Antwerp: Esco, 1976.

Bailey, Peter. *Leisure and Class in Victorian England: Rational Recreation and the Contest for Control, 1830-1885.* London: Routledge & Kegan Paul / Buffalo: University of Toronto Press, 1978.

Balduck, Eli. *Diksmuide, onze trots en onze schande.* Antwerp: Vlaamse Toeristische Bibliotheek, 1968.

Bank, Jan and Van Buuren, Maarten. *1900. Hoogtij van burgerlijke cultuur.* The Hague: SDU, 2000.

Barnum, Phineas Taylor. *The Life of P.T. Barnum, including his golden rules for money-making.* Buffalo: Courier Co., 1888.

Baty, Gaston. *Rideau baissé.* Paris: Bordas, 1949.

Beacham, Richard. *Adolphe Appia. Theatre Artist.* Cambridge: Cambridge University Press, 1987.

Beck, Annelies. "IJzerbedevaart" in: *Nieuwe Encyclopedie van de Vlaamse Beweging.* Tielt: Lannoo, 1998, 1503-1514.

Beck, Annelies. "De IJzerbedevaarten" in: Guy Leemans et al., eds. *Vlamingen komt in massa. De Vlaamse beweging als massabeweging.* Ghent: Provinciebestuur Oost-Vlaanderen/ADVN, 1999, 149-169.

Benjamin, Walter. "Paris: Capital of the Nineteenth Century". *Perspecta*, 12 (1969), 163-172.

Bennett, Tony. *The Birth of the Museum.* London: Routledge, 1995.

Benvindo, Bruno and Peeters, Evert. *Scherven van de oorlog. De strijd om de herinnering aan WOII.* Antwerp: De Bezige Bij, 2011.

Bernaerts, Jan. "A.K.V.T. en 'het Nationaal Tooneelverbond'". *De Standaard*, 1 June, 1927.

Blanc, André. *Histoire de la Comédie-Française.* Paris: Perrin, 2007.

Blockmans, Wim. "Beziel tot hooger Leven! Sociaal-democratische cultuurpolitiek in Nederland tijdens het interbellum" in: Jan Berting et al., ed. *Mensen, macht en maatschappij.* Meppel/Amsterdam: Boom, 1987, 189-209.

Blommaert, Philip. *Geschiedenis van de rhetorykkamer: De Fonteine te Gent.* Ghent: Gyselynk, 1847.

Bochow, Jörg. *Das Theater Meyerholds und die Biomechanik.* Berlin: Alexander, 1997.

Boon, Jan. "De Toneelrenaissance in Vlaanderen". *Dietsche Warande en Belfort*, 24 (1924), 963-966. <corpustoneelkritiek.org/cti/html/1924-00-00_boon.html>.

Boon, Jozef, C.Ss.R. *Spreekkoor en massa-tooneel. Ontwikkeling, theorie, praktijk.* Sint-Niklaas: Van Haver, 1937.

Bordwell, David. *On the History of Film Style.* Cambridge (Mass.): Harvard University Press, 1997.

Bowlt, John. "Constructivism and Russian Stage Design". *Performing Arts Journal*, 1 (1977) 3, 62-84.

Box, Erik. *De derde Arbeidersolympiade in 1937 te Antwerpen.* MA thesis. KU Leuven, 1986.

Brasillach, Robert. *Animateurs de théâtre. Dullin, Baty, Copeau, Jouvet, Les Pitoëff.* Paris: Corrêa, 1936.

Braun, Edward, ed. *Meyerhold on Theatre.* London: Methuen, 1969.

Braun, Edward. *The Director and the Stage: From Naturalism to Grotowski.* London: Methuen, 1982.

Brown, Frederick. *Theater & Revolution: The Culture of the French Stage.* New York: Viking Press, 1980.

Buck-Morss, Susan. *Dreamworld and Catastrophe: The Passing of Mass Utopia in East and West.* Cambridge (Mass.): Harvard University Press, 2001.

Buffalo Bill. *An Autobiography of Buffalo Bill.* New York: Cosmopolitan Book Corporation, 1920.

Bürger, Peter. *Theorie der Avantgarde.* Frankfurt am Main: Suhrkamp, 1974.

Bürger, Peter. *Theory of the Avant-Garde.* Minneapolis: University of Minnesota Press, 1984.

Burt, Ramsay. *The Male Dancer: Bodies, Spectacle, Sexualities.* New York: Taylor & Francis, 2007.

Carlson, Marvin. *The Theatre of the French Revolution.* Ithaka: Cornell University Press, 1966.

Carlson, Marvin. *Theories of the Theatre.* Ithaka: Cornell University Press, 1984.

Clark, Jon. *Bruno Schönlank und die Arbeitersprechchorbewegung.* Cologne: Prometh, 1984.

Claudel, Paul. *La Messe là-bas* (1919) in: Paul Claudel. *Œuvre Poétique.* Paris: Gallimard, 1957.

Cohen, Gustave. "Expériences théophiliens." *Mercure de France*, 48 (1937) 273, 453-476.

Cohen, Gustave. "Les Théophiliens." *The French Review*, 12 (1939) 6, 453-458.

Coppieters, Diana. "Clemens De Landtsheer" in: *Nieuwe Encyclopedie van de Vlaamse Beweging.* Tielt: Lannoo, 1998, 1787-1788.

Corbey, Raymond. "Ethnographic Showcases, 1870-1930." *Cultural Anthropology*, 8 (1993) 3, 338-369.

Craig, Edward Gordon. *On the Art of the Theatre.* London: Heinemann, 1911.

Crombez, Thomas. "The Sovereign Disappears in the Voting Booth: Carl Schmitt and Martin Heidegger on Sovereignty and (Perhaps) Governmentality" in: Erich Kofmel, ed. *Anti-Democratic Thought.* Exeter: Imprint Academic, 2008, 101-121.

Crombez, Thomas and Hoet, Ciska. "Cerebraal doorgevoerde tendenskunst. Over het breukkarakter van massatoneel tussen de wereldoorlogen" in: Lars Bernaerts, Carl De Strycker and Bart Vervaeck, eds. *Breuken en bruggen: moderne Nederlandse literatuur / Hedendaagse perspectieven.* Ghent: Academia Press, 2011, 227-240.

Crombez, Thomas and Vanhoeck, Liesje. "De bouw van het Openluchttheater Rivierenhof te Deurne (1953) en het discours rond stad, land en gemeenschapskunst." *Stadsgeschiedenis*, 4 (2009) 1, 45-60.

Daly, Ann. *Done into Dance: Isadora Duncan in America*. Middletown: Wesleyan University Press, 1995.

Daniels, Barry and Razgonnikoff, Jacqueline. *Patriotes en scène. Le Théâtre de la République (1790-1799)*. Vizille: Musée de la Révolution Française, 2007.

Debord, Guy. *La Société du spectacle*. Paris: Champ Libre, 1971.

De Ghein, Rik. "De zeven bedevaarten van Remi" in: *Remi Van Duyn 1910-1982, portret van een Vlaming*. Roeselare: Huldecomité Remi Van Duyn, 1994, 95-112.

De Gruyter, Domien. *Boekje open! Het toneelleven in Antwerpen rond Wereldoorlog II*. Antwerp: Paradox Pers, 1996.

De Gruyter, Jan Oskar. *Dr. Jan Oskar de Gruyter 1885-1929. Zijn levenswerk*. Antwerp: De Sikkel, 1934.

De Leeuwe, H.H.J. "Dalsum, Albertus Wilhelmus van (1889-1971)" in: *Biografisch Woordenboek van Nederland*. Vol. 3. The Hague: Instituut voor Nederlandse Geschiedenis, 1989. <http://www.historici.nl/Onderzoek/Projecten/BWN/lemmata/bwn3/dalsum>.

De Lentdecker, Louis. "IJzerbedevaart" in: *Encyclopedie van de Vlaamse Beweging*. Tielt: Lannoo, 1973-1975, 700-706.

De Loore, Paul. *Dr. Jan Oskar de Gruyter (1885-1929). Vernieuwer van het toneelleven in Vlaanderen*. Unpublished dissertation. Ghent: Rijksuniversiteit Gent, 1978.

De Maeyer, Aloïs. "Hoe wordt het spreekkoor omschreven." *Tooneelgids*, 15 April, 1933, 115-116.

De Man, Hendrik. *Het sosialisme als kultuurbeweging*. Amsterdam: Arbeiders Jeugd Centrale, 1928.

Demedts, André. "Levensverhaal van Antoon Vander Plaetse" in: *Huldeboek Antoon Vander Plaetse 60 jaar*. Tielt: Lannoo, 1964, 27-61.

Deneckere, Gita. "De macht van de straat. Flaminganten in beweging. Theoretisch-methodologische beschouwingen" in: Guy Leemans et al., eds. *Vlamingen komt in massa. De Vlaamse beweging als massabeweging*. Ghent: Provinciebestuur Oost-Vlaanderen / ADVN, 1999, 25-35.

Derks, Marjet. *Heilig moeten. Radicaal-katholiek en retro-modern in de jaren twintig en dertig*. Hilversum: Verloren, 2007.

De Ronde, Th. "Het Lam-Godsspel te Gent. Op interview bij Herman van Overbeke." *Tooneelgids*, 16 (1931) 14, 2-3.

d'Estrée, Paul. *Le Théâtre sous la Terreur 1793-1794*. Paris: Émil-Paul Frères, 1913.

De symbolen van de IJzertragedie. Bedevaart naar de graven van den IJzer. Diksmuide, 1949.

De Vleeschauwer, Herman [H.J.D.V.]. "Het spreek- en bewegingskoor II". *Jong Dietschland*, 13 February, 1931, 91-92.

De Vleeschauwer, Herman [H.J.D.V.]. "Het spreek- en bewegingskoor III". *Jong Dietschland*, 20 March, 1931, 172-173.

De Wever, Bruno. "Vlaamsch Nationaal Verbond (VNV)" in: *Nieuwe Encyclopedie van de Vlaamse Beweging*. Tielt: Lannoo, 1998, 3380-3387.

Dozy, M. G. "Openluchtspel te Salzburg. Jedermann, das Spiel vom Sterben des Reichen Mannes." *Elsevier maandschrift*, January 1936, 376-385.

Dumont, Wouter. "Fenomenologie van de massa-manifestaties in België in de jaren dertig". *Revue belge d'histoire contemporaine - Belgisch tijdschrift voor nieuwste geschiedenis*, 29 (1999) 1-2, 145-226.

Dupont, F. "Herman Van Overbeke en het openluchtspel". *Toneelleven*, 6 (1938) 36-37, 479-482.

Durnez, Gaston. "Clemens De Landtsheer" in: *Encyclopedie van de Vlaamse Beweging*. Tielt: Lannoo, 1973-1975, 824-826.

Eichberg, Henning. "Das Fest der Bewegung. Arbeitermassenspiel und NS-Thingspiel" in: *Manifestations sportives nationales et internationales: mises en scène politiques. Table ronde*. Dijon, 2007. <http://www.sdu.dk/~/media/Files/Om_SDU/Centre/C_isc/Q_filer/qHE2009Nr5.ashx>

Elias, Hendrik Jozef. *Vijfentwintig jaar Vlaamse Beweging 1914-1939*. Antwerp: De Nederlandsche Boekhandel, 1969, 4 vols.

Eliot, T.S. *Selected Essays*. London: Faber and Faber, 1972.

Etty, Elsbeth. *Liefde is heel het leven niet. Henriette Roland Holst 1869-1952*. Amsterdam: Balans, 1997.

Festbuch zur Ersten Internationalen Arbeiter-Olympiade. Frankfurt: Union-Druckerei & Verlagsanstalt, 1925.

Fischer-Lichte, Erika. *Kurze Geschichte des deutschen Theaters*. Tübingen: Narr, 1993.

Fischer-Lichte, Erika. *Theatre, Sacrifice, Ritual: Exploring Forms of Political Theatre*. London: Routledge, 2005.

Florquin, Joos and Verschaffel, Hilde. "Overbeke, Herman van" in: *Nieuwe Encyclopedie van de Vlaamse Beweging*. Tielt: Lannoo, 1998, 2365-2366.

Foster, Hal, ed. *The Anti-Aesthetic: Essays on Postmodern Culture*. Washington: Bay Press, 1985.

Foucault, Michel. *Discipline and Punish: The Birth of the Prison*. London: Allen Lane, 1977.

Fuchs, Georg. *Die Schaubühne der Zukunft*. Berlin: Schuster und Loeffler, 1905.

Fuchs, Georg. *Die Revolution des Theaters. Ergebnisse aus dem Münchener Künstler-Theater*. Munich: Müller, 1909.

Fuchs, Georg. *Die Sezession in der dramatischen Kunst und das Volksfestspiel*. Munich: Müller, 1911.

Funke, Erich. "Der Sprechchor als Kunstpädagogisches Mittel". *The German Quarterly*, 14 (1941) 2, 103-111.

Geysen, Lode. "Het spreekkoor." *Toneelgids*, September 13, 1932.

Geysen, Lode. *Spreekkoren*. Roermond: Romen, 1934.

Groeneveld, Ben. *Lekenspel*. Amsterdam: AJC, 1935.

Grube, Max. *Geschichte der Meininger*. Stuttgart: Deutsche Verlags-Anstalt, 1926.

Guilbert, Laure. *Danser avec le IIIe Reich. Les danseurs modernes sous le nazisme*. Brussels: Editions Complexe, 2000.

Heynickx, Rajesh. "Van cultuurproduct naar productcultuur. De beiaard als cultuurintegrerende factor bij Vlaamse katholieken van 1918 tot 1958" in: Marnix Beyen, Luc Rombouts and Staf Vos, eds. *De beiaard. Een politieke geschiedenis*. Leuven: Universitaire Pers Leuven, 2009, 127-144.

Hoffmann, Ludwig and Hoffmann-Ostwald, Daniel. *Deutsches Arbeitertheater 1918-1933*. Berlin: Henschel, 1972, 2 vols.

Hooze, Robert; Tollebeek, Jo and Verschaffel, Tom, eds. *Mise-en-scène. Keizer Karel en de verbeelding van de negentiende eeuw*. Ghent: Museum voor Schone Kunsten, 2000.

Hornauer, Uwe. *Laienspiel und Massenchor. Das Arbeitertheater der Kultursozialisten in der Weimarer Republik*. Cologne: Prometh, 1985.

Huldeboek Anton Vander Plaetse 60 jaar. Tielt: Lannoo, 1964.

Hunningher, Ben. *Een eeuw Nederlands toneel*. Amsterdam: Querido, 1949.

Janssens, Jeroen. *De Belgische natie viert. De Belgische nationale feesten van 1830-1914*. Leuven: Universitaire Pers Leuven, 2001.

Jay, Martin. *The Dialectical Imagination: A history of the Frankfurt School and the Institute of Social Research, 1923-1950*. Berkeley: University of California Press, 1996.

Ketelsen, Uwe-Karsten. *Heroisches Theater. Untersuchungen zur Dramentheorie des Dritten Reichs.* Bonn: Bouvier, 1968.

Leach, Robert. *Vsevolod Meyerhold.* Cambridge: Cambridge University Press, 1993.

Levinson, André. *La danse d'aujourd'hui.* Paris: Blond et Gay, 1924.

Lunel, Ernest. *Le Théâtre et la Révolution.* Paris: Daragon, 1909.

Malamud, Margaret. "Roman Entertainments for the Masses in Turn-of-the-Century New York." *The Classical World*, 95 (2001) 1, 49-57.

Marx, William, ed. *Les arrière-gardes au XXe siècle. L'autre face de la modernité esthétique.* Paris: PUF, 2004.

Meire, Frans. *De Leeuw van Vlaanderen.* Merksem: Uitgeversfonds Lode Geysen, 1939.

Missinne, Lut. *Kunst en leven, een wankel evenwicht. Prozaopvattingen in Vlaamse tijdschriften en weekbladen tijdens het interbellum 1927-1940.* Leuven: Acco, 1994.

Molema, Jan and Leemans, Suzy. *Jan Albarda en De Groep van Delft. Moderniteit in een behoudende omgeving.* Heijningen: Jap Sam Books, 2010.

Mortelmans, Hans. "Hendrik de Man en het culturele discours binnen de sociaal-democratische arbeidersbeweging in Vlaanderen (1920-1940)" in: Jan Art, Bart De Nil and Marc Jacobs, eds. *Een mens leeft niet van brood alleen. Bouwstenen voor een culturele arbeidersgeschiedenis (1800-1940).* Ghent: Amsab, 2005, 212-237.

Moynet, Georges. *Trucs et décors. Explication raisonnée de tous les moyens employés pour produire les illusions théâtrales.* Paris: Librairie Illustrée, 1893.

Moynet, Jules. *L'envers du théâtre. Machines et décorations.* Paris: Hachette, 1873.

Naerebout, Frits G. *Attractive Performances. Ancient Greek Dance: Three Preliminary Studies.* Amsterdam: J.C. Gieben, 1997.

Naremore, James and Brantlinger, Patrick. *Modernity and Mass Culture.* Bloomington: Indiana University Press, 1991.

Nijkeuter, Hendrik. *De 'pen gewijd aan Drenthe's dierbren grond': literaire bedrijvigheid in de Olde Lantschap, 1816-1956.* Diss. Universiteit Groningen, 2001.

Niven, William. "The Birth of Nazi Drama? *Thing* Plays" in: John London, ed. *Theater under the Nazis.* Manchester: Manchester University Press, 2000, 54-95.

Nodier, Charles. "Introduction" in: René-Charles Guilbert de Pixerécourt. *Théâtre choisi de G. de Pixerécourt.* Nancy: Pixerécourt, 1841, ii-iii.

Nörtemann, Gevert. *Im Spiegelkabinett der Historie. Der Mythos der Schlacht von Kortrijk und die Erfindung Flanderns im 19. Jahrhundert.* Berlin: Logos Verlag, 2002.

Notteboom, Bruno and Lauwaert, Dirk. *Edmond Sacré. Portret van een stad.* Brussels/Ghent: Mercatorfonds/STAM, 2011.

Otterloo, Annie van. "De Jonge Spelers: schets van een toneelgezelschap" in: E. Alexander, R.L. Erenstein and W. Hagendoorn, eds. *Scenarium 6: Toneel in crisis en bezettingstijd.* Zutphen: Walburgpers, 1982, 82-107.

Pearson, Roger. *Voltaire Almighty: A Life in Pursuit of Freedom.* New York: Bloomsbury, 2005.

Peeters, Evert. *De beloften van het lichaam. Een geschiedenis van de natuurlijke levenswijze in België, 1890-1940.* Amsterdam: Bert Bakker, 2008.

Peeters, Frank. *Jan Oscar de Gruyter en het Vlaamse Volkstoneel 1920-1924.* Leuven: Peeters, 1989.

Peeters, Frank. "22 augustus 1909. Openlucht-voorstelling van *Philoktetes* door de Vlaamsche Vereeniging voor Tooneel- en Voordrachtkunst te Sint-Martens-Latem" in: Robert L. Erenstein et al., eds. *Een theatergeschiedenis der Neder-landen.* Amsterdam: Amsterdam University Press, 1996, 568-573.

Peeters, Frank. "Apologie voor een weeskind, of het melodrama gewroken. Plaatsbepaling en herijking van een populair theatergenre in de Nederlandse theatergeschiedenis" in: Lucia van Heteren et al., eds. *De ornamenten van het vergeten.* Amsterdam: Amsterdam University Press, 2007, 29-42.

Pius XI. *Ubi Arcano Dei Consilio: Encyclical of Pope Pius XI on the Peace of Christ in the Kingdom of Christ.* <http://www.vatican.va/holy_father/pius_xi/encyclicals/documents/hf_p-xi_enc_23121922_ubi-arcano-dei-consilio_en.html>, 1922.

Projectgroep Literatuursociologie. *Links Richten tussen partij en arbeidersstrijd.* Nijmegen, 1975.

Putman, Willem. *Tooneeldagboek 1928-1938.* Antwerp: Globus, 1938.

Rancière, Jacques. *The Emancipated Spectator.* London/New York: Verso, 2009.

Rees, Terence. *Theatre Lighting in the Age of Gas.* London: Society for Theatre Research, 1978.

Reichl, Johannes M. *Das Thingspiel. Über den Versuch eines nationalsozialistischen Lehrstück-Theaters (Euringer, Heynicke, Möller).* Frankfurt: Mißlbeck, 1988.

Reiss, Benjamin, *The Showman and the Slave: Race, Death, and Memory in Barnum's America.* Cambridge (Mass.): Harvard University Press, 2001.

Remi Van Duyn 1910-1982. Portret van een Vlaming. Roeselare: Huldecomité Remi Van Duyn, 1994.

Roedemeyer, Friedrich Karl. *Vom Wesen des Sprech-chores.* Kassel: Bärenreiter, 1931 (originally Augsburg, 1926).

Roland Holst-Van der Schalk, Henriette. *De voorwaarden tot hernieuwing der dramatische kunst.* Rotterdam: Brusse, 1924.

Rombouts, Luc. "Klok en beiaard. Van signaal tot symbool" in: Marnix Beyen, Luc Rombouts and Staf Vos, eds. *De beiaard. Een politieke geschiedenis.* Leuven: Universitaire Pers Leuven, 2009, 9-22.

Rousseau, Jean-Jacques. *Letter to d'Alembert and Writings for the Theater. The Collected Writings of Rousseau.* Vol. 10. Transl. by Allan Bloom, Charles Butterworth and Christopher Kelly. Hanover: University Press of New England, 2004.

Ruitenbeek, Henny. *Kijkcijfers. De Amsterdamse Schouwburg 1814-1841.* Hilversum: Verloren, 2002.

Rulof, Bernard. *Een leger van priesters voor een heilige zaak. SDAP, politieke manifestaties en massapolitiek, 1918-1940.* Amsterdam: Wereldbibliotheek, 2007.

Saerens, Lieven. "Het Wendepunkt (1933-1940)" in: Peter Anthonissen et al. *Ast Fonteyne, 1906-1991. Een kwestie van stijl.* KADOC Artes 4. Leuven: Universitaire Pers Leuven, 1999, 99-126.

Schönlank, Bruno. "Proletarische Sprechchöre." *Vorwärts*, 43 (1926) 127, 17 March, 1926, reprinted in: Jon Clark. *Bruno Schönlank und die Arbeitersprechchorbewegung.* Cologne: Prometh, 1984, 180-181.

Schoonderwoerd, Nicolaas H.G. *J.T. Grein, Ambassador of the Theatre 1862-1935: A Study in Anglo-Continental Theatrical Relations.* Assen: Van Gorcum, 1963.

Schwartz, Vanessa R. *Spectacular Realities: Early Mass Culture in Fin-de-Siècle Paris.* Berkeley: University of California Press, 1998.

Shklovsky, Viktor. "Art as Technique" in: David Lodge, ed. *Modern Criticism and Theory.* London: Longmann, 1988, 16-30.

Sluga, Hans. *Heidegger's Crisis: Philosophy and Politics in Nazi Germany.* Cambridge (Mass.): Harvard University Press, 1993.

Solterer, Helen. "Performer le passé: Rencontre avec Paul Zumthor" in: J. Cerquiglini-Toulet and Ch. Lucken, eds. *Paul Zumthor ou l'invention permanente.* Recherches et Rencontres : Publications de la faculté des lettres de Genève 9. Genève : Faculté des lettres, 1998, 117-159

Springhall, John. *The Genesis of Mass Culture: Show Business Live in America, from 1840 to 1940.* New York: Palgrave Macmillan, 2008.

Stuiveling, Garmt. *Henriette Roland Holst.* Amsterdam: De Bezige Bij / The Hague: Nederlands Letterkundig Museum en Documentatiecentrum, 1977.

Styan, John L. *Max Reinhardt.* Cambridge: Cambridge University Press, 1982.

Stynen, Andreas. *Een geheugen in fragmenten. Heilige plaatsen van de Vlaamse Beweging.* Tielt: Lannoo, 2005.

Talhoff, Albert. *Totenmal. Dramatische Chorische Vision fûr Wort, Tanz, Licht.* Stuttgart: Deutsche Verlagsanstalt, 1930.

Thomé, Christine. "Les chœurs parlés de la Jeunesse Ouvrière Chrétienne dans l'entre-deux-guerres" in: *Entre poésie et propagande. Charles Plisnier et les chœurs parlés en Belgique.* Exhibition catalogue. Mons: Fondation Jacques Gueux, 1997, 41-58.

Tillich, Paul. *Masse und Geist. Studien zur Philosophie der Masse.* Berlin: Verlag der Arbeitsgemeinschaft, 1922.

Toepfer, Karl. *Empire of Ecstasy: Nudity and Movement in German Body Culture 1910-1935.* Berkeley: University of California Press, 1997.

Tollebeek, Jo. "De Guldensporenvieringen" in: Guy Leemans et al., eds. *Vlamingen, komt in massa. De Vlaamse beweging als massabeweging.* Ghent: Provinciebestuur Oost-Vlaanderen / ADVN, 1999, 37-63.

Tollebeek, Jo et al. *België. Een parcours van herinnering.* Amsterdam: Bakker, 2008, 2 vols.

Tolstoj, Vladimir; Bibikova, Irina and Cooke, Catherine, eds. *Street Art of the Revolution: Festivals and Celebrations in Russia 1918-1933.* London: Thames and Hudson, 1990 (org. Moscow: Iskusstvo, 1984).

Tretjakow, Sergei. *Feld-Herren: Der Kampf um eine Kollektivwirtschaft.* Berlin: Malik-Verlag, 1931.

Triau, Christophe. "Choralités diffractées. La communauté en creux." *Alternatives théâtrales,* (2003) 76-77, 5-11.

Tromp, Marlene, ed. *Victorian Freaks: The Social Context of Freakery in Britain.* Columbus: Ohio State University Press, 2008.

Van den Boorn, Els. *Mannus Franken, mensch en kunstenaar.* Amsterdam: De Mannus Franken Stichting, 1979.

Van den Woestijne, Karel. "Tooneel in Vlaanderen." *Nieuw Rotterdamsche Courant,* February 23, 1925, 420-427. <http://www.corpustoneelkritiek.org/cti/html/1925-02-25_vandewoestijne_tooneelvlaanderen.html>.

Van der Logt, Ad. *Het theater van de nieuwe orde. Een onderzoek naar het drama van Nederlandse nationaalsocialisten.* Amsterdam: Aksant, 2008.

Van der Logt, Ad. "De Eerste Wereldoorlog in het Nederlands theater van het interbellum" in: Henk van der Linden et al., eds. *De Grote Oorlog. Kroniek 1914-1918.* Soesterberg: Aspect, 2011, 223-292.

Vande Winkel, Roel and Biltereyst, Daniël. *Filmen voor Vlaanderen. Vlaamse beweging, propaganda en film.* Ghent: Bijdragen Museum van de Vlaamse Sociale Strijd, 2008.

Van Dijk, Terenja and De Rynck Patrick. *Belichte stad. Over dag, licht en nacht.* Tielt/Ghent: Lannoo/STAM, 2010.

Van Gaal, Rob. "13 juli 1924. Albert van Dalsum houdt een voordracht in het Oolgaerthuis te Arnhem: Expressionistisch toneel in Nederland" in: R.L. Erenstein et al., eds. *Een theatergeschiedenis der Nederlanden.* Amsterdam: Amsterdam University Press, 1996, 616-625.

Vanhaesebrouck, Karel. "Geen rijker kroon dan eigen schoon? De programmatiepolitiek van Staf Bruggen en Hendrik Caspeele in bezettingstijd." *Wetenschappelijke tijdingen op het gebied van de geschiedenis van de Vlaamse beweging,* 62 (2003) 1, 48-64.

Van Kerkhoven, Marianne and Mallems, Alex. "Joris Diels. In de bedding van de traditie." *Etcetera,* 3 (1985) 10, 54-59.

Van Kersbergen, J.A. "Midwinterzonnewende". *Nieuw Nederland,* Febr. 1940, 571.

Van Overbeke, Herman. "Kantteekeningen bij de expressionistische insceneering van Verschaeve's *Judas.*" *Pogen,* (1924) 4, 195-197. <http://www.corpustoneelkritiek.org/cti/html/1924-04-00_vanoverbeke.html>.

Van Schoor, Jaak. *Een huis voor Vlaanderen. Honderd jaar Nederlands beroepstoneel te Gent.* Ledeberg/Ghent: Erasmus, 1972.

Van Schoor, Jaak. "Teirlinck en de Russen (1921-1932)" in: Peter Benoy and Jaak Van Schoor, eds. *Historische avant-garde en het theater in het interbellum.* Brussels: ASP, 2011, 99-110.

Verdoodt, Frans-Jos. "Allen daarheen! Over massabeweging en Vlaamse beweging" in: Guy Leemans et al., eds. *Vlamingen komt in massa. De Vlaamse beweging als massabeweging.* Ghent: Provinciebestuur Oost-Vlaanderen / ADVN, 1999, 13-22.

Verkade-Cartier van Dissel, Eline Francoise. *Eduard Verkade en zijn strijd voor een nieuw toneel.* Zutphen: De Walburg Pers, 1978.

Viollet-le-Duc, Eugène. *Dictionnaire raisonné de l'architecture française du XIe au XVIe siècle.* Vol. 8. Paris: Librairies-Imprimeries réunies, 1860. <http://fr.wikisource.org/wiki/Dictionnaire_raisonné_de_l'architecture_française_du_XIe_au_XVIe_siècle>.

Vogt, Karl. *Praxis des Sprechchors mit Regiebuch des Chorspiels 'Der Krieg'.* Berlin: Der Sturm, 1929.

Vondung, Klaus. *Magie und Manipulation. Ideologischer Kult und politische Religion des Nationalsozialismus.* Göttingen: Vandenhoeck & Ruprecht, 1971.

Von Schramm, Wilhelm. *Neubau des Deutschen Theaters. Ergebnisse und Forderungen.* Berlin: Schlieffen, 1934.

Vos, Staf. *Dans in België, 1890-1940.* Leuven: Universitaire Pers Leuven, 2012.

Vos, Staf. "Waanzin of kuur? Het dansende lichaam tussen afwijking en ideaal" in: Christel Stalpaert and Evelien Jonckheere, eds. *Het spel voorbij de waanzin: een theatrale praktijk?* Ghent: Academia Press, 2010, 105-126.

Wagner, Richard. *Gesammelte Schriften.* Ed. Julius Kapp. Leipzig: Hesse & Becker, 1914.

Wils, Lode. "Grammens, Flor" in: *Nieuwe Encyclopedie van de Vlaamse Beweging.* Tielt: Lannoo, 1998, 1348-1350.

Worp, Jacob Adolf. *Geschiedenis van den Amsterdamschen Schouwburg 1496-1772.* Amsterdam: Van Looy, 1920.

Worrall, Nick. *Modernism to Realism on the Soviet Stage: Tairov - Vakhtangov - Okhlopkov.* Cambridge: Cambridge University Press, 1989.

Wulf, Joseph. *Theater und Film im Dritten Reich.* Gütersloh: Sigbert Mohn Verlag, 1964.

Žižek, Slavoj. "Heiner Müller Out of Joint" in: Slavoj Žižek. *The Universal Exception.* London: Continuum, 2006, 42-61.

COLOPHON

Final editing
Luc Vints

Copy editing
Lieve Claes

Layout
Alexis Vermeylen

All translations from Dutch, French and German were made by the editors unless otherwise noted.
The editors wish to thank Sarah Bekaert and Ciska Hoet for their invaluable assistance.

KADOC
Documentation and Research Centre for Religion, Culture and Society
KU Leuven
Vlamingenstraat 39
B - 3000 Leuven
http://kadoc.kuleuven.be

Leuven University Press
Minderbroedersstraat 4
B - 3000 Leuven
Belgium
+32 (0)16 32 53 45
info@lup.be
www.lup.be